The Misunderstood Miracle

Cornell Studies in Political Economy

Edited by Peter J. Katzenstein

Collapse of an Industry: Nuclear Power and the Contradictions of U.S. Policy, by John L. Campbell

Power, Purpose, and Collective Choice: Economic Strategy in Socialist States, edited by Ellen Comisso and Laura D'Andrea Tyson

The Political Economy of the New Asian Industrialism, edited by Frederic C. Deyo

The Misunderstood Miracle: Industrial Development and Political Change in Japan, by David Friedman

Politics in Hard Times: Comparative Responses to International Economic Crises, by Peter Gourevitch

Closing the Gold Window: Domestic Politics and the End of Bretton Woods, by Joanne Gowa

The Philippine State and the Marcos Regime: The Politics of Export, by Gary Hawes

Pipeline Politics: The Complex Political Economy of East-West Energy Trade, by Bruce W. Jentleson

The Politics of International Debt, edited by Miles Kahler

Corporatism and Change: Austria, Switzerland, and the Politics of Industry, by Peter J. Katzenstein

Small States in World Markets: Industrial Policy in Europe, by Peter J. Katzenstein

The Sovereign Entrepreneur: Oil Policies in Advanced and Less Developed Capitalist Countries, by Merrie Gilbert Klapp

International Regimes, edited by Stephen D. Krasner

Power, Protection, and Free Trade: International Sources of U.S. Commercial Strategy, 1887–1939, by David A. Lake

State Capitalism: Public Enterprise in Canada, by Jeanne Kirk Laux and Maureen Appel Molot

The Business of the Japanese State: Energy Markets in Comparative and Historical Perspective, by Richard J. Samuels

Europe and the New Technologies, edited by Margaret Sharp

Europe's Industries: Public and Private Strategies for Change, edited by Geoffrey Shepherd, François Duchêne, and Christopher Saunders

National Styles of Regulation: Environmental Policy in Great Britain and the United States, by David Vogel

Governments, Markets, and Growth: Financial Systems and the Politics of Industrial Change, by John Zysman

American Industry in International Competition: Government Policies and Corporate Strategies, edited by John Zysman and Laura Tyson

The Misunderstood Miracle

Industrial Development and Political Change in Japan

David Friedman

Cornell University Press

Ithaca and London

First published 1988 by Cornell University Press.

International Standard Book Number (cloth) 0-8014-2073-3
International Standard Book Number (paper) 0-8014-9479-6
Library of Congress Catalog Card Number 87-47855
Printed in the United States of America
Librarians: Library of Congress cataloging information appears on the last page of the book.

The paper in this book is acid-free and meets the guidelines for permanence and durability of the Committee on Production Guidelines for Book Longevity of the Council on Library Resources.

Contents

Acknowledgments

This book is the product of my curiosity about industrial alternatives and the choices we might make to achieve a productive yet just society. It grew out of my introduction to new theoretical work in the United States and Europe, which suggested to me that the ideas and analyses conventionally applied to explain and prescribe for economic development may be too limited. The Japanese case, I believe, lends additional support to a growing conviction in political economic studies that our future options are considerably greater than are usually imagined.

In writing this book, I am acutely aware of how much I depended on the guidance, support, and criticism of others; very simply, I could not have completed it without the kindness and concern of my teachers and friends. I mention here only a few of the people and institutions who helped me. My research was funded by a University of California Regents' Fellowship, a Massachusetts Institute of Technology University fellowship in the Department of Political Science, a three-year National Science Foundation graduate fellowship, and, for research in Japan, a Fulbright Fellowship funded by a grant from the Takahashi Zaidan. I am deeply grateful to these institutions for making it possible for me to complete this book.

In Japan, I wish to acknowledge the patient consideration provided me by Ōmori Wataru, Nakamura Takafusa, Kumon Shumpei, and Horiuchi Akiyoshi, all of Tokyo University, and Kiyonari Tadao of Hōsei University. Sugiyama Kazuo, Murakami Masahiro, and Kawashima Yuzo of the Japan Machine Tool Builders Association provided me with invaluable historical materials and introductions to many machinery producers. Tanabe Toshihiko, director of MITI's

Industrial Machinery Division, and his staff provided me with market share and investment data. I also thank Takami Takahashi, president of Minebea Inc., for making his staff available for interviews, especially Ikeda Nobuo, who patiently answered my queries regarding his firm's operations. The Kokumin Kinyū Kōkō and the Sakaki *Shōkōkai* were instrumental in permitting me to visit factories in Nagano Prefecture. Finally, although I am not able to thank each firm individually, I am very grateful to all of the equipment manufacturers and users whom I interviewed and visited to research this book.

In the United States, I owe a large debt to individuals who have, by example and by direct interest in my work, given me far more support and consideration than I deserve: Peter Almquist, Marie Anchordoguy, Suzanne Berger, Peter Brekke, Walter Dean Burnham, John Dower, Don Erway, Peter Gourevitch, Leslie Helm, Gary Herrigel, Peter Katzenstein, Toshihiro Nishiguchi, Hugh Patrick, T. J. Pempel, Michael Piore, Mark Ramseyer, Tracy Strong, and John Zysman. I thank especially Richard Samuels, David Laitin, and Charles Sabel for the innumerable times they have counseled or tried to educate me. Though the errors and mistakes in this book are entirely my own, whatever quality it has is due in no small measure to the influence of these three individuals. I cannot thank them enough for their kindness and concern over the years.

I am grateful to Cornell University Press and editor Roger Haydon for the publication of this book. I also thank Jenny and Peter Ladefoged for providing me with a quiet place to write up my results after Japan. Elizabeth Friedman had the unenviable task of reading the manuscript to try to reduce my typing and grammatical errors; I am, if possible, even more indebted to her than before. Finally, I thank Lise Friedman, to whom I owe more than I can ever say.

DAVID FRIEDMAN

Los Angeles, California

The Misunderstood
Miracle

CHAPTER ONE

Explaining the Japanese Miracle

This book addresses the reasons for the spectacular growth of Japanese manufacturing industries in the period beginning with the mid-1950s and ending in the late 1970s. It focuses on the machine tool industry in Japan from about the time of the Great Depression to the present. I argue that often overlooked or misinterpreted political and industrial developments made it possible for Japanese manufacturers to build goods more flexibly than producers elsewhere. The widespread growth and development of firms seeking production flexibility provided the country's industries with significant competitive advantages at home and abroad. This argument calls for substantial revisions in most contemporary explanations of Japanese success.

Understanding the reasons for Japanese economic development is one of the most serious challenges for students of comparative political economy and industrial policy makers, for no theory of development and no strategy for promoting growth can ignore the country's postwar advance. Striking cases of economic success play an important role in the way other societies analyze their own problems, critique their established beliefs, validate new ideas. In practice Japan is especially important, because its remarkable achievements in such sectors as automobiles, electronics, and automation stand in stark contrast to the manufacturing crisis that continues to grip the United States and most of Western Europe. In clarifying the reasons for rapid Japanese expansion, we improve our ability to interpret and respond to circumstances elsewhere.

In this chapter I discuss two major explanations offered to account for Japanese growth. The theories hold that extensive bureaucratic regulation, or that market forces alone, led to Japanese industrial expansion.[1] Both arguments assume that Japan succeeded mainly by enhancing efficiency and lowering production costs; the question they ask is, What accounts for this efficiency advantage? The two perspectives have each generated valuable research on Japan, and their efforts have promoted useful debate about political economy and industrial policy. But in the final analysis, I argue, neither can adequately explain many important features of Japan's industrial system. One problem is that throughout the high-growth period, small and medium-sized manufacturers increasingly assumed large if not dominant roles in Japanese industry. Another is the extent to which Japanese competitive strategy in domestic and global markets was shaped by an effort to break up mass markets into smaller, specialized segments through continuous product modification and new product development. Both of these important features of Japanese industry receive little attention in contemporary accounts. Because no theory provides a satisfactory explanation or description of Japanese development, none can serve as an accurate basis for discussing industrial options or problems in other countries.

Japanese manufacturing growth resulted, I believe, from the dramatic expansion of smaller producers throughout the nation's economy. Special circumstances in Japan, which I discuss in detail later, enabled smaller-scale producers to implement more flexible manufacturing strategies than those which were possible for firms that pursued mass production alone. The result was to enhance the ability of Japanese manufacturers to adopt extensive, continuous product changes more easily than producers in other countries. This flexible manufacturing and ability to modify products was, in my view, an even more important factor in Japanese expansion than the efficiency gains emphasized by other observers. Indeed, if the Japanese had in fact organized their economy as most popular explanations suggest—reducing costs by coordinating, integrating, or consolidating production—the country's rapid expansion might not have occurred at all. Consequently, my argument takes odds with the conventional interpretation of Japan's economic success and its policy implications.

In this chapter I discuss in detail the two main theories advanced to account for Japanese industrial success. Each of these perspectives is founded on a surprisingly limited view of potential industrial opportunities and options. New research in the United States and Europe offers a novel way of interpreting industrial growth, one that bears directly on the problem of explaining Japanese expansion. Building on this research, I construct an alternative way of understanding Japanese manufacturing growth. Finally, I sketch how we might assess the validity of the competing claims about Japan: apply each theory of industrial success to the problem of explaining the historical growth of the Japanese machinery industry.

Japanese Economic Triumphs: Two Contemporary Arguments

The impressive scope of Japan's postwar economic recovery has stimulated considerable discussion. Broad generalizations about the many arguments that have been advanced will necessarily do injustice to some of their nuances, but we can nevertheless identify two main perspectives that have dominated thinking about Japanese development. One argument, which I call the *bureaucratic regulation thesis,* is that the economic bureaucracy, particularly the Ministry of International Trade and Industry (MITI), directed the development of the high-growth economy. The other, which I shall call the *market regulation thesis,* is that Japanese development was the result mainly of market forces; government activity provided at most a favorable environment for industrial expansion by manufacturers who were responding primarily to market cues. Most contemporary explanations of rapid Japanese development can be reduced to one of these two theses.

The bureaucratic regulation thesis holds that the Japanese state provided domestic producers with the support and guidance they needed to achieve competitive advantages in global markets. One version simply points to subsidies or trade barriers as the source of success; Japanese costs were artificially or unfairly reduced through intervention. More sophisticated accounts contend the economic bureaucracy set up production allocation plans or sanctioned cartels that led to a more rational and hence lower-cost industrial system.[2] Indeed, some observers believe that the state, expecially MITI, effectively planned and directed the transformation of the Japanese economy from its comparatively backward, war-torn condition in the late 1940s to its present status as an industrial giant.[3]

Several features of Japanese political and historical experience provide the bureaucratic regulation thesis with an initial plausibility. Japan is widely perceived as a late-developing nation, industrializing behind much of Europe and North America. Late-developing states, modern political economic theory suggests, tend to establish strong, intrusive bureaucracies, putting into place deliberately the economic infrastructure that emerged more or less spontaneously in nations that developed earlier.[4] Japan is nearly always classified with other late developers such as France as a "strong state," and the influence of late development on Japanese economic institutions has been the theme of many influential studies.[5] Historical generalizations based on the notion of late development have tended to validate the idea that the Japanese bureaucracy must have played an active and even a dominant role in promoting growth.

Indeed, Japanese agencies such as MITI *have* sponsored a staggering array of legislation and applied considerable informal pressure in an effort to control the economy. The existence of highly intrusive, industry-specific measures since at least the Depression corroborates the notion that Japanese economic growth must have been the product of bureaucratic organization.[6] Studies that proceed from this assumption have been able to demonstrate pervasive bureaucratic regulation in most of the sectors that contributed to industrial expansion throughout Japan's high-growth period, and so many observers attribute economic success to the planning and control of Japanese bureaucrats. As one observer has suggested, "Most of the ideas for economic growth [in the postwar period] came from the bureaucracy, and the business community reacted with what one scholar has called 'responsive dependence.' The government did not normally give direct orders to businesses, but those businesses that listened to the signals coming from the government and then responded were favored with easy access to capital, tax breaks, and approval of their plans to import foreign technology or establish joint ventures."[7] The need to catch up with earlier developers made it imperative that Japan build a bureaucracy capable of planning for and implementing an efficient, modern industry. It is because Japan responded to this challenge successfully, according to the bureaucratic regulation thesis, that it enjoyed rapid economic growth.

The idea that bureaucratic control of the economy was crucial in generating growth has stimulated some provocative research on Japan, but the argument has basic problems. One is methodological: most studies simply assert that a given policy led to desired economic outcomes, assuming that the promulgation of a regulation or a law is the same as proof of its effectiveness. Indeed, in most accounts the actual behavior of manufacturers themselves is not examined at all.[8] The difficulty here is obvious. In any given case directives or legislation might have been wholly superfluous to what industrialists actually did to produce growth. Moreover, it is possible that the bureaucracy's policies were either initially proposed by, or even foisted on, the regulators by firms that the regulators were supposed to be controlling.

The failure to show that state control caused growth independently and effectively is the most serious objection to the bureaucratic regulation thesis. Yet because of extensive though superficial evidence of bureaucratic intervention, and the degree of success the Japanese have enjoyed, the argument retains its appeal. It has been particularly important in legitimating the idea that direct government intervention to organize the economy might be a necessary response to economic crisis in other nations. If a strong state led to sustained growth in Japan, the logic runs, might not the same response be necessary to achieve a similar outcome elsewhere—to catch up to the *Japanese?*[9] I believe that this view is seductive because of our implicit assumptions about industrial options in general, and I set out and critique these assumptions in the next section.

The market regulation thesis holds that Japanese economic successes were the normal result of incentives toward profitable economic activity which were generated by the market. Japanese manufacturing grew so rapidly because industrialists were disciplined by the market and met its challenges effectively. The argument is supported by evidence of considerable competition in Japanese domestic markets, where tremendous rivalry leads to cutthroat competition among manufacturers. Furthermore, national budget expenditures appear to impinge on the private economy much less in Japan than in other countries.[10] To many writers, this evidence suggests a freely operating market system in which the most efficient producer gradually emerges in the course of economic competition. Thus, the market regulation thesis rejects the idea that bureaucratic control might bring benefits because of the distortions state intervention would create in an efficiently operating market.[11] Consequently, the theory's proponents interpret bureaucratic initiatives in Japan as providing at best a supportive environment for growth. The real source of Japan's rapid growth was the ability of industrialists to respond to natural market cues.

Japanese economic research guided by the market regulation thesis has produced invaluable material concerning the pace and nature of the country's industrial development.[12] Applied to the issue of explaining rather than describing Japanese economic successes, however, the thesis encounters problems. The most serious objection is that references to market efficiency really provide no explanation for Japanese growth at all. If Japanese producers did a better job of responding to market demands, we need to know *why* they were more capable than manufacturers elsewhere. If the market operated more efficiently in Japan and hence disciplined producers more effectively, we again need to know why this was so. In this book I will show that "political factors"—in a special sense defined below—provided necessary background conditions for Japanese industrial successes. The market itself was a political creation. If we do not examine the foundations on which the market capacities and market structures affecting Japanese industrial development were built, we cannot attain an accurate and satisfactory comprehension of the nation's achievements.

The market regulation thesis tends to assume that economic activity is basically the same in all countries. Economic successes are thus the result of one nation's ability to play the industrial game better than others, either because it possesses a more efficient market or because its industrialists respond better to market challenges. Such a view downplays or even ignores significant differences, both in government initiatives and in industrial structure, between Japan and other countries.[13] Nor is it sensitive to such a striking phenomenon as the spectacular numerical expansion of small and medium-sized firms in Japan throughout the high-growth period.[14] As we will see, the influence of such firms in Japanese manufacturing has been dismissed as a product of retarded development and as a regrettable but comparatively unimportant form of exploitation practiced by larger, more modern firms. Similarly, many other compelling features of the Japanese economy have been ignored or explained away as incidental.

The market regulation thesis remains compelling, I believe, because most people unconsciously accept its assumption that industrial competition is fundamentally the same in all countries. If all industrial nations face basically the same challenges, then it is natural to ascribe success to the ability to meet these challenges. Hence the notion that Japanese markets are more efficient or the country's industrialists more attuned to rational market requirements has intuitive appeal. Much the same logic supports the bureaucratic regulation thesis. Both perspectives share a view of industrial development as progressive refinements in manufacturing efficiency; they disagree only on why the Japanese were apparently able to promote more advanced industrial practices.

The following sections discuss at length the consequences for both arguments if their basic assumptions about industrial growth should be false. There are compelling reasons for rejecting most of the assumptions the theories accept. If we do so, there are grounds for constructing a radically different account of the reasons for Japanese industrial achievement.

Industrial Convergence and Explanatory Theory

There are fundamental objections, as we have seen, to both the market regulation and the bureaucratic regulation theses. Each has problems of proof and of logic; neither typically examines Japanese economic expansion at the level of individual firms or factories. Yet the two theories continue to exert overwhelming influence on studies of Japan. What can account for this vitality? The answer is that both theories are given plausibility by a set of unstated assumptions about industrial convergence.

Although neither approach makes explicit reference to an underlying belief in economic convergence to sustain its arguments about Japanese success, both theses require convergence in order to sustain their picture of Japanese development. They exhibit a remarkable agreement about how economies develop and about the limited effect politics can have on industrial expansion. Both theories accept that in all countries subject to roughly similar technological circumstances, industrial practices will tend of necessity to converge; politics merely affects the speed with which industrialists are able to implement the most efficient practices.

Empirical evidence from Japan profoundly challenges these assumptions. I will show that during the high-growth period, Japanese manufacturing, in contrast to manufacturing in the United States, became decentralized. Apparently there is no necessary convergence between economies of more or less the same level of development. Furthermore, we will see that the Japanese compete as much by changing products and breaking up mass markets as on price grounds (the dominant competitive strategy in the United States). The importance of product competition in Japanese industry indicates that the country's manufacturers may have been pursuing goals different in kind from those adopted elsewhere. Together these observations call for a rejection of the convergence thesis and a new explanation for Japanese successes.

Industrial convergence is the idea that firms, industries, and national economies will tend over time to become more and more similar.[15] It is premised on the belief that there is one, most efficient solution to the problem of organizing individuals, capital, and raw materials to produce goods. The rigor of domestic and international competition, it is thought, creates a Darwinian struggle between companies and nations in which the most efficient producers triumph over the rest. Other manufacturers need first to emulate and then to surpass the most efficient producers in order to survive. Industrial history is thus the successive refinement of manufacturing techniques leading toward greater efficiency; indeed, most of us take for granted that the progression from primitive industry through feudalism, the industrial revolution, and the expansion of mass production to, in our age, factory automation expresses a natural expansion of the human ability to make goods efficiently. Every time a group of pioneering industrialists discovers the next method of increasing output and reducing costs, the rest of the world is compelled to follow.

Some form of this convergence thesis is essential to conventional explanations of Japanese success. Convergence excuses the typical absence of detailed manufacturing analysis because it guarantees, in a sense, that firm behavior or industry organization cannot vary significantly. All countries or producers in similar sectors eventually have to adopt the same manufacturing methods. Convergence also provides the logical foundation for the questions that researchers in both explanatory traditions pose. It leads to the assumption that competition is fundamentally an efficiency race; firms, sectors, and nations succeed or fail as a function of whether or not they anticipate and implement the most efficient manufacturing solutions. Consequently, *what* successful nations accomplish is never really in doubt: Japan grew rapidly because it was the most efficient producer. Research is therefore limited to *how* Japan became so adept at manufacturing. And this in turn has generated two main responses, one stressing the effects of a prescient bureaucracy, the other the discipline of an efficient market.

Industrial convergence is the basic principle that makes comprehensible the notion of a state-led response to late development, suggesting that whole societies need to adopt intrusive state institutions to catch up with the earlier developers.[16] That is, the same Darwinian struggle that forces firms to copy what industry leaders are doing or fail also requires that tardy developers make institutional innovations to meet industrial challenges from overseas. The pressure to achieve efficiency forced Japan to build a powerful bureaucracy, which then systematically inculcated reforms or innovations in production. This account of the Japanese bureaucracy and economy is informed by the history and process of industrial competition as shaped by convergence theory, and so is the account of presumed beneficial effects of state intervention. The argument is that industrial competition is fundamentally about cutting costs by improving efficiency; all producers look to discover and implement essentially the same techniques and strategies. Through subsidies, cartels, and planning the state gave Japanese manufacturers an edge by reducing costs that elsewhere the producers bore directly. Intervention thus produced a more efficient industrial system in Japan.

The market regulation thesis is also based on the notion of convergence.[17] It assumes that manufacturers everywhere, given similar industries and resources, will organize production the same way. In all cases, one most efficient solution will exist. This belief in an optimal solution to production problems makes sense only if one accepts that competition is limited to cutting costs through a small range of techniques. Moreover, it is through unfettered competition that this optimal production solution will be discovered, just as in the broader theory of industrial convergence, economic struggle creates a natural selection in which only the fittest—the most efficient—manufacturers survive. In sum, Japan's more effective market environment led to efficiency advances and hence to success.

Both arguments thus depend on convergence; indeed, there is a surprising amount of *agreement* between these two nominally opposed theories. They both view industrial competition as a matter of enhancing production efficiency. Each starts with the conviction that Japan succeeded because it solved the problem of inducing efficiency gains better than other nations. Furthermore, both approaches view the political process as something that leads to the creation of rules or the allocation of resources affecting the way industrialists organize production. What governments and bureaucracies do is establish laws regulating, for instance, labor or cartels—rule creation—or supply firms or industries with subsidies, loans, and other resources directly. Politics (battles over which rules or resources should support which individuals, firms, or industries) can only enhance or retard the development of manufacturing efficiency in the economy. The sole point of contention between the two arguments is whether political involvement was beneficial in the presumed triumph of efficient manufacturing in Japan. The bureaucratic regulation argument believes government initiatives were crucial; the market approach discounts such a claim. It is on this rather limited question, and on the identification of particularly efficient manufacturing practices resulting from either state activism or market discipline, that contemporary debate about Japan has turned.

If, in fact, compelling evidence existed that Japanese successes were based on a refining of techniques common to producers everywhere, such a focus of controversy might well exhaust the range of fruitful research possibilities. But even a cursory comparison of Japan with the United States, its principal competitor, indicates basic problems with the assumption that all economies are basically the same everywhere. During Japan's high-growth period the structure of its manufacturing industries appears to have broadly *diverged* from that of the United States. Japanese production increasingly took place in smaller firms, which employed the vast majority of the country's manufacturing work force and accounted for close to 60 percent of the national value added. In the United States, by contrast, the number of small firms stabilized as the largest producers employed most of the work force and accounted for close to 65 percent of manufacturing value added. Such evidence casts doubt on the notion that efficiency gains alone were the key to Japanese development; rather, it looks as though industrialists in America and Japan were organizing their economies according to radically different ideas about how best to produce goods. The product strategies of American and Japanese manufacturers also differed; U.S. producers sought stable product lines and economies of scale, whereas the Japanese were likely to change what they made, both more extensively and frequently. Both pieces of evidence resonate uneasily with the idea of convergence.

Consider first the divergence in the structure of American and Japanese manufacturing.[18] At the height of Japan's economic expansion, between 1954 and 1977, the number of manufacturing firms doubled from 429,000 to 720,000. Over the same period, the number of American manufacturing firms grew only slightly, from 288,000 to 350,000. Over time, these statistics show, Japanese manufacturing decentralized in smaller factory units, whereas the United States production was centralized in very large firms. By 1977, though its value was only 30 percent that of the United States, Japanese manufacturing took place in twice as many enterprises. The scale of Japanese production, averaged against total output, was close to one-sixth that of the United States.

This result cannot be explained away as a skewed statistical effect produced by a large number of insignificant, petty firms in Japan. Japanese smaller manufacturers employed the vast majority of the nation's workers and accounted for most of the value added in manufacturing industries. By 1977 over 70 percent of the Japanese workforce was employed in small and medium-sized firms employing under three hundred workers. Just 27–29 percent of manufacturing employees worked in large firms. In contrast, small and medium-sized firms employed just 40 percent of the work force in the United States; about 60 percent of American manufacturing workers, a large majority, worked for large companies. The divergent patterns of U.S. and Japanese employment remained stable between 1954 and 1977. Japanese production workers throughout the postwar period were, for the most part, employees in small and medium-sized firms, whereas those in America were laborers in large firms.

These figures might still be discounted if large firms in Japan, as in the United States, accounted for most of the nation's manufacturing output. Japanese smaller producers would then be a curious but inconsequential anomaly in an otherwise recognizable world of large firms pursuing scale economies. But from 1954 to 1977, the contribution of small and medium-sized firms to Japan's manufacturing value added rose from about 49 percent to close to 58 percent of total manufacturing. In contrast, small and medium firms accounted for approximately 35 percent of American value added in manufacturing, a share that remained steady throughout the postwar era. Thus large firms accounted for 65 percent of U.S. value added as compared with about 40 percent in Japan. Between 1954 and 1977, moveover, while this proportion was more or less stable in America, smaller manufacturers became markedly more important throughout the Japanese economy.

These data undercut the assumption of a basic congruence between industrial states of similar industrial capacity. Even highly aggregated economic statistics illustrate a profound dissimilarity between the world's two industrial giants, Japan and the United States. The assumption of convergence, and the bureaucratic and market approaches based on it, associate "modern" and more efficient production with additional manufacturing concentration and increases in scale. As Japan was registering impressive successes, however, it reversed this expected pattern of growth; the economy decentralized, and average production units *fell* in size. At the very least such evidence calls into question the idea that economic organization must be roughly similar everywhere as nations adopt most efficient solutions in the face of competition. Also, there are grounds for reopening the question of what Japanese producers actually accomplished, for it is possible that Japan's industry was organized along lines antithetical to those which were dominant in the American economy.

More evidence comes from the competitive strategies Japanese firms employed in the high-growth period. In many industries, Japanese manufacturers behaved as if product modification was more important than reducing costs. Certainly in standard components, such as semiconductors and steel, the Japanese competed strongly on the basis of price. During the high-growth period before the 1980s, however, Japanese manufacturers also pursued an aggressive strategy of constantly differentiating products to *break up* mass markets. This strategy poses a problem for any argument based on convergence because the flexible modification of products cuts against greater production efficiency through factory rationalization and scale economies, which convergence assumes to be the basis for industrial competition.

This Japanese orientation toward product modification can be seen even in sectors we think of as inherently mass markets, such as automobiles.[19] Though total Japanese auto production matched or exceeded American output by the late 1970s, Japanese firms continued to produce cars at an average unit volume between three and four times smaller than those of their American counterparts. The reason was that the Japanese wanted to offer a broader range of products for any given market segment. Furthermore, Japanese producers changed their products more extensively and more rapidly than did the Americans; their year-to-year design modifications were much more thorough. U.S. carmakers usually sought only cosmetic changes from year to year and made broad design modifications, which they hoped would suffice for years to come, only at widely spaced intervals. The "downsizing" movement in the wake of the oil crises of the 1970s exemplifies how Americans made wholesale changes only when previous designs proved utterly inappropriate. In contrast, the Japanese propensity to change significant components such as engines and body frames (as opposed to the body metal fitted over the frame) meant that Japanese carmakers manufactured any given component with a much lower lifetime unit volume. The Japanese strategy, in sum, was not so much to reduce costs through economies of scale as to make new products on a flexible basis.

This commitment to what was in effect continuous product development enabled the Japanese to compete on product grounds as well as on price grounds. Harsh experience at home and abroad drove home for Japanese automakers the lesson that they would be unsuccessful even with low prices if they could not also redefine the product niches occupied by foreign producers. One key event was the first Japanese effort to penetrate the American market, in the late 1950s and early 1960s. In that instance, Japanese firms actually did attempt to compete with American firms, by exporting a standard small car. The Americans beat them back by stripping their own low-end models and selling these cars at a temporary loss to keep Japan out of the U.S. market.

The American defensive strategy worked; Japanese firms were forced to quit the United States. Many influential Japanese auto strategists drew the lesson that only by continuously differentiating their products could they avoid price pressures from U.S. firms, which were then much larger. Competing on price grounds alone would be futile; U.S. firms would simply endure losses to preserve market shares. Furthermore, the Japanese firms reasoned, even if they successfully created a new but stable niche, the Americans would eventually drive them from it by developing competing models aggressively priced. The solution was a product line that shifted continually, so that American auto firms would not have a fixed target on which to focus their considerable mass production skills. The result, fortuitously concurrent with the rapid gasoline price hikes of the 1970s, was a successful effort to appeal to U.S. consumers with autos that differed from American models, including recreational vehicles and cars with high fuel-economy qualities, pollution-control capabilities, and the like. Initial failures in international competition led the Japanese to modify their approach to mass production, introducing greater flexibility.[20]

Competition among the Japanese themselves exacerbated this concern with product flexibility. Not only was standardization abandoned as a strategy to deal with the Americans, it also proved impractical at home. First, many of the incentives toward price competition in international markets were minimized in competition between domestic firms. A Japanese producer might enjoy a labor cost advantage over Americans or Europeans, but such cost differentials were more or less equalized at home. Hence incentives to compete by differentiating products were as great as, or greater than, incentives to compete by reducing costs in the huge domestic market.

Second, for reasons that occupy the body of this book, it proved easier for new firms to enter existing markets in Japan than in the United States. And Japanese newcomers almost always made their market entry with significantly new products. In autos one example of this strategy was the micromini cars introduced by Honda and Suzuki in the late 1960s to challenge—successfully—the existing carmakers' share of domestic sales. New entrants broke up or redefined mass markets, leading to extensive product change in Japan as a competitive strategy. In contrast, U.S. auto manufacturing was committed to standardization and thus to cost reduction rather than product change.

In this book I show that the auto industry is but one example of Japan's more general concentration on product rather than price competition. The ability to manufacture flexibly was a dominant part of the industrial strategy of Japanese firms in the high-growth period. Frequently the drive to create new products led the Japanese to define entirely new markets that other nations had overlooked or ignored. Price competition was certainly an important part of Japanese domestic and international strategy, but so too was finding and exploiting market niches. This additional objective does not fit well with traditional understandings of industrial development. Firms in Japan apparently sacrificed scale economies for rapid and extensive product changes more readily than did firms in the United States; the organizational, training, and design costs associated with continuous product change all reduced their price advantages in mass markets. It follows that price efficiency could not have been the sole or even the main concern of many Japanese producers. Hence the notion of convergence assumes a view of competition that is at best too limited.

Statistical evidence of a structural dissimilarity between the United States and Japan is accompanied by a strategic divergence between the two nations. These findings reinforce the idea that some of the assumptions behind the bureaucratic and market regulation arguments may be incorrect. Our cursory examination of Japanese economic structure and competition suggests that the country's successes may not have been based on principles common to all relatively advanced industrial nations, nor were advances in efficiency alone the primary competitive basis of its manufacturers' success. Such conclusions require us to reject the idea of convergence itself; we need a different understanding of how economies develop and grow.

Politics and Economic Change: The Challenge to Convergence

Recent economic history research in Europe and America has led to findings that challenge the idea of a more or less fixed pattern to economic development. Critics of convergence have been motivated by dissatisfaction with the overly rigid treatment of industrial change in the Marxist tradition as well as by an unease with the assumptions behind neoclassical social science. Their most significant proposition is that there were, and there continue to be, several equally plausible, modern, and productive ways of organizing an economy with a given resource base. Societies are not forced by competition toward a single, most efficient outcome. Rather, a complex political process determines what form of production a given industry or country will adopt.

To formulate a new explanation for Japanese successes, I draw heavily on the work of Michael Piore and Charles Sabel, two American social scientists who have been instrumental in weaving together the results of isolated individual research into a coherent argument.[21] Two facets of their work are of particular importance for my purposes: their description of equally possible industrial alternatives, which they refer to as mass production and flexible production; and their view of how politics generates specific industrial outcomes in actual cases. After discussing the distinction between mass and flexible production, I describe Piore and Sabel's conception of politics and how it may be said to determine an economy's form of production. Politics, we will see, has a broad meaning in Piore and Sabel's treatment, and it affects much more than the relative efficiency of the economy: it can completely change the way societies produce goods.

Our starting point is the distinction between mass and flexible production. (I treat the two manufacturing strategies in ideal typical form, exaggerating what occurs in the real world so as to make organizing principles clear.) Mass production is the attempt to produce a single good at the highest possible volume to reduce costs through economies of scale. Flexible production is the effort to make an ever-changing range of goods to appeal to specialized needs and tastes with tailored designs. A mass producer wants to sell a standard product to a wide range of users who sacrifice special requirements for lower price; a flexible manufacturer seeks to create specialized product niches by selling individually tailored goods for which, it is assumed, a consumer will pay a premium.

Mass production and flexible production require different skills in the factory, different strategies of using labor and machines, and different ways of integrating other firms into the manufacturing process. A mass producer wants to fix the design of a product so that costs can be reduced by rationalizing the factory. One way is to break down manufacturing tasks into ever more specific operations until a specialized machine can be substituted for a human worker. Another is to control closely the autonomy and scope of workers who cannot be replaced by machinery, reducing costs through discipline and supervision.

A mass production strategy thus carries several consequences. First, the skill level of the work force continually declines as each laborer becomes responsible for an ever more limited repertoire of operations. The more a good is standardized, the more limited individual responsibilities in the factory become. Second, production machinery becomes more specialized until gradually each piece of equipment is dedicated to a single manufacturing task along the assembly line. Hence as worker skill declines, the machinery becomes more specialized; the entire factory is itself dedicated to volume production of a single good. Finally, the firm has no need to maintain close technical ties with suppliers, because the comparatively static design of its product limits supply issues to the matter of price alone. Once the firm announces part specifications, outside suppliers compete to meet demand, mainly by reducing costs. The mass producer thus runs its factory through a hierarchical system of management, adopting strategies that deskill the work force, require dedicated, single-purpose equipment, and involve arm's-length dealings with other suppliers or manufacturers.

A flexible producer, by contrast, would be crippled by the rigidities inherent in mass production. The essence of flexible manufacturing is to make a wide variety of goods tailored to specific needs. To do so, a flexible producer requires a high level of skill in the work force, to facilitate rapid changes in manufacturing processes and to reduce oversight costs; workers need to be able to make changes on their own, lest the burden on top management inhibit the firm's ability to meet or create new demand. Hence worker supervision is much less extensive than under mass production, and the number of tasks a worker must master is always expanding. Furthermore, because product designs are constantly changing, the flexible producer must rely on general-purpose machinery. Single-purpose machinery would be much too inflexible to permit rapid design shifts, and too costly because dedicated machinery might not adapt to tasks involved in making new goods. Finally, to coordinate parts for new products, or to make it possible to integrate a new part design into a finished product, flexible producers require very close technical contacts with other firms. Frequently they subordinate price issues to design or manufacturing matters. In sum, a flexible firm adopts strategies that require a highly skilled work force operating with minimal supervision, general-purpose machinery, and close coordination with other producers.

This distinction between mass and flexible production is recognized in conventional economics, but the usual approach is to treat flexible manufacturers as remnants of an earlier technology or to regard flexible techniques as regrettably unavoidable in markets that by their nature are too small or shifting to permit scale economies. In most cases, however, mass production seems the obvious solution to production problems. It is simply more efficient than any other way of making goods and hence is the historically dominant form of industrial organization. Competition has forced nation after nation to adopt mass production, whose gradual diffusion is the motor of industrial convergence.

Piore and Sabel dispute this view. They argue that although material and resource constraints may limit the freedom to choose different manufacturing strategies, the degree of constraint involved is far smaller than contemporary development theory supposes. Most cases present a range of equally modern and efficient possibilities, ranging along a continuum from pure mass production to pure flexible production. In real life an industrialist or a factory worker has no fixed criteria for deciding which of several possibilities is "best." Although mass production is efficient with respect to price, for instance, it is ineffective in coping with changing demand. But though a flexible firm might be better able to adjust to demand shifts, it may sacrifice low-cost production and scale economies by pursuing flexible manufacturing. Choosing a type of production depends on how people evaluate the market context around them, but they have no guarantee that they interpret that context correctly. Industrial choice cannot be reduced to the inevitable discovery of the optimal production solution in the face of Darwinian competition.

Instead, because material or market constraints communicate a fundamental ambiguity to individuals involved in industry, Piore and Sabel contend that the choices people actually make must be the product of other factors. The additional criteria brought to bear on manufacturing decisions are people's orientations regarding just or appropriate activity in the factory, the market, and the economy as a whole. Piore and Sabel call the definition of the set of beliefs and rights affecting permissible industrial choices "politics," for that definition results from struggles throughout society to work out a systematic way of structuring social relations. Political events thus include such matters as the resolution of factory control problems between workers and managers, and struggles between firms regarding appropriate market coordination, as well as regulatory debate about the role of the state in the economy. At all levels of society politics shapes the content of the industrial rights and rules to which people resort in deciding how an economy should be organized.

"Politics" as employed in this manner has a special meaning, one that at first glance may seem unfamiliar or counterintuitive. In most of social science, politics is a system that allocates resources and creates rules. Political factors in industrial studies are usually limited to the overt actions of organs of the state, such as the legislature, the bureaucracy, and the like. The economy is thought to be governed by principles beyond the scope of political debate; politics can affect only the relative success of industrialists trying to follow those principles.

If we view politics as the fundamental orientation people possess about justice, appropriate behavior, and rights throughout society, however, even seemingly minor workplace struggles or conflicts between large firms and subcontractors about legitimate association have crucial importance in shaping industrial order. The way individuals, and people collectively in firms, industries, and society as a whole, define the content of the myriad rights bound up in an economy is also political; it is not defined or constrained by material or market circumstances beyond relatively loose boundaries. As the definition of economic rights varies, so too will incentives to adopt some variant of mass or of flexible production. In this view, then, an economic order is the result of countless political choices made more or less consciously throughout the industrial system; it is an artifact of the definition of justice and fairness people adopt as they encounter the workplace and the market.

Consequently, the politics of resource allocation or rule creation (on which most contemporary studies focus) is much less important than the politics affecting the definition of rights in the workplace and throughout industry. If Piore and Sabel are right, to understand an economy we need to examine the creation of ideologies through conflict in areas of society most people do not think of as "political" in the usual sense. Debate about the appropriate use of machinery, or whether workers should have the right to broad training, or the autonomy of small-firm suppliers, may strike many as technical matters. But if we accept that material constraints are looser than the idea of convergence supposes, then we must also accept that fundamental decisions about market strategy and workplace organization must in part result from politics. And if we ignore the creation of ideologies that inform choices about organizing production, then we will be unable to explain or anticipate how a given economy actually operates.

The ideas workers develop about fairness in the factory, for example, will constrain or enhance trust between managers and employees. Combined with the ideological residue of countless other political battles, such ideas will lead to greater or lesser incentives toward mass or flexible production. Workers in one setting may fight to preserve their place in the factory through the retention of specific job classifications, thereby making the attempt to redefine work continually, as in flexible production, more difficult.[22] In similar circumstances other workers may see one of their essential rights as being able to learn new work and plan factory operations autonomously, making it more likely that some sort of flexible production would develop.

The basic claim in this view of politics is that the beliefs workers and managers have about fundamental rights cannot be reduced to material circumstances; beliefs will vary even under identical resource constraints. The basic industrial approach of any society is founded on the definition of the content of rights that bear on the workplace, the interpretation of the market, and relations between firms. Thus the politics between industrial actors are as important as the role or function of the state. National strategies such as protectionism or small business finance will lead to different outcomes in different nations, depending on the definition of the economic rights of the affected industrial actors. In turn, the industrial order itself must be comprehended as the outcome of this definition of rights throughout society, this politics. The difficulty with this argument, discussed below, is how to study the effects and creation of an economic order if politics at so many levels determines the result. For now, however, I note merely that politics can be conceived of as a part of industrial society much more pervasive, and with more profound effects, than the idea of convergence will permit.

Let us now reconsider the idea of convergence which lies behind the bureaucratic and market regulation theses about Japanese success. The idea of convergence begins with the assumption that economies tend to develop toward the same outcome, which is defined by the most efficient way of producing goods within a given set of resource constraints. It holds that there *is* a particular, optimal solution. The economy develops as people respond to problems the market poses. At the same time, however, although industrial development is more or less autonomous, politics—the process by which the action of the state allocates rules or resources—can have an effect. Contemporary observers agree that political decisions can retard or enhance the rate at which most efficient solutions are implemented; debate centers on whether state intervention helps or hinders the quest for efficiency.

But the critique of convergence theory I developed above views the material constraints on industrial choices as basically loose; within broad limits, societies can address the problem of what to produce and how to make goods in different ways. Two general solutions are mass production and flexible production. Both methods of producing goods are efficient and modern, but they involve divergent approaches to factory management, market strategies, and technical development. Because this approach recognizes a much larger range of possible ways to organize an economy, the ultimate outcome depends on the resolution of political battles fought throughout society. "Politics" is the definition of basic ideas about justice, fairness, and propriety as made by individuals and groups involved in production; it encompasses but transcends the idea that politics is something the state does in making rules or distributing resources. Political conflict thus determines the nature of the industrial system itself, the range of possible outcomes between pure mass production and flexible production; it is much more important than merely retarding or enhancing the adoption of "naturally" efficient solutions.

The view of industrial development proposed by Piore and Sabel makes it possible to build a new explanation of Japanese economic achievements, one not based on assumptions of convergence. The bureaucratic and market regulation theses make sense only if we believe implicitly in the idea of industrial convergence. But if in most material settings there are equally plausible manufacturing alternatives, and if the politics defining people's basic sense of fairness and justice promotes the adoption of one industrial system over another, then neither the bureaucratic nor the market regulation thesis is appealing. Both tend to ignore the details of industrial activity in Japan, because they assume factory practices are basically the same everywhere. If this assumption is unwarranted, however, we need to look again at Japan to see whether the country's industrial organization is merely a more efficient version of practices common everywhere or something rather different. Again, in considering politics neither argument looks beyond the state, but if political conflict at the lowest levels of society profoundly affects industrial order, we need to expand dramatically the scope of the "political" in explaining Japanese economic achievements.

Industrial Alternatives and Japanese Economic Success

The main theme of this book is that Japan's economic successes can be explained primarily as the result of a greater diffusion of flexible manufacturing strategies in the country than in other nations. In Japan a large number of manufacturing enterprises produced goods according to flexible principles. In the United States, a contrasting case, both prevailing industrial ideology and actual manufacturing practices have reflected a much deeper commitment to mass production as the basis for organizing the economy. Japan's divergence from industrial strategies that were dominant in the United States was, as I will argue, a very significant, if not the most important, cause of its postwar achievements.

Several competitive advantages resulted from the wider adoption of flexible production in Japan. First, Japanese manufacturers could compete through product differentiation as much as through price differentiations. They could offer goods that appealed to more specialized tastes, thus drawing demand away from the standardized products made by mass producers elsewhere. Such a strategy, as in the Japanese incursion into the U.S. auto market, is effective because mass producers cannot readily change products to meet new demand; their labor, machines, and organization become fixed on manufacturing one basic type of good. The only response a mass producer can make to a product challenge—apart from appealing to the state for trade sanctions against the flexible manufacturer—is to cut prices. But even if lowering prices is economically feasible, it does not guarantee success where flexible firms offer products so appealing that consumers perceive standardized goods as inadequate. Japanese manufacturing was decentralized among many flexibly organized firms, and so Japanese producers could change goods easily and compete by offering new products. The result was a partial breaking up of mass markets into specialized segments, which Japanese manufacturers could exploit and to which mass producers were less able to adapt.

The second advantage was the ability to launch completely new products more easily than producers elsewhere and to create new markets from overlooked technology. This book details many instances in which small Japanese firms launched billion-dollar industries from *American* designs or technology that U.S. industrialists had ignored. The Japanese political economy developed a network of financial and organizational practices that supported the continuous creation of small, flexible firms throughout the high-growth period. Compared to their competitors in other nations, particularly the United States, Japanese entrepreneurs faced low startup costs that made it easier for them to use unexploited technologies in the global marketplace. Hence skilled entrepreneurs with access to underutilized technology could quickly set up operations and enter the market.

The system of small-firm support also affected product innovation in existing enterprises, because the diffusion of flexible firms in Japan made it less costly even for large and established manufacturers to adopt new designs or ideas. Most large firms spread production among smaller-scale suppliers, each of which was pursuing, to a greater or lesser extent, flexible production strategies. The overall costs of new product development were thus reduced because firms could adapt more readily to new parts designs or even generate such designs themselves. In contrast, the high startup costs and rigidities imposed by mass production in America cut against rapid implementation of new designs or technologies. More flexible startup or existing firms in Japan could handle products with initially unclear or apparently limited appeal. The result was that Japanese manufacturers brought into the market opportunities overlooked or too costly to explore elsewhere, frequently generating enormous profits.

Third, the flexible sector in Japan created demand for unique goods, in turn promoting the continued expansion of flexible techniques while providing specialty firms with lucrative markets. This effect was particularly pronounced in the machinery industries, where the growth of Japan's smaller-scale manufacturers brought equipment makers to build such unique products as small computer-controlled lathes, milling machines, and machining centers. In some cases the new equipment itself became hugely successful in international markets; unique Japanese demand led to the creation of valuable global markets. But an additional benefit was the advancement of the small-scale sector's ability to realize its strategic objectives. Each time new machinery was tailored to meet the needs of Japan's flexible users, the overall ability of domestic firms to continue to pursue product competition or to create new markets was enhanced. And because specially designed equipment made the flexible sector more competitive, it fostered the small firms' capacity to pay for even more exotic and useful tools. Demand for better manufacturing products thus created a cycle in which the ability to use new equipment technology spurred the overall flexibility and strategic competitiveness of Japanese manufacturers.

Fourth, the Japanese economy in general was enabled to adjust better to demand cycles and economic crises; responses were more stable and less socially disruptive than elsewhere. The expansion of small-scale flexible firms in Japan gave manufacturers a wide range of options for coping with the demand shifts, materials shortages, foreign competition, and other disruptions that chronically plague industry. Japanese firms could not only cut prices or curtail production but also shift production to sectors less affected by economic reversals or stimulate demand by creating new markets. And by relying on product design as well as price cutting to deal with crises, the more flexible firms could reduce their exposure to wage pressure from lower-cost producers abroad. Foreign manufacturers, even those that possessed cost advantages, could not bring a cheaper, directly competitive product to market because designs were shifting continuously. In contrast, firms adapted to mass production were very rigid; they could respond to economic disruptions only by lowering prices to try to stimulate sales, by reducing operations, resulting in layoffs and costly excess capacity, or by cutting wages.

Because Japanese producers could respond to demand shifts with a greater variety of tactics, the country was affected much less than the United States by postwar economic disturbances. This effect was particularly pronounced during the two oil crises, as chapter 4 shows: Japanese firms were able to profit from demand shifts in autos and electronic machinery, while American firms were plunged into adjustment struggles they have yet to resolve. (A prototypical form of Japan's postwar combination of flexible and mass producers had also permitted more effective responses before the war, as during the Great Depression.) In addition, as manufacturing flexibility helped insulate Japanese manufacturers from price challenges mounted by low-cost foreign producers, so it also reduced the stiff cost competition faced by mass producers elsewhere. Adjustment crises were more easily managed in Japan because of the responses made possible by the expansion of smaller-scale, flexible manufacturers throughout the economy. Thus, in turn, labor conflict and corporate disruption were minimized.

A fifth advantage of flexibility for Japanese manufacturing was the striking gains in product quality that the country's producers achieved. The emphasis on producing new and changing goods contributed to more expert manufacturing. As discussed above, workers in flexibly organized factories must be much better trained than their counterparts in mass-production firms. In a more flexible economy, as a consequence, blue-collar workers must have a better grasp of the manufacturing process and must be able to find solutions to problems independently. Indeed, comparative labor surveys have consistently shown that in equivalent jobs, Japanese workers *are* much better trained and more independent than American employees.[23] One would expect a more highly skilled and autonomous work force to produce better-quality goods, and that is what happened.

Moreover, changing output to meet or stimulate new demand requires that each firm, enterprise, or division within a larger factory become expert in specific manufacturing operations. Though flexible firms by their nature seek to adopt new or unexplored manufacturing techniques, they tend to specialize within a range and to amass expert knowledge of manufacturing processes within their particular specialty. They develop unequaled expertise in applying manufacturing technologies to new uses or product designs. In the ideal type of a flexible economy, finished goods are assembled from individual parts each of which is made by an expert firm with the highest level of skill in its field. To the extent that Japanese manufacturing approached this ideal, it did so by promoting accuracy and quality through the specialization and high levels of worker skill necessary to implement flexible production strategies on a wide scale.

Finally, the support mechanisms for small manufacturers dramatically enhanced rates of market entry. In effect, barriers to the creation of manufacturing firms were lower in Japan. In any given sector existing producers constantly faced challenges from new firms seeking a share of the market. This intense competition is discussed in detail in chapters 4 and 5; for now the important point to note is that the dynamics of rapid market entry reduced some of the price disadvantages involved in flexible production. One would expect the sacrifice of scale economies inherent in flexible manufacturing to impose a significant cost burden on the Japanese. But in addition to lower wage and capital rates—which in any case, I will suggest, played a much less important role than is usually imagined—the intensity of competition reduced production cost penalties as well. Consequently, Japanese manufacturers could offer goods with specialized characteristics at prices that did not sigificantly reduce affordability.

Thus the extensive development of flexibility in Japanese manufacturing led to numerous competitive advantages that help account for rapid industrial expansion. Nevertheless, it is important not to overstate the differences between Japan and other nations. Of course, Japanese industries and firms engage in mass production and compete on price grounds. Nor is flexible production unique to Japan. All national economies preserve some mix of manufacturing systems; differences between nations are matters of degree. In industries such as computers and specialty steel, American production has been marked by flexible principles; parts of Italy, Germany, and France have seen the emergence of industrial regions composed of firms even more flexible than those in Japan.[24] Indeed, certain European manufacturers have been successful against the Japanese precisely because they compete more effectively on the basis of flexible production strategies, such as product differentiation; they beat the Japanese at their own game.

Yet during the high-growth period the Japanese achieved much of their success in autos, electronics, and machinery, industries that most European and American producers thought of as "natural" mass markets. Mass production techniques were first refined to produce goods for these markets in the United States and were later adopted, albeit with significant modifications, by the Europeans.[25] The Japanese economy developed in such a way as to preclude the ready implementation of mass production, even though a major objective of the bureaucrats was to emulate the American model. Consequently, industries treated as mass markets in other countries preserved the flexible alternative in Japan.

Japanese manufacturing was so heavily influenced by flexible production principles for reasons that lie in the contextual politics of the country's industrial development. If, as Piore and Sabel argue, political events structure economic order, then the greater expansion in Japan of small-scale firms pursuing flexible strategies was the product of a definition of rights and substantive justice accepted throughout Japanese society. In this book I point to only a few important events that created such rights: the resolution of conflicts regarding bureaucratic influence in the economy and its effect on the allocation of financial resources; the changing relationship between large firms and small suppliers; the definition and development of career goals involving self-employment by blue-collar employees in smaller firms; the coordination struggles between members of industry "cartels"; and the growth of geographical regions of high-tech, small-scale manufacturers. Each of these events led the individuals, firms, and institutions involved to define an appropriate or "just" way of structuring economic relationships. Together with many other events we will be unable to discuss, these episodes formed a set of substantive rules and rights, which led to the creation of institutions and practices that fostered a greater degree of flexible production in Japan than elsewhere.

Many readers might prefer a more precise correlation between particular outcomes and specific causal factors. But politics as defined by Piore and Sabel makes it impossible, indeed misleading, to identify some single set of factors that completely explains the Japanese case. They argue that political struggle throughout society cumulatively defines the rights that structure an economy toward either mass or flexible production. A focus on only one factor, for example a government strategy or a style of firm management, would be inconsistent with this understanding of politics. If we do not take note of all developments defining rights and affecting behavior elsewhere in the economy, any single factor or even set of factors cannot lead to a predictable outcome. Yet to allude to these collateral influences without systematically linking them to a larger theory would make every explanation ad hoc.

Does not such a claim appear to make *any* effective argument about causal factors impossible? If specific factors cannot be identified to explain particular results, how can the argument be tested? My account of Japan can be evaluated against competing claims first by learning how the Japanese economy actually operates and then by trying to organize findings into a coherent scheme of explanation. The test of a theory is whether it can accommodate findings consistently, ignores them, or makes them inexplicable. If we view Japan as a place where opportunities for flexible production were great, and then relate factory practices, regulatory battles, and industry strategies to this development, I believe we can achieve a consistent account of the nation's economic success. Furthermore, the advantage gained by accurately describing and explaining many important features of the Japanese economy far outweighs any difficulty in providing a complete causal account of its development.

In sum, both the bureaucratic and the market regulation theses assume that Japanese industry is basically the same as elsewhere, only more efficient. By contrast, I argue that Japanese industry diverged from other cases: the flexible manufacturing option was developed more fully in Japan. I challenge both the claim of the bureaucratic regulation thesis that the state coordinated the attainment of greater efficiency in Japan, and the contention of the market regulation thesis that competitive cues alone led to an optimal outcome. Rather, the cumulative effect of political developments throughout Japanese society made it impossible for the state to coordinate the economy as bureaucrats wanted; at the same time those developments also provided the political, social, and financial prerequisites for the competitive market behavior that the Japanese exhibited. That is, the bureaucratic regulation thesis is substantially wrong, the market approach incomplete. It is only by viewing Japanese development as the consequence of myriad political struggles affecting industrial rights that important features of the Japanese industrial system may be addressed, let alone explained.

The Development of the Japanese Machinery Industry

One way to assess the validity of the arguments proposed to account for Japanese economic achievement is to apply them to a representative case. Obviously it would be impossible to treat in any detail the entire industrial history of Japan; in dealing with aggregate statistics, policies, and economic strategies we would lose analytical clarity. A more manageable scheme is to see how well each argument explains one representative instance of Japanese economic growth to build a more general interpretation from the results. In this book I focus on the Japanese machine tool industry.[26] I assess the extent to which each explanation can account for the rapid development of numerical controlled (NC) or computer-guided machinery in the country.[27] For several reasons this industry is especially suited for studying different theories of Japanese success.

The growth of the Japanese machinery industry exhibits all of the traits generally associated with the country's advance. Machine tool output in Japan increased spectacularly from 1930 to 1983, as Figure 1.1 shows. Over that period the Japanese machine tool sector recovered from near total devastation to a position of global dominance. Machinery production experienced a small wartime expansion in the 1940s, and spectacularly increased between 1955 and 1983 as output rose from ¥3.4 billion to ¥800 billion. The machinery industry is thus one of the typical "miracle" sectors of the postwar Japanese economy.

The machinery industry achieved these gains, moreover, by transforming low-tech products copied from foreign designs into unique goods. It did so with the most sophisticated electronic equipment, and the central development was the diffusion of NC tools in the 1970s, when Japanese producers recorded their biggest gains. By 1981, as Figure 1.2 illustrates, NC machinery accounted for 51 percent of the value of Japanese output. Upgrading and new product definition were thus important in machinery. And just as with smaller, fuel-efficient cars, so product innovations in machine tools brought about export successes. By the late 1970s exports accounted for more than 40 percent of the value of the industry's output, and 70 percent of export volume was NC equipment.[28]

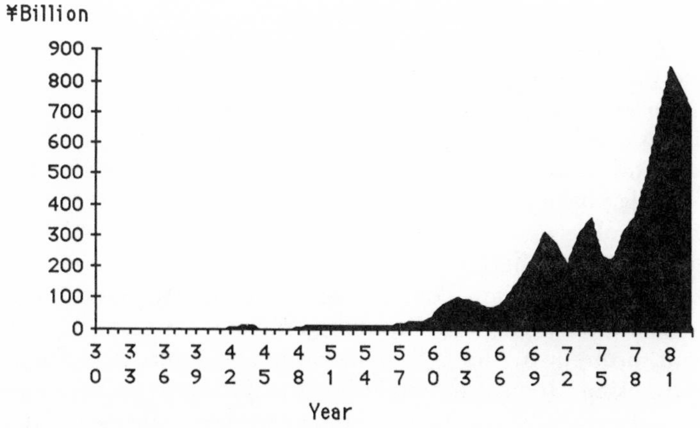

Figure 1.1. Japanese Machine Tool Output, 1930–1983 (in ¥ billion)
SOURCE: Compiled from Nihon Kōsaku Kikai Kōgyōkai (Japan Machine Builders Association), *Hahanaru kikai: San-jū nen no ayumi* (Mother machines: A 30 year history) (Tokyo: Seisanzai Marketing, 1982), pp. 47 and 99.

In sum, the Japanese NC machinery industry has much in common with other sectors that achieved postwar successes. A handful of electronics and machinery firms made their initial NC products in the early 1960s, religiously copying American designs. But Japanese manufacturers concentrated on developing small, easily programmable, general-purpose machines catering to small-scale, flexible operations. U.S. manufacturers all but ignored this market; they viewed NC

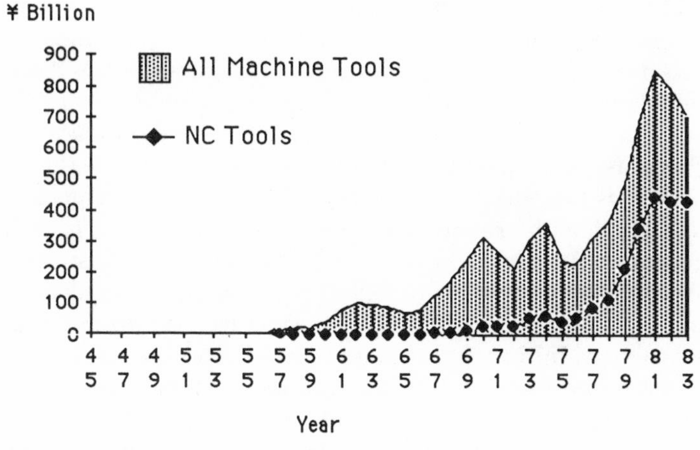

Figure 1.2. NC Share of Total Japanese Machine Tool Output, 1945–1983 (in ¥ billion)
SOURCE: Same as for Figure 1.1, pp. 112–113.

equipment as a big-ticket specialty item for large clients who could afford the price.[29] At home and abroad Japanese NC machine tools turned out to be a smash hit.

Japanese product innovations profoundly affected the American machinery industry, which, like U.S. leaders in autos, steel, electronics, and all too many other cases, had once enjoyed global prestige and regular balance of payments surpluses. In 1982 the American machine tool sector recorded its first payments deficit, which topped $1 billion. As in other affected industries, the industry's national organization, the Machine Tool Builders' Association, asked for import relief, charging Japan with dumping and unfair practices. A related law suit, brought by the U.S. firm Houdaille Industries, was an uncompromising attempt to show that the Japanese government had organized a machine tool cartel that had targeted America with devastating effect.[30] Those who viewed Japanese successes as a function of illicit efforts to cut costs rallied around the Houdaille action; the firm's lawyer, Richard Copaken, was featured in the introductory chapter of *The Japanese Conspiracy,* a book widely used in congressional debate by the so-called Japan-bashers in industry and government.[31]

NC machine tools thus form a perfect example of a common pattern in American-Japanese trade competition. American entrepreneurs develop new technologies that have several possible product applications. U.S. producers rapidly settle on one standard notion of how to use the new technology. In contrast, after a short learning period Japanese firms, using the same basic technology, begin to enter domestic and international markets with products that appeal to overlooked groups of consumers. As Japanese firms convert latent demand into secure product niches, they expand their market share and begin to challenge American firms directly. U.S. companies cannot to meet the new competition; as America suffers setbacks, the result is a highly charged international atmosphere.

NC tools are a representative case of Japanese economic success, and a focus on the industry makes it possible to evaluate the competing theories advanced to account for Japan's achievements. Their history exhibits the rapid introduction and redefinition of new technology characteristic of Japanese advances and the adjustment problems this strategy posed for U.S. firms. Why did the Japanese machinery sector grow as it did? Did bureaucrats push producers toward new products, for instance, NC tools, while centralizing production to enhance economies of scale? Can we comprehend developments in the Japanese machinery industry as the product of "natural" market forces? Or did contextual politics provide for the expansion of more flexible firms in Japan, thus leading to the ability to build new products while simultaneously creating a market for their use?

There are further good reasons for studying the machine tool industry. The industry has been subject to all of the major policy initiatives commonly cited as generating the Japanese miracle, and so it is particularly useful for investigating the bureaucratic regulation thesis. In the 1930s machinery producers (together with the aircraft, steel, petroleum, automobile, shipbuilding, and light metals industries) were the target of special legislation that aimed to centralize industries for military purposes.[32] These industries would later comprise the core of postwar Japanese manufacturing; the prewar legislation was the bureaucracy's first concerted attempt to shape the economy.

In the postwar period machinery producers again were affected by government economic policies. From 1956 to 1971 the industry was subject to the Temporary Measures for the Promotion of the Machinery Industry Law, which authorized MITI to plan, set up cartels, and use fiscal incentives to promote selected industries. The law was extended three times. After it finally expired, a new bill was passed, the Temporary Measures Law for the Advancement of Designated Electrical and Machinery Industries which was in force from 1971 to 1978. This law, which listed machine tools as one of its targets, again provided MITI with a panoply of powers to promote various industries. Finally, in 1978, the Temporary Measures for the Promotion of Information Machinery Law was passed. The bill's language tempered MITI powers of regulation, because of trade friction, but once again the law was designed to promote special equipment, and among the targets it listed were NC machines.

That the machine tool industry has been a part of almost every major regulatory effort in Japan since the 1930s, when industrial policy first emerged, allows us to focus on the history of an *industrial sector* rather than the history of policy legislation. To study policies in isolation from the industrial and political context in which they were formed and administered is to assert what must be proved—that legislation administered by MITI is evidence of successful, independent government guidance. But if we do not carefully examine industrial politics and concrete market responses, we cannot exclude counterarguments. For example, policies may have been passed by the legislature but ignored by recalcitrant private interests. Or the policies may have been designed by the firms they were supposed to control, so that the bureaucracy was an intervening rather than an authoritative actor. Finally, even if MITI did independently design and administer policies, industrial transformations in the economy may have been due to factors completely divorced from government activities. The fact that the bureaucratic regulation argument cannot exclude any of these hypotheses is its greatest weakness.

A good example of this problem is Chalmers Johnson's influential work *MITI and the Japanese Miracle.* Johnson argues that because the locus of Japanese economic decision making is in the bureaucracy, the nation's economy is ultimately political in nature. But his exclusive focus on MITI precludes his appreciation of the political roots of industrial planning. The government, he claims, can wield the power of an "absolutist state" as its "elite bureaucracy . . . makes most major decisions . . . controls the national budget and is the source of all major policy innovations."[33] In this view, MITI's policies have no background; they spring fully formed from the desks of the relevant industrial bureau.

Yet Johnson's research is filled with instances where political opposition led to the transformation of MITI's plans or their wholesale rejection. He shows that business came to dominate prewar regulatory institutions after only token bureaucratic resistance; that even in the midst of war private firms shot down proposals for military economic leadership; that after the war severe political opposition sank a number of MITI structural or trade initiatives, most notably in the auto industry; and finally, that the bureaucracy suffered an unbroken string of failures trying to obtain legislative approval for expanded powers.[34] Carefully examined, the record Johnson himself provides gives little support for the idea that MITI and its predecessors guided development. Indeed, it seems more likely that at best, policies resulted from a compromise forced on the bureaucracy, or even that business constrained the state. Johnson's research design, a historical account of MITI's internal politics, cannot falsify any of these propositions.

To avoid such problems, I examine the historical interaction between the Japanese bureaucracy and the machine tool industry from the 1930s to the present. In the development of a particular industry it is possible to compare what actually took place in the economy with bureaucratic efforts to modify business behavior, and so to determine the effectiveness of policies. It is also possible to find out who actually makes policy and how the contents of various initiatives come to be defined. By studying the machinery sector in detail we can assess how bureaucratic plans were implemented, what influence they exerted on industrial growth, and where they came from.

The machine tool industry is also important because the development of NC equipment is clearly linked to the phenomenal influence of small firms in Japan. The expansion of small, flexible firms is crucial; it demands to be explained in any account of Japanese development. The challenge is especially great in the machinery sector, where medium-scale firms predominate; among the 1,918 firms involved in Japanese machine tool production in 1982, only thirty-three

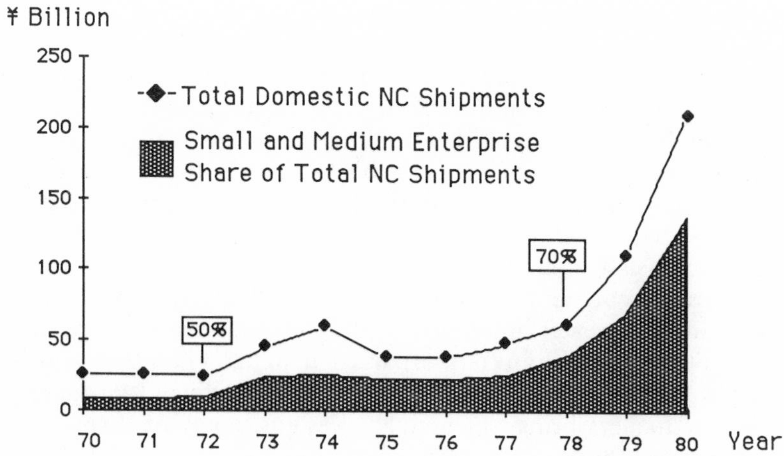

Figure 1.3. Share of Small and Medium Enterprises in NC Domestic Sales, Japan, 1970–1980 (in ¥ billion)
SOURCE: Compiled from Kokumin Kinyū Kōkō Chosabu. (People's Finance Corp. Survey Group); *Nihon no chūshō kigyō kōgyō, no. 10* (Japan's small business manufacturing, no. 10) (Tokyo: Chūshō Kigyō Research Center, 1982), p. 10.

employed more than three hundred employees.[35] Moreover, most of these large companies were separate internal divisions of huge enterprises such as Mitsubishi, which had established smaller, specialized manufacturing operations.

Much more compelling is the fact that small and medium-sized Japanese enterprises purchase close to 70 percent of total domestic NC output; the industry's main consumers are small-scale factories. In the United States, where increasing factory scale is thought to correlate with greater technical capabilities, NC machine tools were produced primarily for the largest corporations, which alone were thought to have the skills necessary to use them. Hence in the United States the idea that small businesses could use NC equipment looked like an illiterate buying the complete works of Shakespeare, and that attitude prevailed until Japanese importers proved it false. In contrast, the Japanese focused their NC machinery production on small firms. Figure 1.3 shows that by 1972, 50 percent of domestic sales were to smaller firms, a proportion that rose to 70 percent by 1978. Furthermore, growth across the decade was almost entirely attributable to expanded sales to small enterprises.

Even more surprising is the extent to which extremely small firms purchased NC equipment. If we consider 1982 NC sales in Japan to large firms (300 employees and more), medium firms (30-299 employees), and small firms (fewer than 30 employees), over one-quarter went to small firms. Another 33 percent was accounted for by medium firms, and just 40 percent by large firms.[36]

The influence of small manufacturing enterprises makes the Japanese NC industry ideal for assessing the strength of the market regulation thesis. If it was market cues that primarily induced equipment successes in Japan, we must explain why firms in Japan responded to new technology where those in the United States did not. If the market structures of the two nations differed, why did these differences not diminish as optimal manufacturing and marketing solutions became apparent? And if incentives for small-scale NC development were indeed greater in Japan, why did Japanese small manufacturers but not their American counterparts demand and how they were able to pay for sophisticated tooling? Furthermore, why did Japanese machinery makers bring out new NC designs, many of them initially offered to U.S. producers who spurned them?

The small-scale sector in Japanese manufacturing highlights two difficulties in the market regulation thesis: the failure to distinguish the Japanese economic structure adequately from other cases, and the failure to provide reasons for observed market phenomena. It is only by appreciating how broad contextual factors transformed and strengthened the role of small firms in the economy that we can make clear Japanese industrial success.

Finally, the NC machine tool sector is important because changes in machine tools indicate more general manufacturing trends throughout the economy. Machine tools are capital goods that other companies buy to make the products they sell. If Japanese NC tools differ systematically in design or application from those in the United States, then we may generalize more widely about the two economies. An economy in which machinery designs are primarily dedicated to a single purpose reflects the greater diffusion of mass production; general-purpose equipment suggests a more flexible approach. Like a fossil record, the development of NC machine tools is suggestive of a wider history—in this case, of the production ideology operating in the economy at large. The development of NC tools in Japan, I will show, reflected small-firm expansion and the integration of flexible manufacturing practices into mass production.

In this book I describe the machinery industry's expansion in Japan from the Great Depression to the present. In some cases evidence culled from the machinery case directly refutes crucial contentions of the two standard explanations of Japanese success—the arguments are factually wrong or insufficient. In addition, the history of the industry's growth makes it clear we should interpret Japan's economy as the product of many political events throughout society which permitted greater manufacturing flexibility. This argument consistently explains the widest range of economic phenomena in Japan.

I focus first on the bureaucratic regulation thesis. Can some form of state control explain what happened in the machinery market both before and after World War II? Chapter 2 examines government attempts to cartelize, consolidate, and coordinate production from the Great Depression to wartime. Though the Ministry of Commerce and Industry (MCI), MITI's predecessor, clearly wanted to exert control over machinery producers, it was unable to do so, despite the wartime emergency. Indeed, its policies were frequently counterproductive. In particular, efforts to curb market entry and promote American-style mass production by large firms actually enhanced the decentralization of the prewar economy, preserving the very firms the state wanted to merge or eliminate.

Chapter 3 examines postwar laws passed in what many observers have taken to be a successful attempt by bureaucrats to direct domestic firms toward high-profit markets. But if "regulation" means the ability of the state independently to set a market plan and then to implement its vision, the bureaucracy again failed. Not one postwar market or production plan came close to being realized; the machinery industry grew in a pattern the reverse of what the bureaucracy sought. MITI's longstanding desire was to build up economies of scale through cartels, restrictions on market entry, and consolidation. Instead, Japanese machinery makers fragmented the market: new entrants flooded high-tech equipment sectors, existing firms flatly refused to coordinate or consolidate production.

Chapters 2 and 3 illustrate the considerable market dynamics that surrounded the spectacular revival of Japanese machine tool production after the war. They also show how political events—internal conflicts in machinery industry groups, battles between large and small firms, prewar struggles for market power between the military, the bureaucracy, and private enterprises—began to shape the substantive rights of producers in the Japanese economy. These chapters demonstrate more than just the failure of the bureaucratic regulation thesis; they show how seemingly limited political conflicts were associated with the emergence of small-scale flexible firms.

In Chapter 4 the analysis shifts to assess the market regulation thesis, by addressing the problem of Japanese small-firm manufacturers. The predominance of small firms in Japan seems to undermine a central assumption behind the argument that Japanese industry is basically the same as manufacturing elsewhere only more efficient. One tradition of research, widely accepted in Japan and followed by outside observers, explains away the extensive role small firms play in the Japanese economy by treating small producers as less modern than, or as exploited by, the large ones. This, the "dual structure" argument maintains that small firms in Japan are technically less adept and survive only because large firms, which tightly control them, use them to produce cheap components.[37] If true, the argument would sustain the idea that large firms seeking scale economies are the optimal or most advanced production unit. Small producers could be characterized as inefficient remnants of earlier periods of Japanese industrial development, preserved only for their ability to squeeze labor and provide cheap parts.

Several political events, as we will see, especially in the late 1950s, counteracted tendencies in the Japanese economy to institutionalize a dual structure. Instead, they generated a climate that fostered widespread flexible manufacturing by independent small firms, firms that frequently possessed, within their specialties, greater technical abilities than large companies. The definition of rights and substantive opportunities produced by these events created an economic system that permitted rapid entry into profitable sectors, increased the independence of small manufacturers, and allowed the widespread adoption of flexible manufacturing. The dual structure receded, and in its place emerged flexible, technically advanced, and comparatively self-reliant enterprises.

The market regulation argument cannot be accepted, therefore, because it cannot accurately describe the small-firm manufacturing system in Japan, nor can it explain how this system developed. The ability of smaller-scale factories to compete, grow, and build new markets, an absolutely crucial feature of Japanese expansion in machine tools and in the economy as a whole, was predicated on political factors. As rights and substantive ideas about "just" economic practices were elaborated, so a financial, manufacturing, and regulatory climate emerged that sustained the flexible option to a greater extent in Japan than elsewhere. This result, however, did not simply precipitate from the market; it was as a result of politics (as defined above) that alternative industrial options flourished more readily in Japan. The market, then, was itself a special outcome of background circumstances.

Chapter 5 looks at the way the Japanese political context produced greater incentives toward flexible production in a specific case: Sakaki township in Nagano Prefecture. Sakaki, in the hinterlands of Honshu's central mountain range, was historically a poor agricultural village; today it is the world's largest per capita user of NC machinery. Situated on farms and in orchards are scores of family-owned workshops containing the most sophisticated industrial equipment. The objective of this chapter is to understand how the general growth of flexible manufacturing opportunities in Japan affected development in a particular and especially unlikely instance.

As a crucial case Sakaki also allows me to highlight another important part of the process of sustaining flexible firms in Japan: the widespread emergence of regions of small manufacturers that collectively enhanced their individual vitality. Regional cooperation provided Sakaki and other areas with the ability to resist wage squeezes by large firms, promoted the technical advancement of local manufacturers, and facilitated the access to capital that small firms needed to purchase new equipment. The creation of effective regional institutions was, once again, "political"; it required that the rights of individual firms and collective rights be defined with reference to general ideas about economic and substantive justice. Thus the growth of flexible manufacturing regions was yet another part of the process by which political events made possible the market capacities of Japanese producers.

In Chapter 6 I draw together the results of my analysis. The rapid advance of the machinery industry and the emergence of NC tooling in the 1970s cannot be explained by either the bureaucratic regulation thesis or the market regulation thesis. The state was either ineffective or dominated by producers; the market itself was a product of political context. Neither thesis accurately describes or explains many significant structural and strategic features of the Japanese economy, and the same objections apply to work that combines the two arguments.

If, however, we accept that Japan may have diverged from the mass production model of industrial development, then we reopen questions ignored or closed in other accounts. Is differential industrial performance based on flexible operations as well as on mass production? In the machinery industry, flexible firms promoted the development of new equipment. Furthermore, the general support for small firms' operations in Japan gave machine tool makers the ability to meet demand by shifting production or encouraging new market entrants. We can understand that support only by considering the politics surrounding industry—that is, the creation of rights both before and after the war. My argument is not limited to the machinery case; it applies to many other important sectors as well. In sum, one source of Japanese success was the competitive advantages that its manufacturers enjoyed as a result of their flexible operations.

I stated at the outset that explaining Japanese economic achievements tells us as much about ourselves as about Japan. If contemporary accounts are inadequate, so too is the policy debate based on them. General recommendations about appropriate economic policy based on bureaucratic or market explanations are, I will show, untenable. Japanese experience supports neither the view that other countries must construct an intrusive regulatory apparatus "like Japan's" to promote efficiency, nor the idea that the market should be left unregulated to enhance competitiveness. Instead, Japan's flexible manufacturers suggest a much more interesting set of options. I believe there is a real lesson to be learned from Japan: the idea that redefining economic or social rights and providing support for overlooked manufacturing options can revive or sustain an economy. That lesson suggests that the possibilities for rebuilding a manufacturing economy are at once more promising and more difficult to achieve than contemporary theories tell us.

Chapter Two

Early Regulation of the Machine Tool Industry

Evidence of state control over the machine tool industry should be particularly marked in Japan prior to World War II. The country was preparing for war, an undertaking that frequently demands state coordination. The government was increasingly dominated by nationalists who were receptive to economic intervention as a means of building up the military and were subject to only the most modest electoral constraints. Finally, business was on the defensive; assassinations of industrial leaders and their political allies were commonplace by the late 1930s. Under such conditions the bureaucracy should have been able to control the economy with ease.

Yet government regulatory efforts were ineffective. Industrial transformations commonly assumed to have been the result of state policies never took place; policies designed to produce one outcome led to another; and economic adjustments congruent with policy goals occurred for reasons unrelated to bureaucratic intervention. The Japanese economy in the 1930s and 1940s should be an easy matter for the bureaucratic regulation thesis. But in fact centralized economic authority did not coordinate industrial growth.

Early regulatory initiatives may be divided into three main periods. The first was marked by planning; the government undertook research on the structure of the economy. It began with the creation of the Resources Bureau (Shigen Kyoku) in 1927 and led to the establishment of the Ministry of Trade and Industry (MCI) in 1929.[1] After the passage of the Major Industries Control Law, the MCI administered an attempt between 1931 and 1939 to consolidate and centralize militarily important industries.[2] This effort first involved general attempts to cartelize the economy and later moved toward industry-specific legislation. Finally, World War II prompted the development of industry control associations (*tōseikai*), intended to regulate minutely the industrial behavior of firms in specific sectors according to a general plan.

In evaluating Japanese business-state relations from 1927 to 1945, proponents of the bureaucratic regulation thesis argue that prewar government activity was the first step toward a system of economic controls that the postwar period would recreate. In the early 1930s policies were designed to induce the huge financial and trading conglomerates, the *zaibatsu,* to enter machinery, electronics, and other heavy industries to create economies of scale. Initially the state was directly to coordinate the rationalization of heavy industries. However, the political strength of the firms involved led to a system in which bureaucrats provided financial incentives while industrialists controlled actual economic activity. Then, as the wartime emergency deepened, the bureaucracy again tried to increase direct control over the economy, pushing for greater consolidation of large firms and seeking to eliminate small producers through attrition or by forcing them to subcontract to large companies. The *zaibatsu* managed to defend themselves and limit state power. But by the outbreak of war, in this version of history, government intervention, though only partially successful, had created a heavy machinery sector that had achieved economies of scale. And after Japan's defeat the bureaucracy, having absorbed the lessons about fragmented economic stewardship it had learned from conflict with the *zaibatsu,* set up a system of regulation that was more effective and hence produced rapid growth. Thus the postwar miracle was fostered by MITI in a reincarnation of the prewar system of regulation pioneered by the MCI.[3]

In the machinery industry, however, as I will show, planning, cartels, industry-specific measures, and the *tōseikai* did not result in centralized manufacturing dominated by either government or big capital. The prewar government and the *zaibatsu* were locked in a power struggle that prevented either side from implementing its favored industrial policy. Furthermore, bureaucratic policies, even those which matched the strategic interests of *zaibatsu* affiliates, did not force small businesses out of manufacturing; the prewar "adjustment" policies that aimed to centralize production at the expense of small factories succeeded only to the extent that materials shortages or bombing eliminated whole sectors, large and small firms together, as in textiles. Where materials were available, as in the weapons industries, small firms not only flourished but insinuated themselves into the *tōseikai,* the institutions that were supposed to manage their demise.

There is common agreement that "industrial policy" in Japan dates from the mid-1920s, just before the Great Depression. Previous government economic policies were for the most part shaped by political or international concerns, such as managing the nation's balance of payments. An early state presence in heavy and extractive industries had been eliminated in the 1880s in a celebrated series of sales of state interests to the *zaibatsu*. Large capital cliques more or less independently ran the financial, extractive, and commodity markets, whereas very small firms produced final goods for actual sale on the market. But the Depression, coupled with rising militarism, brought the state to experiment with interventionist policies designed explicitly to reshape the economy.[4]

Four major groups affected the development of prewar industrial policy. First the bureaucracy, in which the MCI was the locus of detailed industrial planning, was composed of two groups with different views of economic development and the role of the state. One faction, which advocated a "soft" approach to government policy, wanted to use the power of the state to stabilize the activities of private firms. Its adherents believed that unrestricted price wars, labor competition, and the like had caused the Depression; they sought a consolidation of sectors to reduce competition, stable prices, and the orderly division of product lines to assure an economic scale of production. Members of this faction included the MCI minister, Yoshino Shinji, and this group legitimated the objective of controlling "excessive competition" as a policy goal in Japan.

A younger cadre of bureaucrats typified by Yoshino's protégé Kishi Nobusuke, who would later become the wartime MCI minister, a convicted war criminal, and an influential postwar prime minister, adopted a "hard" view of government intervention. The more radical among them came to be known as reform or "new bureaucrats," a phrase applied to officials heavily influenced by Nazi thought, and they demanded a bureaucracy acting for the good of the country to control the rapacious behavior of private interests. This group wanted to use state power to force efficient scales of production on the economy and to ensure that labor and management were disciplined. They were antagonistic to the *zaibatsu* and sympathetic to militarist ideology; many of them served in Manchuria, where the military government gave them the heady experience of complete economic authority. From the hard faction Japan received the idea of rationalization as structural or managerial transformations enforced by an authoritative bureaucracy.[5]

The second group was the military, together with the cluster of economic planners the militarists employed in Manchuria and at home. The militarists had a complex, perhaps contradictory view of the economy. To support the military build-up they sympathized with the MCI's efforts to consolidate and encouraged the more radical bureaucrats in their efforts to centralize production. But they diverged from the MCI in one respect: the military wanted to create new *zaibatsu,* coordinated by individuals sympathetic to their political and social ideology, rather than control existing enterprises. Indeed, many industrialists, for instance Ayukawa Gisuke, founder of Nissan, a so-called new *zaibatsu,* became influential partly because of their close connections with the military. Also the military wanted to boost domestic production of war matériel because it feared an embargo of goods or basic commodities. Opposed to import dependence, it wanted to use the state to direct the economy toward domestic manufacture.[6]

At the same time the military's opposition to the *zaibatsu* led it to style itself a defender of the small, traditional workplace. While militarists were seeking large factories for munitions, they were also advocating a populist resurgence of small-scale manufacturers. I return to this development in chapter 4; here I only note the fact of the military's strong support for small firms. This support went beyond rhetoric; in armaments sourcing, and in the letting of contracts, the military did help redirect production away from large firms toward the economic periphery. For example, it stipulated that a certain percentage of all government contracts be diverted to rural producers.[7]

The third group was the *zaibatsu.* The *zaibatsu* often were not unified and competed one with another. Nor was their economic presence as vast as many have assumed. Indeed, as late as the mid-1930s direct *zaibatsu* presence was extremely rare in the consumer goods sectors we associate most strongly with Japanese postwar advances—autos, machinery, and electronics. And even in heavy machinery, steel, shipbuilding, and textiles, *zaibatsu* involvement remained low until the late thirties. In 1934, for instance, firms of five hundred or more employees had just a 38 percent share of total production in all manufacturing sectors; in spinning their share was 49 percent, in chemicals just 28 percent, and in raw metal production 57 percent. And of course many of the larger firms counted in these statistics were not *zaibatsu* companies. Furthermore, careful historical studies by Nakamura Takafusa show in almost all manufacturing sectors a very marked trend toward *deconcentration* from the 1920s to the mid-1930s.[8] *Zaibatsu* economic domination was most advanced in finance, raw materials, and primary manufacturing such as pig iron and steel. When *zaibatsu*-affiliated firms required manufactured products such as automobiles, machine tools, and electrical equipment, they imported them from overseas.[9]

Small businesses were the fourth and final group. Small-scale factory operators opposed the *zaibatsu* and were especially concerned with reforming the financial system, because of the concentration of investment capital in the hands of the combines. *Zaibatsu* reluctance to enter manufacturing sectors often forced small firms to rely on their material wholesalers for expensive, if not exorbitant, financial support. Small factories were excluded from *zaibatsu* capital sources and starved for operating funds. Not only did this condition lead to a strong (and successful) movement to reform the financial system, as we shall see in chapter 4, but it also generated the very first bureaucratic "industrial policy" measures in the 1920s.

The interplay between these four major groups in the initiation and application of policies had as its net effect on prewar regulation the failure of any effort to coordinate or consolidate production; the MCI achieved none of the objectives it sought. The history of the machinery industry demonstrates how and why prewar industrial policy was ineffective.

The Initial Expansion of Machine Tool Firms

The machine tool industry immediately prior to the Great Depression typified the general state of Japanese manufacturing. There were no *zaibatsu* affiliates involved in production, and import reliance was approximately 50-60 percent of the market, a staggeringly high level.[10] The two observations are related: the lack of Japanese investment capital limited supply, so domestic machinery or consumer goods needs had to be met through imports. Trade was dominated by the *zaibatsu,* which, as brokers for foreign goods, had little incentive to build up Japanese manufacturing capacity (which would threaten their profits from imported goods). Japan machinery manufacturers faced intense competition from foreign producers and indifference from domestic investors.

Despite these problems, a growing number of Japanese entrepreneurs were generating a modest expansion in the machine tool industry by the 1920s. Machine tool firms were established in two main ways. One was for individuals, usually former factory employees, to begin production on a trial basis for their original employers and then to become independent manufacturers. The other was for large companies to create independent firms out of their specialized machinery departments.

The first path is exemplified by Ikegai, named for its founder, which by 1930 was the largest machine tool firm in Japan. In the 1880s Ikegai began work as a teenager in a military plant. He then took a job as a machinist in a private factory, where he used and studied American-style lathes. In 1889 he set up as a subcontractor to his former factory and he built his first lathe, modeled on English designs. His attempts to establish himself as a machinery maker were hampered by stiff foreign competition and a restricted market. He survived by accepting a variety of subcontract and specialty production orders; his company's products between 1895 and 1910 included electric lightbulbs, water sluices, rolling machines, and parts for the military during the Russo-Japanese War. Increases in demand spurred by World War I finally allowed Ikegai to specialize in machine tools. Other firms founded by entrepreneurial machinists or technicians include Shin Nippon Kōki, whose founder was an assembly worker in the 1880s, and Karatsu.[11]

Of firms that developed along the second path, Okuma, a successful maker of noodle machines in the 1890s and early 1900s, is typical. World War I provided the firm with a chance to use its machinery expertise in a new field—weapons tooling. It spun off its noodle business and began a division dedicated to machine tools, concentrating on lathe production. The sharp drop in machinery demand that the post–World War I depression and import boom brought forced the firm back into manufacturing noodle machinery, but Okuma retained its facilities for machine tool production throughout the 1920s. Another example is Niigata Machinery, situated on the remote Sea of Japan side of the central mountains, originally a repair shop for Nippon Oil. In 1896 Nippon Oil received an order for fifty lathes from the military in Niigata, which wanted to make use of the repair facility's equipment. Though Nippon Oil merely lent its machinery, the military contract proved the feasibility of independent machinery production. The company spun off its repair shop as Niigata Machinery in 1910, when the demand boom prior to World War I led to sustained growth. Niigata, Okuma, and Tokyo Gas, a utilities firm, were all machine tool firms that originated as parts of larger concerns.[12]

Ikegai, Karatsu, Niigata, Okuma, and Tokyo Gas were the five largest firms engaged in machine tool production through the mid-1930s. They were sometimes known as the Big Five, a misnomer if their operations were measured against the manufacturing scale of their global competitors but an accurate description of their influence in the Japanese machinery industry. Yet the Big Five accounted for only a portion of total Japanese machinery production. Indeed, prewar machine tool manufacturing involved hundreds of smaller enterprises. These firms were usually part-time manufacturers of machine tools, surviving in slack periods by subcontracting or producing other goods.

Table 2.1. Growth in Machine Tool Firms by Size, 1932–1938

Size of Firm (by number of employees)	1932	1933	1934	1935	1936	1937	1938
5–30	360	428	534	661	631	824	1531
31–100	27	57	77	86	120	151	354
101–500	9	6	7	14	16	41	83
500+	1	2	3	4	4	5	10
Total	397	493	621	765	771	1021	1978

SOURCE: Chokki Toshiaki, "Nihon no kōsaku kikai kōgyō no hatten: Katei no bunseki" (diss., Tokyo University, Economics Department, 1963), p. 152. (An analysis of the development of the Japanese machine tool industry).

The growth in smaller machinery manufacturers, as shown in Table 2.1, was quite dramatic, nearly quintupling in number from 1932 to 1938. Particularly impressive were the gains registered by extremely small firms. Moreover, as government surveys ignored companies with five or fewer employees, which probably outnumbered all other firms combined, the statistics understate the activity of small businesses in the prewar machine tool sector. Even between 1937 and 1938, though large firms registered considerable growth for reasons detailed below, small firms kept pace; in the same period, for instance, firms in the smallest size class for which statistics were collected increased in number by 180 percent.

As World War II approached, the Japanese machine tool industry was not the focus of *zaibatsu* attention, because of the import strategies and investment reluctance of the large combines. Industry relations with the bureaucracy were for the most part handled by the five largest machinery producers working as a group. The market was highly cyclical, and imports were running at approximately 50 percent of total domestic production. Production was split among hundreds of smaller producers.

The Growth of Regulatory Initiatives: Planning

Government began paying formal attention to the machine tool industry, and indeed to industrial policy for all of Japan, with the establishment of the Resources Bureau or Shigen Kyoku in 1927. This agency, which reported to the cabinet, was charged with surveying various industries to inform bureaucrats and politicians about the state of the Japanese economy. It was born out of the worsening economic conditions of the late 1920s, which legitimated a direct state interest in the economy. At the same time the militarists wanted to develop policies to counter the influence of the *zaibatsu* while putting the economy on a war footing through a general expansion of manufacturing. The Resources Bureau was originally conceived as a device to identify problem areas in the economy; corrective measures would then be taken. However, the *zaibatsu* greatly weakened the bureau's power. Proposed authority for military planning was defeated, and the bureau was reduced to a minor cabinet advisory board with ambiguous authority and a staff of only five employees. It was limited by the Resources Survey Law (Shigen Chōsa Hō) of 1929 to carrying out the first regular industrial surveys in prewar Japan.[13]

Its mandate required the Resources Bureau to describe the condition of various industries of strategic interest to the military and the economy, and then to suggest policies that would rectify perceived problems. The bureau did so by convening a commission (*shingikai*) at which selected industry representatives discussed their activities and prospects with bureaucrats. This phase of discussion or policy research lasted from the late 1920s to the mid-1930s, when other institutions usurped planning and survey functions.

The machine tool industry's interaction with the Resources Bureau began in 1929 and lasted until 1937. Because of the fragmentation of the industry, the bureaucracy came to rely on the five largest firms for its insights concerning machinery policies. Bureau findings were heavily influenced, if not totally determined, by the Big Five companies though the effectiveness of government strategies hinged on the responses of machine tool producers not represented in the *shingikai*.[14] And, as we shall see, the reaction of unrepresented firms doomed bureau initiatives.

The first assessment of the machine tool industry was published by the Resources Bureau in 1929. It identified two concerns: Japan's excessive import reliance, and problems with the types of machines that domestic firms produced. Both industrial representatives and militarists strongly emphasized the problem of imports. Domestic producers wanted to halt the flow of foreign, mainly American, equipment that competed directly with their own copies of those tools. The military was concerned that any embargo on essential imported equipment in response to contemplated military action in Asia would catch Japan unable to manufacture its own machinery, crippling the armaments sector. Thus the report argued for support to enhance domestic production.

The Resources Bureau reviewed the output of the major firms, dividing their product lines into eleven categories, such as grinding, turning, and boring machines. The report concluded that Japanese tools were all ordinary, standard equipment for general-purpose machinery. Imported equipment was of the dedicated variety, of use in mass production. This was a matter of considerable concern to the military, which sought special-purpose machinery to build military vehicles, aircraft, and armaments. As a result of military requirements, in 1929 the Resources Bureau decided to redirect Japanese machine tool production from general-purpose to war-related specialty machines.

With the growing strength of the military and the wartime preparations of the 1930s, we should expect the Resources Bureau's policy goals to have had a marked effect on machine tool development. They did not. Though backed by the military, the economic bureaucracy, and the largest machine tool firms, the bureau's efforts for nearly a decade did not lead to a single set of concrete guidelines, let alone an effective measure. Despite the threat of machine tool embargoes after the Manchurian invasion of 1931, the Resources Bureau was reduced as late as 1935 to repeating its dire warnings of 1929—without providing any remedies.

The goals of transforming production and reducing imports were not attained. Imports continued to keep pace with domestic production; the value of imports was 53 percent of domestic output in 1933 and 46 percent in 1937. At the same time military economists grew increasingly alarmed at the lack of development of specialty machine tools. Not only was production centered on general-purpose machinery but, as Table 2.1 showed, hundreds of smaller firms were entering the market with their own, often idiosyncratic designs. Military planners, seeking standardized machinery for rapid wartime conversion, found this particularly worrying.

The reason for this lack of action was the political struggle among various interests in the machine industry. Users, producers, and different branches of the bureaucracy could not agree on what, if any, action should be taken. In an effort to solve this problem, the Resources Bureau convened a Joint Survey Research Discussion Group (Chōsa Kenkyū Kyōgikai) in February 1935, which included the Big Five, representatives from various other bureaucracies, and a contingent from Tokyo University. At the first meeting of this group it was proposed that special standards be set for all machine tools—an idea that fell short of moving from general to specialty machines but that would nevertheless make all tools produced in Japan roughly interchangeable. This objective appealed to the military, which sought standardized equipment, and to the bureaucracy, which wanted to promote scale economies. At the same time the proposal would give domestic firms that could meet product specifications for standard-type tools an advantage over their competitors; this appealed to the Big

Five firms, which faced increasing competition from what they called "inferior," smaller firms.

The bureaucracy was so reliant on industry sources that it turned the actual task of writing product specifications over to the Big Five, which in turn divided the machine tool market into segments according to each firm's area of expertise. A special Machinery Members Group (Kikai I-In Kai) of company representatives gave Ikegai the task of drafting specifications for radial ball lathes; Tokyo Gas, milling machines; Okuma, step lathes; Niigata Metal Manufacturing, gear lathes; and Karatsu, vertical boring machines. The push toward standardization gave these firms the opportunity to establish their own machinery designs as national standards. The specifications they developed came to be known as the S-Type (for "standard-type") machine tools.

Implementation of even this modest proposal for industrial development was delayed two years, until it appeared in a Resources Bureau report of April 1938. The report was passed to the Planning Agency (Kikaku-In), a cabinet organ set up by the now powerful interventionists in government to establish industrial targets for wartime production. The Planning Agency issued the S-Type specifications in July to compel standardization among the growing number of smaller firms.

The smaller machine tool firms killed the proposal. Many argued their products were superior to those produced by the larger firms that had written the S-Type specifications. Others rejected the idea that they should build to someone else's design. Some small firms admitted the S-Type machines were beyond their capabilities. As a result, the S-Type tool designs were never adopted by the smaller firms for which they were developed—in fact, in an ironic twist, the S-Type campaign led to further fragmentation of the market. The only party in Japan to use the S-Type specs was the National Railways. The Resources Bureau had persuaded the Railways Ministry to underwrite experiments to help produce the S-Type designs the Big Five had developed, hoping that if so important an industrial force were to embrace the designs, other firms would follow. As it became clear that S-Type designs would not be available from domestic producers, and that the Big Five could not possibly meet railway machinery demands on their own—railway orders for machine tools amounted to close to 25 percent of total domestic machinery demand—the National Railways began making machines itself. A major consumer thus withdrew from the very market the bureaucrats and the Big Five firms wanted to expand.[15]

By 1937, then, the bureaucracy had failed to restructure the machine tool sector thought to be so critical to Japanese military and industrial capacities. But war with China and the reality of a major embargo gave greater weight to the interventionist-minded "new bureaucrats" within the MCI and their military allies in government. To supplement the Resources Bureau, the cabinet convened a Resources Commission, which addressed findings related to major industrial issues immediately prior to legislative activity. Commission attention signaled a higher level of concern; where the bureau had been hamstrung from the start by *zaibatsu* pressure, the cabinet-level commission had greater leeway to adopt whatever policies the prime minister and his advisers saw fit. With this development began a new type of regulatory initiative—a cartel scheme.

The Introduction of Cartels and Industry Licensing

Under pressure from the military and civilian bureaucrats in the MCI, a Tenth Special Resources Commission was convened in June 1937 to debate the problems of the machine tool industry. It produced a series of steps for promoting domestic manufacture. First, the commission set an output target for the industry of ¥130-400 million by 1941. Next, the commission argued in favor of strong bureaucratic efforts to promote the technical development of machine tools made in Japan. Reflecting military concerns, it emphasized the need to move production toward the specialty, mass production–oriented tooling required for armaments. Finally, it insisted that import reliance must be reduced and demanded efforts to promote the use and growth of domestic machine tools. These recommendations were transmitted directly to the prime minister on June 30, 1937.[16] The Resources Commission's report became the basis for a special Machine Tool Industry Law. The 1937 China Incident, and with it the high probability of American reprisals, led the government to accelerate the law's passage through the Diet. In April 1938 the law came into effect. It was the first real attempt to respond to problems that had been identified nearly a decade earlier by the Resources Bureau.

The government came to adopt a series of industry-specific control laws in the late 1930s. Special legislation was promulgated for petroleum in 1934, automobiles and fertilizer in 1936, gold, synthetic petroleum, and iron and steel in 1937, mineral production, electric power, aircraft, and machine tools in 1938, light metals and shipbuilding in 1939, and coal distribution and synthetic chemicals in 1940.[17] It is usually argued that these laws represent a major extension of state authority into the private sector. However, as we shall see, they were actually an effort to respond to earlier regulatory failures. The specific industry laws were shaped by the ineffectiveness of previous strategies.

The Major Industries Control Law of 1931, the main previous attempt to regulate the economy, was based on 1920s' legislation that sought industrial groups or unions (*kōgyō kumiai*) among small firms. It encouraged firms in certain industries to set up self-regulating cartels to promote both price and output stability. The law's provisions were simple: under Article I, if half of the producers in a given "major industry" set up a marketing, sales, or pricing plan, they had to report the details of the plan to the government, which gave it legal sanction; under Article II, if two-thirds of all the firms in an industry agreed to the plan, then the MCI could, at its own discretion, require all producers to abide by it. The law also provided for a Control Committee to review plans submitted to the MCI, with the possibility that the MCI might modify or abrogate certain parts of the agreement.[18] The government thus approved regulatory schemes designed by firms that then ran cartels backed by the threat of government sanctions.

The Major Industries Control Law came into effect in August 1931, its content determined by the contemporary balance of power between state-control and private-control groups. On the interventionist side were the military, the MCI, and small firms. Opposing them were the *zaibatsu,* which initially viewed the proposal for state-sanctioned cartels with alarm. *Zaibatsu* power on the committees that debated the law and the still weak position of the military and its "new bureaucrat" allies permitted the state to sanction only those actions which private firms developed among themselves. The industrial combines cut a deal with the more moderate advocates of state control: the bureaucrats' goals of concentration and market control would be achieved by private actors with state blessing. The most radical interventionists were defeated and private interests were defended, although the government was accorded a measure of oversight powers.[19]

In many manufacturing sectors the law led to the creation of "cartels," that is, price, marketing, or production agreements officially submitted to the government. Some observers have argued that these cartels centralized the economy to the benefit of the *zaibatsu,* that the law amounted to big capital's triumph over the bureaucracy and the whole Japanese economy.[20] But careful analysis suggests that the cartels operated so ineffectively that they could not even enforce agreements in the interests of the *zaibatsu* that were supposed to be their main beneficiary.

The Major Industries Control Law emasculated government authority, making it impossible for cartelized firms to police their agreements. In particular, the government was unable to exercise the formal power to enforce agreements made by two-thirds of firms against all companies in an industry. Only one case of Article II application was reported by a contemporary observer, in 1938; modern research indicates perhaps three instances when cartels numbered, by various estimates, in the hundreds.[21] Thus companies that did not obey the agreements were free to price and produce as they chose.

One large, recalcitrant firm could destroy the coordination necessary for cartelized behavior. And in most cartel agreements, the number of recalcitrant firms was significant. Though there was close to 100 percent incorporation of firms in cotton or silk, the metals industry cartels almost never included even 50 percent of the manufacturers. In the cartels for angle steel, steel bar, wire rods, and steel plate, as many firms stayed outside the agreements as were in the group. In copper plates all fifteen firms refused to join a cartel authorized by the government. In carbon bisulphide and sulphuric acid the ratio of outsiders to participants was two to one in the first instance, five to one in the second.[22]

Within the cartels, members found no ready agreement on the application of principles. Opportunities to cheat were legion. One popular method was to take advantage of military control of Manchuria, where enormous investments were taking place but where the military refused to let mainland laws be applied. Many companies adopted cartel objectives to hamper their competitors' advantages in Japan while covertly expanding operations in Manchuria for reshipment to the home islands.

In other cases, battles over sales quotas or prices between members transformed the problems of market competition into intracartel struggles but did not eliminate them. As G. C. Allen observed of the period, "The cartel, in Japan as elsewhere, has often been merely the result of the maneuvering of rivals for positions of advantage in the competitive struggle." Inter-*zaibatsu* competition, he felt, had weakened the cartelization scheme; though the Depression had led to initial efforts to consolidate, natural antipathy between business interests reduced the power of restraint agreements:

> The policy of industrialists themselves towards cartelization has not been without ambiguity. During the period of Depression the leading industrialists as a whole were favorably disposed to cartels and to government encouragement of them; since in this way the "weak selling" of smaller rivals could be checked. But wherever cartelization led to the domination

> of an industry by one or more powerful financial cliques, then there was a demand in those quarters for a relaxation of government control. Further, some cartels, especially since recovery set in, have formed the battleground of rival groups. In some cases violent struggles concerning production or sales quotas have taken place among these groups within the cartels. In other cases, a powerful firm has preferred to stand outside the cartel, to which its rivals belonged, and to expand its output under the shelter of the restrictions which the cartel imposed on its member firms. Thus, while it may be admitted that cartels have reduced competition in some industries, a large number of industries may be found in which cartels have served as a medium for the struggle of rival interests.[23]

The large business interests most affected by the cartels wanted to use the government to insulate them from both foreign and domestic competitors without infringing on their own autonomy.

The bureaucrats were not happy with the law. Their bargaining position had deteriorated from 1931, when the effects of the Depression seemed to make businesses somewhat responsive to the notion of state involvement in the economy, but by 1934 even cartelized firms were pushing for a rollback of bureaucratic power. Moreover, the militarists were disappointed that attempts to regulate the *zaibatsu* had instead been transformed into institutions that assisted big capital without actually reshaping the economy. Many who opposed the *zaibatsu* argued that the cartels were out of control.[24]

These pressures led to the application of the Major Industries Control Law in a new manner. Government would *license* firms in a specific industry, giving them priority in the distribution of financial benefits, equipment, and orders. By creating a set of preferred firms, the government would gradually induce consolidation in a given sector. The result was a series of specific industry control laws. The development of this legislation is often cited as evidence of creeping statism; firms would need explicit recognition from the state to operate.[25] However, just as large private interests had affected the operation of the cartels, so the licensed firms shaped the terms and application of the special industries laws. In most cases, the government was forced to sacrifice such objectives as industry consolidation for narrow company interests, for example increasing prices for licensed goods or reducing foreign competition.

The first application of specific industry laws was the Petroleum Industry Law of 1934. In its original form the law called for expropriation of company assets and comprehensive regulation by the state. Severe opposition from the affected firms watered the plan down to the point where the government merely licensed the companies to which it would extend benefits, a position, one analyst suggests, "that preserved the largest measure of independence for private capital while establishing its protection from foreign competition."[26] Interventionists wanted to consolidate and control the petroleum industry through the 1934 law, but they were brought to accept the preservation and support of the very companies they sought to transform.

Another instance in which domestic firms used the specific industry laws to reduce foreign competition was the Automobile Industry Law of 1936. The law was heavily influenced by Nissan, an auto firm headed by Ayukawa, a powerful "new *zaibatsu*" industrialist supported by the military; for a time he oversaw all industrial operations in Manchuria.[27] Ayukawa helped persuade the government that the Ford and GM subsidiaries operating in Japan posed a threat to military preparedness; if an industry law licensed only domestic firms, it would force the foreigners to leave. Only Nissan and Toyota received recognition from the government, eliminating foreign auto production in Japan. But the consequence was that Japanese motor vehicle technology stagnated, and the military had to rely on poor-quality domestic equipment for its needs.[28] The spirit of the law was sacrificed for the benefit of politically savvy Japanese industrialists.

The Machine Tool Industry Law of April 1938 also failed to bring about the market outcomes that state control sought. Machinery firms possessing over two hundred machine tools, and specialty firms with over fifty machine tools, would receive licensed status from the government. These licensed firms were permitted to write off new machinery investments over a five-year period to increase scale; they were provided with subsidies to expand operations, exempted from duties on imported equipment they needed for their operations, and exempted from state, profit, and income taxes for five years. The government also pledged to provide depreciation assistance of up to 60 percent of the value of the machinery involved and to permit stock debentures of up to double the value of paid-up capital. Finally, the law also exempted licensed firms from restrictions on pricing and materials increases imposed by Japanese commercial law.[29]

Negotiations among the bureaucracy, industrialists, and the military shaped the content of the Machine Tool Industry Law. The decision to license machinery firms by the number of tools they possessed, for instance, was the product of intense struggles between the Big Five firms—most of which did not at the time meet the two hundred minimum for machine tools—and the MCI. The Big Five, under tremendous pressure from smaller producers, whose numbers had swollen to 1,900 by 1938, wanted legislation that would freeze out these new competitors.[30] Licensed and nonlicensed tiers of firms distinguished by scale of tooling would limit competition.

The MCI's overriding aim as the law's administrator was to promote the expansion of scale production in the industry. Prewar bureaucrats thought that only large firms could promote technical advances, and they viewed the market competition associated with small producers as destabilizing. But the bureaucracy was not convinced that traditional machinery firms could meet domestic needs; it wanted to push them toward a greater scale of operations while offering incentives for new, larger firms to enter the market. New entrants and older firms would have to meet the two hundred standard to qualify for benefits, while nonlicensed firms would either have to merge or go out of business. Either outcome would consolidate production.[31]

The military agreed with the MCI on the need to increase scale economies, although it was concerned less with the growth of big enterprises, which it associated with the *zaibatsu* it mistrusted, than with the development of standardized war equipment. Large producers, it felt, would develop products with internally consistent parts. The military also wanted to promote the specialty manufacturing needed for weapons production. The larger machine tool factories that the MCI sought to encourage, however, were producing only general-purpose machines; smaller companies occupied the special-purpose niches. Consequently, the military pushed the MCI to modify its two hundred tool test so that specialty producers with only fifty tools could also become licensed firms.[32] Smaller specialty producers would then qualify for various government incentives under the law.

As the Machine Tool Industry Law was being promulgated, a series of other laws and rules reinforced the general push toward centralization. The machine tool sourcing rule, created in 1938, prohibited companies with thirty or more tools from selling to any buyer other than the government without MCI permission. Another, based on the Emergency Capital Regulation Law of September 1937, stipulated that any firm wishing to begin or to halt machinery production must obtain from the MCI a license to do so.[33] Both acts were explicitly aimed at small producers and sought to build up the armaments industries; the limits on new entrants and the encouragement of consolidation to sell to the lucrative military market would either force small firms out of the industry or make them increase their scale.

Was the Machine Tool Industry Law, as administered by the MCI, successful? Observers who have adopted the bureaucratic regulation thesis suggest that the law did entice big capital into heavy industry, thus creating economies of scale.[34] And indeed, a flood of new companies, some with *zaibatsu* capital affiliation, began to enter the sector with the passage of the Machine Tool Industry Law. Between July

Table 2.2. Firms Licensed under the Machine Tool Industry Law, 1938–1940

Company name	Type of company	Date licensed
Okuma	Big Five firm	July 1938
Hitachi Machine Tools	Reorganized firm	"
Ikegai	Big Five firm	"
Niigata	Big Five firm	"
Toyo Precision Machinery	Reorganized firm	"
Tsujo Manufacturing	Reorganized firm	"
Nissan Precision Machinery	New company	October 1938
Toyo Machinery	New company	"
Toshiba Machine Tools	New company	"
Osaka Wakayama Metals	New field	"
Dai Nihon Weapons	New company	December 1938
Karatsu Metals	Big Five firm	February 1939
Shinobara Machinery	Existing firm	"
Osaka Machinery	New field	"
Mitsubishi Electric	New company	"
Tokyo Machinery	New company	"
Jinbara Manufacturing	New company	December 1939
Toyoda Machinery	New company	November 1940
Okamoto Machine Tools	New field	"
Mitsui Machine Tools	New company	"
Osaka Iron Machinery	Reorganized	"

SOURCE: Same as for Table 2.1, p. 137.

1938 and November 1940, twenty-one companies and twenty-four factories were licensed (see Table 2.2). Of these, four firms—Hitachi, Mitsui, Toshiba, and Mitsubishi—were directly funded with *zaibatsu* capital, and several others obtained indirect *zaibatsu* financing. However, if we carefully examine the dominant strategies of licensed firms we find that the scale economies promoted by the Machine Tool Industry Law were in practice often illusory. Consider the very first set of licensed firms of July 1938. The six initial licensees were all either existing machine tool firms or reorganized companies in which two or more smaller factories combined to meet the two hundred tool limit specified by the law. They were attracted by the debenture and tax breaks offered to licensed firms. Many of the reorganized firms were backed by *zaibatsu;* Hitachi Machine Tools was funded by Hitachi Manufacturing, Toyo Precision Machinery was financed by Mitsui, and Tsujo was affiliated with the Yasuda commercial house.

The rush to qualify for state-sponsored benefits motivated many firms to make uneconomical investments or to merge incompatible, often physically separate assembly operations under a single operational banner. Okuma, for instance, engaged in what were later disparaged as "undisciplined" (*kakekomi*) purchases of machinery to make the limit; the company had 117 machines in 1936, over 200 by 1938. Ikegai qualified only by counting two factories in Mita and Kanagawa which were several miles apart. Operations divorced in this manner could not contribute to economies of scale at the factory level. Finally, the reorganized firms supported by *zaibatsu* were often patched together more to achieve nominal compliance with the law than to increase volume or quality. Hitachi, for instance, was an amalgam of several companies, including the machinery division of Tokyo Gas, located in Omori and Kawasaki, and its operations were spread over several geographically separate plants.[35]

This pattern of development extended to the second wave of licensees of October 1938, in which "new companies" predominated. The establishment of these new firms often resulted from the strategic calculations of larger manufacturing concerns. Some firms, for instance, wanted to use the financial provisions of the law to fund their internal tooling requirements; Toshiba and Nissan, and later Dai Nihon, Mitsubishi, Toyoda, and Mitsui were all cases in which the machinery divisions of large concerns were spun off as "separate" machine tool firms and financed under the liberal stock, depreciation, subsidy, and tax provisions of the Machine Tool Industry Law. Others sought government machinery research grants for their parent interests, in effect subsidizing corporate tooling. The "new" companies rarely contributed to national product development or the military market. Though Nissan, for instance, accounted for about 9 percent of total output from licensed firms by 1940, suggesting some development of scale economies, Mitsubishi, Toyoda, and Toyo each accounted for less than 3 percent of total production by licensed firms in 1941.[36]

The last category of licensees involved firms shifting to machine tool production though their real expertise was in other fields. Osaka Machinery was a spinning machine producer, for example, Tokyo Machinery made printing equipment, and Jinbara manufactured hydraulic generators. In each of these cases, material or capital shortages eliminated demand in the major markets of the firms involved. Because the Machine Tool Industry Law was so heavily geared toward subsidizing investments, it gave large machinery manufacturers in other fields a way to ease the burden of market adjustment. Most of these firms tried to preserve their technical skills in their original markets by making machine tools on equipment better suited for other uses, thus maintaining their fundamental technology in the hope of future improvements in demand. Thus these "new field" companies entered the machine tool market as a defensive move financed by the government. Under the law, large-scale companies in declining sectors found a subsidized shelter from adverse market conditions; they were not "induced" to shift to metal machinery production.

Even the law's most ardent supporters recognized the fundamentally hollow character of the license scheme. One Japanese scholar in the 1930s, who had written forcefully about the regressive character of small producers, supporting a policy that would stimulate centralization in the industry, lamented the law's results. The government had sought to enhance the production efficiency, output, and technology of machine tools in Japan, he observed, but "when the government's current machine tool industry policies are examined, they are not able to achieve their fundamental target through reorganization. For example, in order to promote technology the Machine Tool Industry Law was promulgated. With it came a 'large scale industry' orientation in policy. But although we have a 'large scale industry' based on the Law, the purpose of this industry has not been the promotion of technology."[37] The licensing of firms did not lead to expected results in production, efficiency, or technological advances.

After the promulgation of the Machine Tool Industry Law, however, the proportion of production achieved by the licensed firms did appear to increase. Between 1939 and 1941, as illustrated in Figure 2.1, licensed company production rose from 27 percent to 47 percent of the total value of output. These numbers suggest that the consolidation scheme was working, that the MCI policy of freezing out smaller firms was proving successful.

But several factors overstate the share of the bigger companies; indeed, the evidence points more to the surprising resilience of small-scale firms in the face of concerted bureaucratic hostility and wartime contingencies. The most important distorting element was price inflation caused by the fact that the licensed firms themselves ran the pricing mechanisms set up under the law. Under the legislation, licensed companies were organized into the Japanese Machine Tool Manufacturers Organization (JMTMO) in 1938. Standing committees in the organization submitted price specifications for MCI approval, which was generally automatic in cases of standard classes of machines. "New" tools—even slightly modified models—were priced according to what the manufacturer submitted to the JMTMO. Furthermore, to enhance the trend toward scale increases, the government set the prices it paid for its machinery according to the size of the manufacturing firm: the bigger the firm, the higher the price. If the price of an "A" group machine tool—produced by JMTMO members—was ¥10,000, the same tool made by a medium-sized firm

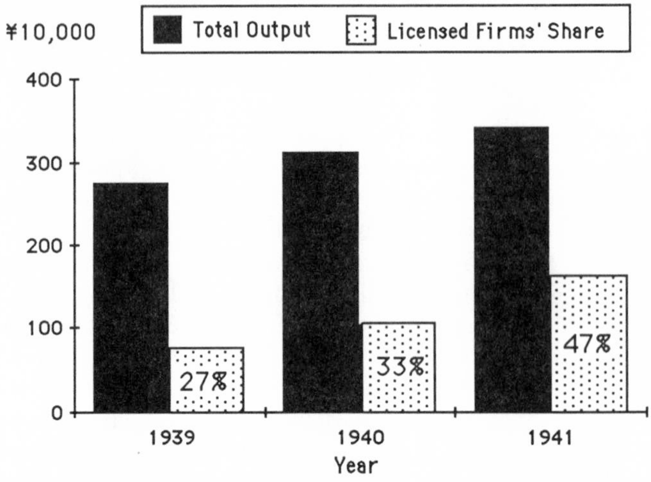

Figure 2.1. Share of Licensed Firms in Total Machine Tool Output, by Value, 1939–1941
SOURCE: Nihon Kōsaku Kikai Kōgyōkai (Japanese Machine Tool Builders Association), *Hahanaru kikai: San-jū nen no ayumi* (Mother machines: A 30 year history) (Tokyo: Seisanzai Marketing, 1982), p. 46.

would be priced as a "B" tool at ¥7,500, smaller firms in a "C" group would get ¥5,000, and so on.[38]

By 1941 JMTMO members were receiving over three times what other companies could charge for lathes, twice as much for milling machines, and three times as much for grinders. Overall, licensed companies were paid about double the price that nonlicensed companies received. In fact, the primary product of the Machine Tool Industry Law was price inflation (see Figure 2.2). Though the major goal of the law was to expand machinery output, production measured as the number of machines peaked in 1938 at 67,260 and had actually fallen about 20 percent by 1944. Nevertheless, the value of output of the industry rose 300 percent in the same period.

Indeed, if we consider the *number* of machines rather than the *value* of output, licensed firms accounted for a much smaller share of production than value statistics indicate. In 1943, their best year, licensed companies made just 35 percent of Japanese machine tools, and their share fell back to 31 percent by 1944 (see Figure 2.3). Thus even with the Machine Tool Industry Law, the emergence of new companies, strong bureaucratic support, and a wartime emergency, 70 percent of the country's machine tools were produced by unlicensed firms.

A second factor affecting apparent consolidation was the growing reliance of licensed firms on subcontracting. Licensed companies re-

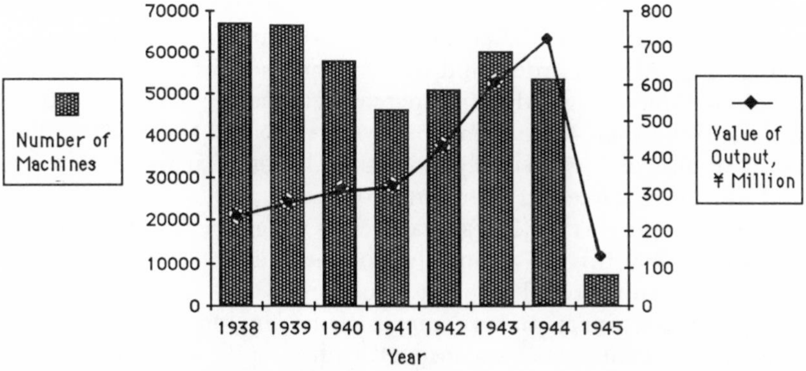

Figure 2.2. Price Inflation and Machinery Output in the Machine Tool Sector, 1938–1945
SOURCE: Same as for Figure 2.1, p. 47.

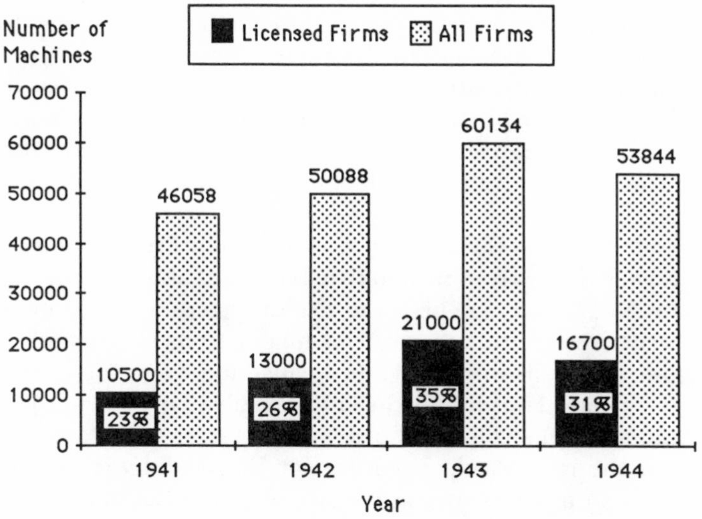

Figure 2.3. Share of Licensed Firms in Machine Tool Production, 1941–1944 (Number of Machines)
SOURCE: Sugiyama Kazuo, "Kōsaku kikai kōgyō no genjō to ikusei no mitchi" (The current situation of the machine tool industry and the road to growth), reprinted in Nihon Kōsaku Kikai Kōgyōkai (1982), "*shiryō*" sec., p.12. This, the first postwar White Paper on the machine tool industry, was published by the *gyōkai* in 1951.

ceived priority in the placement of orders from the government, the major purchaser immediately before and during the war. Because of a huge gap between orders and real capacity, however, licensed firms in all manufacturing industries increasingly met demand by shifting orders to the small-scale firms they were supposed to supplant. The increase in orders was simply more than licensed firms could meet, and they were forced to farm out production.

One example was the Nakajima aircraft conglomerate. By 1944, as the war clearly turned against Japan, the military was desperately seeking to centralize all airplane production into one or two huge groups of machinery makers, metals firms, engine companies, and other components makers associated with aircraft. Late in 1944 the Homare Group, named for the airplane Nakajima produced, was created as a supposedly integrated aircraft firm with Nakajima at its core. The Homare Group was not a single firm; rather, it was composed of machinery producers who entered the airplane market as their own markets collapsed because of material, capital, or demand shortages, drawn by the resources the military was diverting to aircraft. In turn, as the military concentrated on (largely one-man, suicide-mission) aircraft, in a last-ditch effort to forestall defeat, Nakajima was swamped with orders it could not fulfill. It became dependent on smaller firms. Subcontracting rose from about 33 percent—already very high—in the middle of the war to over 40 percent by 1945.[39] In fact, reliance on subcontracting was one of the features that distinguished Japan from other wartime economies; one reason commonly advanced for the Japanese defeat is lack of rationalization because small firms had captured so much of the machinery market by the end of the war.

The same process is evident in machine tools. Prewar subcontracting averages varied from firm to firm but ran at about 20 percent per company.[40] The average began to rise dramatically, however, as orders were directed to licensed firms unable to meet demand. Table 2.3 shows shortfalls in production relative to orders for Ikegai and Tokyo Gas (later Hitachi) for the last available years, 1937–1938. For both companies the volume of orders in 1937 was twice capacity; one year later the ratio was 333 percent for Ikegai and 222 percent for Tokyo Gas. Companies such as Ikegai and Tokyo Gas, burdened with orders that vastly outstripped their maximum capacity, had to rely on outside purchases to meet demand.

Thus the "big company" policy central to the Machine Tool Industry Law neither produced scale economies nor enhanced output. Nor did it halt the flourishing growth of small producers. The sourcing and capital laws promulgated in conjunction with the industry law

Table 2.3. Shortfalls in Machine Tool Production Ability, 1937–1938 (in ¥ 1,000)

	1937		1938	
Company	Orders	Capacity	Orders	Capacity
Ikegai	10,000	5,000	20,000	6,000
Tokyo Gas	12,000	6,000	20,000	9,000

SOURCE: Nihon Kōsaku Kikai Kōgyōkai (Japan Machine Tool Builders Association), *Nihon kōsaku kikai kōgyō hattatsū no katei* (The process of Japan's machine tool industry's growth) (Tokyo, 1951), p. 127.

itself strongly favored consolidation, but evidence suggests that despite the effort to eliminate them, small firms were able to protect themselves and even expand operations.

One set of data, from the Small and Medium Industry Survey Group, covers the total number of firms and employees in the machinery, tooling, and equipment industries between 1938 and 1942. The survey, one of the few published under wartime secrecy laws, covers machine tool firms and related industries. Because legislation affected general machinery sectors in much the same way as the machine tool industry itself, however, the survey provides us with an important clue as to the fate of small machinery businesses. If government policies were effective, we should expect to see a decline in the number of machinery companies. In fact, the number of machinery industry factories *grew*, from 17,750 in 1938 to 25,097 in 1942 (a 141 percent increase), as employment more than doubled (see Table 2.4). This growth is particularly impressive because in wartime the total output of the machinery industry stagnated or even fell; more firms and more employees were crowding into a shrinking market. Because the vast majority of these firms were small companies, the survey

Table 2.4. Changes in Employment and Firms in the Machinery Industry, 1938–1942

	1938	1939	1940	1941	1942
Number of Factories	17,750	23,150	24,990	25,601	25,097
Number of Employees	990,000	1,352,000	1,541,000	1,702,000	2,084,000

SOURCE: Chūshōkigyō Chōsakai Hen (Small and Medium Enterprise Survey Group), *Chūshōkigyō no hattatsū (2): Chūshōkigyō kenkyū vol. VII* (The development of small and medium enterprises (2): Small and medium enterprise research vol. VII) (Tokyo, Chūshōkigyō Chōsakai, 1962), p. 55.

indicates that small enterprises actually expanded as the state tried to consolidate the industry.

This finding is broadly confirmed in a survey conducted by the Eastern Japan Machine Tool Council between 1942 and 1945. The Eastern Japan survey did not cover very small firms, so it understated the total number of active firms by a large margin—firms of 5 to 30 workers, as noted earlier, accounted for 1,531 of the total of 1,978 companies engaged in machine tool production in 1938. But the survey does provide a good measure of growth in middle-level firms, those not among the twenty-one licensed companies. Its results show that the number of medium-sized machine tool firms increased 33 percent between 1942 and 1944, from 353 to 446 enterprises. The increase was halted only in 1945, when factories were destroyed by allied bombing and materials shortages became critical.[41]

In sum, the license scheme apparently failed, as did efforts regarding technical and volume promotion connected with the Machine Tool Industry Law; as total output fell, price inflation rather than increased quality and scale economies was fostered. Finally, small businesses were not prevented from entering the market; where resources were available, small enterprises flourished. The same pattern of bureaucratic and policy failure may be observed in the establishment of the *tōseikai.*

THE *TŌSEIKAI* AND THE ATTEMPT TO COORDINATE WARTIME PRODUCTION

In 1941 the government, under pressure from the military, began to push for the consolidation of strategic military industries into groups that it intended to manage through a system of centralized control. These groups were called *tōseikai* or control councils. The government would establish basic objectives, and the oversight bodies created for each industry *tōseikai* would see to it that member firms obeyed the bureaucracy's plans. Machinery, rolling stock, armaments, and other important *tōseikai* could then be effectively directed toward wartime production. Eventually *tōseikai* were set up in several war-related industries in 1941–1943 to try to increase scale economies in weapons production, eliminate small firms (the goal of the bureaucrats), and regulate the *zaibatsu* (the aim of the military).

The bureaucracy did not control the *tōseikai,* as even contemporary historiography, which viewed the period as one of big business domination of the economy, more or less recognized. But the expansion of small firms in those machinery sectors under the purview of the *tōseikai* suggests that the *zaibatsu* were not in complete control of industry either. Indeed, smaller producers insinuated themselves into the regulatory network that was supposed to destroy them. The smaller producers registered particularly impressive successes in obtaining raw materials—whose allocation was the most important function of the *tōseikai*—and thus blunted wartime economic policies and *zaibatsu* objectives.

Controversy still exists over the *tōseikai*. Were they the apex of state control or, instead, the consolidation of monopoly interests? One view holds that the control councils represented an expansion of state authority, with disastrous results; each time the bureaucracy interfered with the economy, it was driven to additional meddling to undo its previous damage.[42] Similarly, the government's wartime controls have been interpreted as a tragic coda to the Japanese rejection of the principles of free enterprise.[43]

A much more common attitude interprets the *tōseikai* as the ultimate triumph of big business; one scholar notes that the control councils "were utterly dominated by the *zaibatsu*." That observation echoes in arguments that there was "surprisingly little government interference" in the Japanese economy during the war, and the assessment that wartime regulation was so scattered among conflicting private, bureaucratic, and military interests that eventually it was "disastrous for Japan's war effort."[44] T. A. Bisson, a member of the U.S. Occupation Forces, offered an unusually blunt evaluation of control of the *tōseikai:*

> The provisions of the Major Industries Association Ordinance, authorizing establishment of the Industrial Control Associations [*tōseikai*], were basically dictated by the business interests and deliberately intended to round out their cartels. . . . On the central issue the details are too clear to permit of any misunderstanding. The government was not asserting its control against the will of the monopolists, but was acting on terms set by the *zaibatsu* and in directions desired by them. Still less did the militarists impose their will on the business leaders. The whole history of Tojo's relationship with the *zaibatsu* before and after the Pacific War negatives any such conclusion. In the crucial struggle, beginning with Tojo's request for special powers in January 1943 and ending with the final agreement which enabled the Munitions Ministry to inaugurate its activities on January 15, 1944 the *zaibatsu* held out for unconditional victory and won it. During the latter half of this period, which lasted for a full year, the *zaibatsu* were engaged in a maneuver that can be characterized, without unduly stretching the facts, as a sitdown strike. If the Army/Navy/Air Force General Headquarters were to insist on retaining administrative control over an expanded aircraft production program,

> involving complete mobilization of the industrial giants of the Japanese economy, the monopolists were simply not interested. They became willing to play ball when the administrative authority was vested in a Munitions Ministry controlled by their men and operating within the framework of a Munitions Company Act to which they subscribed.[45]

The idea that the *zaibatsu* controlled the wartime industrial councils has emerged as the dominant interpretation of this phase of economic policy.

These accounts have glossed over an obvious problem: Why should a wartime economy be subject to intense private pressures or to competition among various branches of the government? If Japan had a strong state capable of bureaucratic control, why did wartime crises not produce the kinds of institutions that wielded authoritative management even in America? Moreover, such accounts assume that wartime industrial regulation was a matter of conflict between the *zaibatsu* and the military or civilian bureaucrats alone. But if this is so, why did smaller firms strongly influence the growth of machinery, aircraft, and armaments industries, the very focus of wartime contention?

The machinery *tōseikai* were in fact shaped by much more than power struggles between "new bureaucrats" and big capital. Indeed, they became the center of competition for scarce materials among large, medium, and small producers. Wartime shortages forced all producers to struggle to assure themselves of the raw materials they needed for their operations. The various machinery *tōseikai* grew out of a metals distribution program, and in the final analysis they could not and did not exclude small firms. Rather, small enterprises pushed themselves into the distribution network and came to share control of the *tōseikai* themselves. Presence on the *tōseikai* ensured small firms that they would be allocated raw materials, which in turn helps explain their rapid growth and subcontracting influence even as the state, the military, and big business—albeit for different reasons—were avidly seeking consolidation.

The machinery industry *tōseikai* were the descendants of a metals distribution system established within the MCI in February 1938, the Metals Control Council (Tekkō Tōsei Kyōgōkai). Metals shortages necessitated a system of allocation. Moreover, the government wanted to ensure that available resources went to munitions production. The Metals Control Council began the actual dispersal of metal stock in July 1938 with a "ticket system"; qualified machinery firms received a card voucher they later redeemed for necessary materials.[46]

Securing increasingly scarce metal stock was among the most important factors affecting company survival immediately before the war. As a result, influence in the Metals Control Council was crucial for manufacturing enterprises. From its inception the council saw intense lobbying efforts by large and small firms to gain preferred status in metals distribution. In turn, the bureaucracy sought to use official status as a council member as an incentive to encourage the consolidation of enterprises seeking power on the council.

The first move in the organizational battle was made in May 1938, by larger but non-*zaibatsu* machinery firms. Machinery and electronics producers created an umbrella organization, the Machinery Industries Metals Distribution Association, under which specific sectors were grouped in separate divisions. The Big Five companies were placed in the fifteenth division of the new organization as the machine tool representatives. This new organization was an attempt to obtain MCI authorization to administer the distribution of metals and thus to secure preference for allied members.

But the MCI wanted to force large machinery manufacturers to merge, or at least coordinate production, in exchange for control of materials allocation. In response, the big machinery firms reorganized in October 1938, in what appeared to be an attempt to create a stronger, more integrated control association, as the MCI had requested. In the machine tool division, for example, all licensed or soon-to-be-licensed companies were invited to participate. The new, expanded division called itself the Japan Machine Tool Manufacturers Association (JMTMA), but it was again dominated by the Big Five: a representative from Ikegai was president, and four of the five vice-presidential posts went to Niigata, Tokyo Gas, Karatsu, and Okuma. At the same time the umbrella organization was renamed the Japan Machinery Manufacturers Association. The MCI then tried to turn over the Metals Control Council to this new group.[47]

Large enterprise control of metals distribution might well have been expected to overwhelm the thousands of small machinery manufacturers. Indeed, the president of the JMTMA went so far as to suggest a reorganization plan for small and medium-sized machine tool firms which would have established each JMTMA member as a parent company around which other factories would cluster. The 1,900 or so small-scale machine tool firms would be forced to accept either institutionalized subservience to the larger companies or bankruptcy because of inability to secure materials.[48] The small producers resisted these moves. The heart of their strategy was to organize into regional groups and to use their combined strength to pressure the bureaucracy for access to the metals councils. In 1939 smaller machinery manufacturers formed the New Diversified Industrial Manufacturers Association, an umbrella organization imitating the Japan

Table 2.5. Regional Groups of Small Firms in the National Machine Tool Manufacturers Association, 1940

Name	Number
First Tokyo MTMA	162
First Osaka MTMA	128
Aichi Prefecture First MTMA	45
Shizuoka Prefecture MTMA	24
Niigata Prefecture MTMA	18
Hyogo Prefecture First MTMA	14
Kanagawa Prefecture MTMA	12
Total	403

NOTE: MTMA stands for Machine Tool Manufacturers Association

SOURCE: Nihon Kōsaku Kikai Kōgyōkai (1951), p. 127.

Machinery Manufacturers Association. In July the machine tool branch of the new association was formed, calling itself the National Machine Tool Manufacturers Association. Initially entry was restricted to companies with twenty machines or more, although many members were much smaller but noted for impressive technology.[49] In 1939, 296 firms from seven geographical areas entered the association; by 1940, as Table 2.5 shows, the number of firms had risen to 403. In addition to this effort by medium-sized and selected smaller producers, thousands of very small machinery firms also formed locality-based industrial organizations. Accurate statistics on the growth of these organizations are not available, but by 1939 over a thousand regional groups contained more than 116,000 very small firms.

The combined efforts of small firms brought about another reorganization of the metals distribution system. In late 1939 all of the representative bodies for machinery companies, including machine tool firms, came together under a new group, the Japan Metal Products Manufacturing Amalgamated Union. Large firms were represented in a division called the Japan Machinery Manufacturers Union, which numbered 19 industries and 233 firms. Medium-sized firms made up a division called the New Diversified Products Union, composed of groups from 13 regions involving 69 industries and 2,146 enterprises. The smallest firms were part of either the Diversified Parts Union of 229 industries and 14,023 firms or the City, Town, and Prefecture Manufacturing Union, representing 1,233 regional groups with 116,153 members.

Though the bureaucrats wanted to use access to metals as a tool to force consolidation, the smaller producers had their own voice in the distribution process, so they could secure access to raw materials without meeting state objectives. The small firms forced through the creation of a system of shared interests in which the *zaibatsu* did not even hold dominant power in the *large firm* branch of the Japan Metal Products Manufacturing Amalgamated Union; Big Five firms were the major force. The influence of large firms as a group was anyway reduced by the presence of organizations for smaller producers. Within the distribution system, which became the basis for the machinery *tōseikai* set up in 1942, big capital did not defeat the government and establish monopoly power, nor did the bureaucracy dictate industrial policy. Rather, all affected industrial actors carved places for themselves within the regulatory organization.

The growth of the Japan Metal Products Manufacturing Amalgamated Union coincided with a gradual disenchantment with piecemeal government regulation. With the Machine Tool Industry Law of 1938, the MCI had attempted to increase scale production by licensing, controlling market entry, limiting machinery sales to military clients, and, finally, setting prices. As we have seen, all of these efforts failed. The result was inflated machinery prices paid for with public funds. In March 1941 the industry law was repealed and with it the system of selective licensing. The ad hoc system of price controls, standards, sourcing rules, and regulations concerning market entry was also abolished, and preparations were made to incorporate all machine tool firms into an industry organization or *tōseikai.*[50]

The *tōseikai* were mandated by the Major Industries Consolidation Order (Jūyō Sangyō Dantai Rei) of August 1941. The order called for the creation of coordinated groups in designated industries to "strengthen more effectively the domestic economy" and for the integration of militarily significant industries to promote the war effort.[51] It was based on Article 18 of the National Mobilization Law, a hotly debated measure passed in 1938 that gave the military-controlled government vague, general powers to control the economy in preparation for war.[52] However, the formal powers conferred on the military by the mobilization law were in practice largely rolled back, and the *tōseikai* ended up looking like the ineffective, privately managed cartels of the mid-1930s.

The first *tōseikai* were created in the automobile and rolling stock industries in December 1941. In January of the following year all machinery firms were organized into three overlapping *tōseikai:* an industrial machinery group, an electric machinery group, and a precision machinery organization. These *tōseikai* were given broad authority for pricing, production, and structural policies. They were supposed to be an "external organ" of the MCI, faithfully implementing government policies, but instead, from the very start, private firms acting through the old metals distribution system affected every aspect of the *tōseikai*'s operation.[53]

Most machine tool firms were included in the precision machinery *tōseikai;* 318 of the 381 companies in this group made machine tools. Members were drawn from all three branches of the Japan Metal Products Manufacturing Amalgamated Union, although the groups of large and medium-sized firms had the most power. The *tōseikai* elected its own president, from non-*zaibatsu* affiliated Osaka Machinery, which choice the MCI duly approved in December 1942. The precision machinery *tōseikai* was thus a self-regulating body made up of firms originally brought together under the Materials Control Council of 1939.[54]

Wartime conditions greatly affected all of the machinery *tōseikai,* and they operated only for about eighteen months, from late 1942 to mid-1944. They attempted planning as the cartels of the 1930s had done, but they faced additional problems, among them severe difficulties over resources. Often distribution, still made by a ticket system approved by the *tōseikai,* was inefficient; firms were issued tickets for nonexistent materials. And promises to satisfy military demand for specialty equipment, a problem first identified in the 1929 Resources Bureau report, went unfulfilled. Instead, the *tōseikai* became primarily the focus of competition for scarce resources.

To protect its members from a cutoff in metals supply, for example, the precision machinery *tōseikai* created its own resource company, the Precision Machinery Materials Procurement Stock Company, in June 1943. The company was funded with public monies authorized by the self-regulating *tōseikai.* Its purpose was to secure the various resources that member firms needed by competing against other agencies, among them the military itself, in domestic and international markets. The company could not overcome shortages and trade interruptions, and in 1944 it was disbanded. But its establishment suggests the dominant agenda of the precision machinery *tōseikai:* it was an instrument for obtaining critically needed resources for the benefit of member companies.

In manufacturing the *tōseikai* did not lead to private or state consolidation. In machinery they were, in fact, especially useful for certain groups of smaller firms; by entering the regulatory network, small-scale producers could assure themselves of a share of the metals allocations. The *tōseikai* were one reason why small producers were able to survive and grow during wartime.

Another reason was that the *tōseikai* provided firms with opportunities to escape *zaibatsu* pressure. Because the *tōseikai* were organized along product lines, they cut across the structure of *zaibatsu* power; the combines were conglomerations of firms in different industries. Within the *tōseikai* companies could use group or government contacts to minimize the power of big capital. Thus the *zaibatsu* became increasingly hostile to the *tōseikai,* because their affiliated firms repeatedly justified independent action on the grounds that they were constrained by the decisions of the control associations. But, of course, these firms had a large say in the strategies to which they were "forced" to adhere. As Chokki Toshiaki observes, this consideration may have *reversed* the trend toward *zaibatsu* entry into machinery production that the Machine Tool Industry Law fostered:

> With the creation of the precision machinery *tōseikai,* the movement of big capital toward tie-ups with small and medium machine tool concerns died out. Also, mergers between members of the *tōseikai* fostered by external capital sources ended. The reason for this was that within the precision machinery *tōseikai,* a form of cartel, even small and medium enterprises could maintain their stock of capital, resources, and workers. Moreover, the machine tool firms backed by big capital, in their role as *tōseikai* members, would be subject to cartel-like regulations promulgated by small and medium machine tool firms, and thus their previously close ties with their parent companies would weaken. This gave rise at the time to a notion of "*tōseikai* and *zaibatsu* conflict."[55]

The *tōseikai,* in contrast to the picture painted in conventional arguments, tended to retard both private and public centralization.

Manufacturing *tōseikai* were abandoned in 1944 as increasingly scarce materials were funneled to certain classes of machinery for use by aircraft firms. In response, as we have seen in the case of Nakajima Aircraft, machine tool firms poured into the industry, surviving because lack of capacity forced aircraft contractors to subcontract. Aircraft manufacturing was to have been coordinated by a new Munitions Ministry, staffed by the MCI, which as Bisson argued preserved private interests even as the war effort was failing. Nevertheless, the ministry still sought consolidation; its staff wanted to integrate operations around factories such as the Homare division of Nakajima Aircraft and the Atsuta airplane group of Kawasaki Manufacturing.

Materials shortages scuttled all of these efforts. The planning targets for each of the affiliated aircraft machine tool groups fell short by an average of more than 50 percent. The Homare group never came close to meeting its objectives, while others, like the Atsuta group, were planned much too late in the war and were never implemented. The critical situation in resources is revealed by production statistics: the total number of machines produced fell sharply, from 53,000 units in 1944 to just 7,300 units in 1945.[56]

By the end of the war, in conventional accounts, government policies and *zaibatsu* pressures had forced a reduction in the number of small firms through attrition or consolidation. And indeed the wartime emergency *did* transform the role of small firms, as we shall see in chapter 4. As resource shortages forced them to focus on the manufacture of munitions, small firms began to specialize in subcontracting. Before the war smaller enterprises had built finished goods from mass-produced commodities; after Japan's defeat they turned to making parts for final assemblers.

But did smaller firms suffer more than larger ones at the time of Japan's defeat? The evidence has been exaggerated, and we have seen evidence of the continued vitality of small firms. Furthermore, closures of small factories were the result not so much of policy as of allied bombing patterns, which focused on urban areas where the older, small-factory hamlets were concentrated. Edwin Reubens, one of the few American scholars to study small businesses in the direct aftermath of the war, argued that consolidation policies did not destroy small firms but that allied bombing, coupled with a Japanese military draft that affected male operators of small independent enterprises, did. A decline in production by small firms at the end of the war reflected not the success of prewar policy but rather the effects of wartime physical devastation on Japanese society: "To sum up the history of small plants: they were not much affected by war-time changes until after 1942; as a widespread form of organization they persisted throughout the war; individual units suffered some closings during 1943 and 1944, and suffered widespread destruction during 1945; while the end of the war undoubtedly found a great reduction in the total number of establishments (the reduction being concentrated around the smallest units), the physical and organizational potential for a fairly rapid revival still existed."[57]

The history of the *tōseikai* provides evidence that the bureaucratic regulation thesis misstates the genesis and effectiveness of prewar industrial policy. In all three phases of prewar regulation—planning, cartels, and finally control associations—there is no instance in which bureaucratic or military industrial plans were effective. No policies were implemented without being subject to extreme pressures from private firms. The very formulation of state strategies almost always involved reliance on the regulated parties for data, insight, or advice. And, most dramatically, smaller firms, the target of the consolidation effort, eventually employed the *tōseikai* to assure their own survival. As we will see in the postwar period, such a transformation of policy instruments is not a singular event; rather, it is a consistent feature of Japanese industrial regulation. Strategies were frequently modified so that they actually produced unintended consequences or results contrary to the original goals. The *tōseikai* period does not support conventional arguments about coordinated production in wartime Japan.

Conclusions

In no case of prewar or wartime regulation of the machinery industry did the government achieve its objectives. The major goal of the MCI was to enhance production scale through factory consolidation. Neither the cartel schemes, the license laws, pressure in the materials councils, the *tōseikai,* nor the wartime reorganizations of the aircraft industry produced this result. The firms that were directly subsidized and licensed managed to secure state support without complying with general policy. Small firms found ways of protecting themselves, often by partially coopting the institutions that were to have destroyed them. Production plans such as those for standardized machines, even when authored by big firms, met with no success. As late as 1945 the military was still trying to find a way to force companies to make the tools it wanted for armaments and aircraft.

This record of policy failure is not what the bureaucratic regulation thesis leads one to expect. In order to carry out their policies, strong states need authoritative powers to enforce compliance. Either the prewar Japanese government did not have authority, or it could not independently use the formal powers that were conferred on it. The prewar bureaucracy, even with military backing, lacked the authoritative powers required for effective policy implementation.

Nor did this failure produce a consolidated manufacturing system dominated by the *zaibatsu,* as conventional histories contend. Even though it stimulated some advances by big capital in prewar Japanese machinery and other important sectors, small firms retained and in some instances even expanded their share of the market. Indeed, the comparison between prewar Japan and the United States underscores the fragmented, decentralized nature of the Japanese economy: where in the mid-1930s at most 40 percent of Japanese manufacturing value added was produced by firms of five hundred or more employees, large firms accounted for 70 percent of value added in America by 1929 and 75 percent by the start of the war.[58]

Prewar Japan should be an easy case for the bureaucratic regulation thesis. According to the theory, the government developed interventionist skills while generating scale production facilities and centralized institutions that would be crucial to the postwar expansion. In this interpretation the state was able to coordinate the economy, though frequently the balance of prewar power forced the government to permit the *zaibatsu* to consolidate production on their own. But as we have seen, the establishment of cartel-like groups provided no guarantee that firms would be able to coordinate production or prices, nor did it reduce conflict—it transformed market struggles into debates within an organization, but it did not eliminate them. The same conflicts were later preserved in the structure of the *tōseikai*. Thus the prewar experience offers little support for the notion that state bureaucrats were influential in generating economic change in Japan. Postwar policies, as the next chapter shows, also pose problems for the bureaucratic regulation thesis.

Chapter Three

Economic Regulation and the Postwar Machine Tool Industry

Postwar industrial policies affecting expansion of the machine tool industry demonstrate strong evidence of MITI's inability to control development. Chapter 2 showed that prewar attempts to coordinate production failed because politics constrained the activity of industrial interests such as the MCI, the military, and small and large machinery producers. After the war political struggles between MITI, the Japan Machine Tool Builders Association (JMTBA or the *gyōkai*)—the representative body for machinery producers—and machinery firms outside the association similarly thwarted bureaucratic policy objectives. Consequently postwar economic policy, like prewar efforts, did not consolidate production and restrict the freedom of small firms to enter the market with new designs, as MITI sought. The resolution of conflict about the character of postwar machinery development, I will argue, was one of the political prerequisites for the expansion of flexible manufacturing in Japan.

In the bureaucratic regulation thesis, MITI's postwar economic policies came in several stages. First was a strategy of financial support; MITI directed funds toward key sectors from the mid-1950s to the late 1960s, to rebuild the nation's industrial base. Coupled with this effort was an attempt to establish production and other performance targets for specific industries through planning documents that stipulated concrete objectives. Then, from the 1960s onward, MITI switched to a policy of consolidation. The government responded to imminent capital liberalization mandated by Japanese entry into the General Agreement on Tariffs and Trade (GATT) with cartel schemes, plans to increase economies of scale, and encouragement for rationalization. Finally, in the 1970s MITI transformed many industries, bringing about the integration of electronics and computers within important industrial sectors, which also increased the efficiency of Japanese factories through automation. Trade successes were built on this advantage. In the bureaucratic regulation thesis, then, it was MITI's financial support, planning skills, and consolidation strategies that made it possible for Japan to perfect the manufacturing techniques which led to price and quality advantages over its trading partners.[1]

The machine tool industry was directly affected by each of these phases of Japanese industrial policy. Under the first and second Temporary Measures for the Promotion of the Machinery Industry Laws (1956–1960 and 1961–1965), MITI attempted extensive planning with financial support. In the third term of the Machinery Promotion Law (1966–1970) MITI pressured for the cartelization of machinery production, a goal it continued to pursue in the context of the Temporary Measures for the Promotion of the Electrical Machinery Law (1971–1978). In the latter period of that law, and with the promulgation of the Temporary Measures for the Promotion of the Information Machinery Industry Law (1978 onward), the bureaucracy apparently tried to advance the development of computerized machinery such as NC machine tools.

The machine tool industry provides an important test case for the bureaucratic regulation approach, and I will argue that none of MITI's machinery policies was successful. In the period of planning and financial support output objectives had no effect on industry performance, while government loans did not generate economic expansion. The cartelization phase did not reduce firm entry or market volatility, nor did it rationalize production. In fact, the machinery industry actually intended its cartels to *thwart* MITI's objectives. Finally, NC development and export successes were not the result of government or private efforts to coordinate production and marketing abroad. Rather, they were generated by a domestic demand for new tools which producers in other countries apparently ignored; exports were built on the appeal of new, smaller NC products. As we will see, in no single instance did MITI's policies lead to anticipated market outcomes. This failure helped promote flexible manufacturing in Japan.

The Postwar Recession and the Creation of the *Gyōkai*

Japanese postwar machinery policy was shaped by the industry's economic circumstances in the aftermath of defeat. The extreme economic hardship of 1945–1950 led machine tool firms to organize a representative body, the *gyōkai,* to press for government support. The *gyōkai* was the locus of most major strategic initiatives undertaken to promote the production of machine tools.

Immediately after the war the American Occupation (SCAP) authorities recommended that machine tools be confiscated for reparations payments, and that the machinery and stock at ninety-one machine tool plants be seized. In addition, machine tools in other installations affiliated with military production such as armaments or aircraft were also seized. Through these means SCAP initially appropriated up to 50 percent of the machine tools and machinery manufacturing capacity of the Japanese economy.[2]

Political and market pressures modified the reparations plan. The rebuilding of Japan as a strong ally took precedence over punitive measures, and the U.S. military and Japanese industrialists strongly resisted moves to impound machinery. Furthermore, no agreement could be reached on what should be done with the appropriated equipment. Faced with a reversal of its mandate to dismantle Japanese industry, and under pressure to support the regrowth of manufacturing, SCAP finally decided to distribute the confiscated machine tools to other Japanese factories. The move devastated machinery producers. Of the 590,000 machine tools in Japan in 1945, 220,000 had been seized for reparations; the majority were ultimately distributed to Japanese manufacturers.[3] The result was a tremendous glut of standard machine tools, which crippled the industry's postwar recovery. Not until 1960 would the machine tool industry return to its 1938 benchmarks in annual value of industrial output and annual number of machines produced.

Other SCAP policies exacerbated the problem. Deflationary measures were particularly hard on capital goods producers, as machinery consumers cut back on credit purchases because of high interest rates and made do with older equipment. Between 1949 and 1950 the total number of machines produced fell from 6,680 to just 4,039, the lowest since 1932, while the value of output fell 28 percent despite the persistence of inflation.[4]

The saturation of markets with older Japanese machines helped promote machine tool imports. Large and small users of industrial machinery wanted state-of-the-art equipment for their own recovery, but Japanese producers lacked the sophistication required. Moreover, the effective destruction of their mainstream tooling markets by the distribution of reparations equipment made it impossible for domestic companies to generate capital for the necessary investments in equipment and technology. Japanese equipment users had to look abroad for tools. Imports flooded the market after 1949, when foreign capital restrictions were eased for machinery. In 1950 the value of imports amounted to 29 percent of domestic production; by 1955 imports accounted for 57.7 percent of the domestic market; and as late as 1962 import dependency was still at 32.6 percent.[5]

Domestic oversupply and import penetration led to a severe retrenchment in the machine tool industry. The number of firms surveyed by the Eastern Japan Machine Tool Council fell from a wartime high of 446 in 1944 to 186 in 1946, and to just 21 companies by 1951 as 94 percent of prewar and wartime firms suspended operations.[6] Failures included *zaibatsu* affiliates and smaller independents alike. Demand for domestic machinery was dependent on the procurement policies of large, nationalized industries. For example, over 50 percent of Japanese-made machine tools in 1947 were purchased by the national railways.

Economic distress prompted surviving firms to try to recreate the prewar industry councils or *tōseikai,* to coordinate the interests of the machinery industry. In postwar terminology such industry groups are called *gyōkai.* Industrial *gyōkai* are a prominent feature of the postwar Japanese economy. They are typically composed of the major firms in any given manufacturing sector. In the machine tool *gyōkai,* member companies were either large firms that possessed some special or superior technology or firms that had a history of influence with the bureaucracy or in the industry at large. The machinery *gyōkai* served two purposes: it was the main lobbying organization for the industry, serving as liaison with the bureaucracy; it was also the locus of contacts among members.

The first efforts to organize the machinery industry after the war were undertaken in January 1946, when one hundred machine tool firms from the Tokyo area tentatively established the Japan Machine Tool Council as an umbrella organization. In May 1948 a second council was created to represent firms from Osaka and Kyoto. These councils, though explicitly modeled on the *tōseikai,* were regionally fragmented and contained different members. Whereas wartime *tōseikai* were set up with the explicit participation of the government, moreover, the new councils were independent creations of the affected machinery firms. These councils were not immediately successful. Sentiment ran extremely high against industries associated with armaments; representative groups that resembled the *tōseikai* were, given American antipathy toward wartime institutions, in particular disfavor. Nor could impoverished machine tool firms afford the staff and facilities that the proposed councils required. In consequence, the Tokyo council was dissolved in July 1948, and the Osaka-Kyoto council in May 1949.

Factional splits between regional groups of producers and the problems of financing industrial groups continued to fragment producer organizations. Surviving machine tool firms were generally grouped in one of three different organizations: the Eastern Japan Machine Tool Council (Tokyo) with twenty-seven firms, the Kansai Machine Tool Council (Osaka, Kyoto) with twelve companies, and the Chubu Machine Tool Council with seven members. In August 1948, however, the Kansai and Eastern Japan organizations, the two largest clusters of firms, formally affiliated. Forty surviving tool makers finally agreed to consolidate into a single Japan Machine Tool Builders Association in December 1951. The national machine tool *gyōkai* was born.[7]

The companies in the *gyōkai* were an amalgam of wartime licensed firms, other smaller members of the *tōseikai,* firms with close links to machine tool producers, and some new companies whose management exhibited considerable production and political acumen. The licensed class included the Big Five and such *zaibatsu*-created companies as Hitachi Precision Machinery and Toyo Machinery. The smaller enterprises, including Osaka and Tokyo Machinery, were companies that had switched to machine tools in the materials crises of the wartime era. Firms with close links to tooling producers, either as consumers or as parts manufacturers, included Railcar Manufacturing and Imperial Chuck, which made parts for cutting tools. Finally, the talented new firms were best exemplified by Makino Milling Machine, whose founder built his small machinery company into the leading mill maker in Japan. Subsequently Makino would play an important role in the development of NC technology, the creation of machinery export associations, and reorganization politics.[8]

Though the *gyōkai* was the center of postwar policy debate between government and the machine tool industry, its membership was only a small fraction of Japan's tool companies. In 1955, for example, the *gyōkai* had 55 members while total firms in the industry numbered 264; by 1981 there were 113 *gyōkai* members while the industry as a whole numbered 1,928 firms.[9] Companies not in the *gyōkai* were commonly referred to with an English loan word as "outsider" firms. The reasons for not joining an industry group vary from case to case. Some companies, in the case of Mori Seki, simply distrust the purpose of the group. Others want to maintain independence and so refuse to debate general policies in the *gyōkai.* Many firms are not invited to join because *gyōkai* members do not see them as sufficiently important players in the industry. Until the late 1970s *gyōkai* members accounted for 75 percent of total machine tool output, but in new products the outsider companies were crucial—indeed, the largest NC lathe maker in Japan was an outsider company. Outsider firms were in general a crucial part of the Japanese industry, and they influenced policy debate and practice as well.

The earliest activity of the *gyōkai,* in 1951 and 1952, aimed to move machine tool firms into the network of economic policy–making institutions created by SCAP. In 1952 the JMTBA took over the production of machinery records and other data for use by the occupation authorities. In February it gained a foothold in the procurement bureau that oversaw purchases made by the U.S. Army. It formed contacts with distribution companies based in Japan and in other East Asian markets.[10] In addition, it began to coordinate activity with other machinery industry groups to maximize political power against the bureaucracy. Producers in transport machinery, smaller equipment, precision products, and other allied machinery sectors gradually rebuilt a lobbying network that resembled the three integrated *tōseikai* of the wartime period. Firm membership in two or more *gyōkai* facilitated contacts. By the mid-1950s all of these machinery groups were housed in the Machinery Promotion Building in Tokyo, a symbol of the effort to unify the political clout of machinery manufacturers.[11]

Political pressure for industry relief intensified just before the formal incorporation of the *gyōkai* in 1951. In August the staff of the Eastern Japan Machine Tool Council wrote an internal report entitled "The Current Machine Tool Industry and the Road to Growth." The document summarized the dire position of the industry and suggested the reasons for the recession it was facing. It then turned to proposals for recovery, which centered on the modernization of equipment. The stock of Japanese machine tools was extremely old and technically deficient, the report suggested, and if the machine tool industry was to recovery its vitality and meet the demand for tools in other sectors, it needed promotional strategies to expand machinery markets and support the development of advanced technology.[12]

This document was the first postwar White Paper published by the *gyōkai.* It set a precedent whereby industry itself signaled appropriate policy for the bureaucracy to act upon. Ever since, specialized committees in the *gyōkai* with responsibility for technology, market demand, and finance issues, have submitted reports to MITI's Industrial Machinery Bureau, which holds responsibility for policy in the machine tool sector. Additional ideas or points are clarified in liaison discussion groups between *gyōkai* members and bureau representatives; occasionally, academics or other "neutral" parties attend these discussions. White Papers have preceded major policy initiatives without exception and are the basics on which the bureaucracy has drafted its legislation.

The initial report was used as the basis for discussions in November 1952. Meetings led to a second report incorporating most of the *gyōkai*'s work, "The Current Machine Tool Industry and Recovery Policies," which was submitted to the Industrial Machinery Bureau. On this document the bureau produced a summary of policy objectives in February 1953 entitled "Machine Tool Management Administration Plans: 1953." The "Management Plans" paper was the first comprehensive policy outline for the machinery industry produced by the postwar economic bureaucracy and coincided with the return of Japanese sovereignty. It underlined the need to restrengthen Japanese machinery firms and promised support from the new Japan Development Bank, a public bank established to provide loans that would serve policy goals. It also promised that the government would help offset development costs for advanced equipment technology. The plan further suggested that import duties and taxes be adjusted to promote domestic production of tools and to reduce imports.[13]

Promotional and support measures largely echoed industry requests, but the bureaucracy had additional objectives. The MCI inserted a clause to the effect that it would promote production specialization and increase the scale of operations, a position congruent with its prewar efforts. Next, it linked machine tool development to its goal of enhancing rationalization throughout all manufacturing sectors.[14] Though the MCI meant the consolidation of production in larger firms, the *gyōkai* members understood it to mean demand stimulation measures: firms would be encouraged to buy newer and better machines. The *gyōkai* wanted to use new financial organs for small firms and tax breaks in the proposed Enterprise Rationalization Law to stimulate domestic demand. Eventually its position was adopted; with the market glutted by older tools, only some sort of aid for machinery purchases would create a market from which manufacturers might obtain the cash flow they badly needed. These market stimulation measures were known as "scrap and build" policies, for they encouraged machinery users to exchange their equipment and buy replacements from struggling Japanese manufacturers.[15]

Policies based on the 1953 plan actually did nothing to alleviate the crisis in machine tools. In accordance with scrap and build, the Enterprise Rationalization Law of March 1952 was amended to provide for a 50 percent first-year write-down for thirty-two classes of machinery, to encourage new machinery purchases. But the effects were more than offset by import policy. Users resisted attempts to restrict their purchases to domestic equipment; they wanted support extended to *all* machines, wherever manufactured. Equipment users brought the government to pass the Machine Tool Import Assistance Regulation in late 1952, giving machinery importers subsidies of up to 50 percent of the value of their purchases and generous amortization schedules. The result was that domestic machinery output continued to fall while imports rose.

Slightly more support was provided under a system of experimental research subsidies between 1953 and 1955. Machine tool firms and other manufacturers of industrial equipment were eligible to receive a 50 percent subsidy for experiments leading to advanced machinery. In the three years of this program, approximately ¥280 million was distributed to twenty-eight companies for research related to sixty-one types of machine tools. The research results were published in the public domain. These limited research grants did not, however, produce a recovery; the total amount disbursed under the program was less than 2 percent of capital spending by machine tool firms in the same period.[16]

Japanese machinery industries continued to stagnate, although the Korean War led to a recovery in other sectors, especially those with military applications. But by 1955 changes in the economic bureaucracy made possible by the return of Japanese sovereignty and in the *gyōkai* led to a new, intensified promotional effort. When the occupation authorities disengaged, and with the abolition of the MCI and the creation of MITI in early 1952, the economic bureaucracy avidly began to seek economies of scale that would bring Japanese firms up to the level of volume production achieved by overseas and especially U.S. firms.[17] MITI was thus able once more to attempt the sort of industry promotional policies begun by the MCI before the war.

At the same time the machine tool *gyōkai* had completed its alliance with machinery makers in the electrical, large-scale industrial, automotive, forming, plastics, watch, and other sectors. Together, the groups began to lobby for special legislation to earmark financial assistance for them. In October 1955 the *gyōkai* submitted "A Petition for the Enactment of Legislation Concerning the Recovery of the Machinery Industry" to the Industrial Machinery Bureau. Together with submissions from the other machinery sectors, this petition became the basis for the Temporary Measures Law for the Promotion of the Machinery Industry (Kikai Kōgyō Shinkō Rinji Sochi Hō). The bill was promulgated in 1956 for an initial five-year period; it was extended twice to 1971.[18] The Machinery Promotion Law inaugurated a period of planning and financial support for the machinery industry. In both the planning effects of the legislation and the degree to which financial support enhanced expansion, MITI's goals went unrealized, and bureaucratic control or guidance was ineffective.

PLANNING AND THE MACHINERY PROMOTION LAWS

The Machinery Promotion Law was short, containing only twenty-four articles, usually one sentence each. It provided a bare minimum of statutory direction, leaving details to the bureaucracy.[19] First, it called for the rationalization of designated machinery industries and gave MITI planning authority to meet that goal. MITI was empowered to draft a plan for rationalization of the machinery industry at the recommendation of a council of businessmen and academics. Second, in Article 5 the government promised to commit funds to meet planning objectives. The third part of the law stipulated conditions under which affected firms might take "concerted action." These clauses, clearly modeled on *tōseikai* experience, anticipated interfirm coordination; they called for joint action where necessary to achieve planning goals, production restrictions, quotas, and cooperation in technology development and the procurement of components. Firms contemplating concerted action had to submit reports to MITI, and where joint action was necessary but firms reluctant, MITI was given authority to enforce compliance. The provisions to encourage private cartel schemes and to compel joint action were provided for with virtually the same powers as those in the Important Industries Law of 1931. Finally, the law described the machinery industry council, a group of academics, industry specialists, and bureaucrats who would meet to establish overall policy.

The Machinery Promotion Law was implemented in five-year increments, each governed by a master plan. The first, published in March 1957 for the period 1956–1960, was called the "Basic Rationalization Plan" (Gōrika kihon keikaku); the second, made public in October 1961, covered 1961–1965 as the "Basic Recovery Plan" (Shinkō kihon keikaku); and a final five-year plan was established for 1966–1971.[20] Each plan specified objectives for design improvements, production, exports, equipment investments, production techniques, and industry organization.

Design improvements were technical goals: increasing the rotational speed of lathe engines, for example, or enhancing the overall capacity of Japanese milling machines. The technical improvements that the plan hoped to induce were listed for various machine types. In addition, by comparing international indexes of productivity the plan stipulated target reductions for manufacturing costs. The plans set production and export goals as monetary increases for the five-year period concerned. For example, the first plan wanted overall production boosted to ¥20 billion and exports to ¥4 billion by 1965. Each five-year plan also specified equipment or capital investment goals. Investments were divided into those for "designated machinery," to be encouraged by the plan, and "other machines." In 1956–1960 the total investment target was ¥6 billion; in 1961–1965, ¥85 billion.

Objectives regarding production techniques were either general ideas or specific targets for improvements in manufacturing. The Basic Rationalization Plan merely urged that firms "specialize by type of machine"; the Basic Recovery Plan suggested increases in average lot sizes for special machines, to enhance scale economies. (Lot sizes are the number of units of a particular item made at one time in the same manufacturing setup.) In lathe production, for instance, the plan recommended a minimum lot size of fifty units; below that number, it was felt, cost of production relative to units produced would be too high. Finally, under industry organization, each plan suggested objectives to further the development of machinery production. They called for the "standardization of parts" in an effort to increase scale economies by fostering interchangeable equipment. The first plan also called for the creation of a joint research facility and the establishment of an institution to promote exports. Objectives for each planning category are summarized for the first two plans in Table 3.1.

Government financial support, authorized under the Temporary Measures Law, went to machine tool firms either as loans or as subsidies for research. The most important leader was the Japan Development Bank (JDB), established in 1951 to help provide loans to industries designated by the bureaucracy.[21] It was an independent agency, not under direct MITI control, although it did coordinate its lending with bureaucratic objectives. Approximately 80–90 percent of all government financial support extended to the machine tool industry after the war came in the form of JDB bank loans. The rest was primarily from the Small and Medium Enterprise Finance Corporation, a government-funded institution that made loans to small firms. Of all government support to the machine tool industry from 1945 to 1985, 92 percent was disbursed between 1956 and 1965, a total of ¥7.2 billion, which amounted to less than 5 percent of all machine tool investment in that decade.[22]

MITI granted experiment subsidies directly to individual firms. An extension of the research support program begun in 1953–1955, these subsidies tailed off dramatically. In the mid-1950s, before passage of the Machinery Promotion Law, average yearly expenditures were about ¥90 million, but by 1960 they had fallen to just ¥13 million.[23] One major reason, discussed later, is that Japanese firms were importing technology through tie-ups with foreign firms rather

Table 3.1. Policy Goals for the Machine Tool Industry under the Rationalization and Recovery Plans, 1956–1965

Target	Rationalization Plan: 1956–1960	Recovery Plan: 1961–1965
Rationalization	a. Increase technical capacity of special machinery b. Reduce production costs 20 percent	a. Increase technical capacity of special machinery b. Reduce production costs 15 percent
Production	¥20 billion by 1960	¥135 billion by 1965
Exports	¥4 billion by 1960	¥13.5 billion by 1965
Investment	¥6 billion 1956–1960	¥85 billion 1961–1965
Product Technology	Specialize in particular tools	Produce tools in appropriate lot sizes
Other goals	Standardize parts; joint research	Increase firm size; develop new technology; set up export group; standardize parts

SOURCE: Nihon Kōsaku Kikai Kōgyōkai (Japanese Machine Tool Builders Association), *Hahanaru kikai: San-Jū nen no ayumi* (Mother machines: A 30 year history) (Tokyo: Seisanzai Marketing, 1982), p. 64.

than conducting research themselves, so the need for subsidies was low.

The 1956–1960 Rationalization Plan and the Recovery Plan of 1961–1965 provide excellent opportunities to test the relationship between MITI initiatives and industry outcomes. If the bureaucratic regulation thesis is correct, we should see machinery firms acting largely in accord with planning targets. Furthermore, we should expect MITI itself to develop and enforce its industrial vision through sophisticated market analysis. But as I will show, none of MITI's planning goals was achieved. What is more, MITI developed targets using the most primitive methods, basing policy goals almost entirely on rough estimates and analysis supplied by the *gyōkai.* Consequently the documents that MITI published on machine tool planning do not demonstrate a rationally designed strategy for the industry written by bureaucratic regulators. Instead, and in every dimension, MITI's "planning" was ineffective.

Consider first the actual statistical record of the machine tool industry as compared with the goals set by the 1956–1960 and 1961–1965 plans.[24] If MITI possessed the power to affect industrial outcomes, there should be a fairly good correlation between its stated objectives and what targeted firms actually achieved. Figure 3.1 contrasts the planned reductions in production costs against what the industry actually achieved for all machine tools and for selected individual categories of equipment. The Rationalization Plan called for a 20 percent reduction by 1960, and the Recovery Plan a 15 percent reduction by

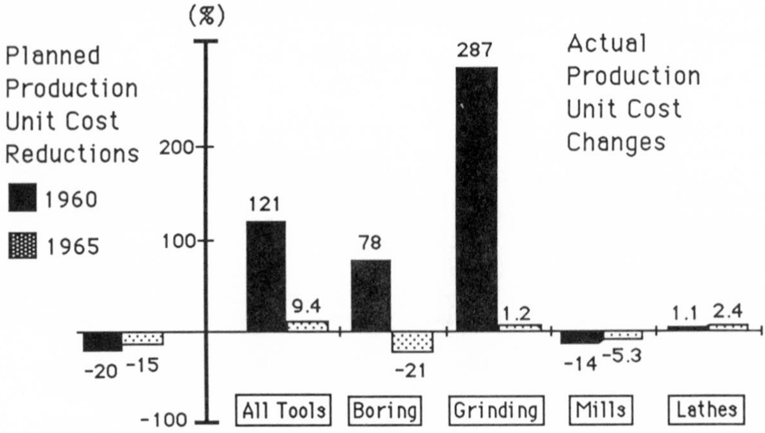

Figure 3.1. Planned and Actual Changes in Production Costs, 1960 and 1965
Source: Same as for Table 3.1, pp. 104–111.

1965; but unit costs actually *rose* for all machine tools, in 1960 by 121 percent and by 9.4 percent in 1965. Production costs also increased for grinding machines and lathes for both years. Only boring machines and mills showed decreases, but the reductions were between 30 percent and 50 percent smaller than targeted. By any measure the plans failed to meet their production cost objectives.

The same is true of production volume targets. The Rationalization Plan sought to boost annual output to ¥20 billion by 1960; the target of the Recovery Plan was ¥135 billion by 1965. But actual results varied wildly from the plans. Output in 1960 was ¥45 billion, or 225 percent of planned value, whereas output in 1965 was only 52 percent of the plan, at ¥70 billion. Again, bureaucratic targets had little effect on industry performance. MITI's export goals in both plans also went unfulfilled. Exports were supposed to have been ¥4 billion by 1960 and ¥13.5 billion by 1965. But exports in 1960 were just 40 percent of the planned amount, and in 1965 they were only 66 percent. Both plans also established investment targets for machine tool firms. They set their goals as investment volume in designated (preferred) tools and in other tools for the full five years of each plan. The total for 1956–1960 was to have been ¥6 billion and for 1961–1965, ¥85 billion. Once again planning goals were widely different from what nominally "regulated" firms achieved. Actual investment was 296 percent of the plan in the first period, when economic conditions were relatively good, and only 53 percent of target in the second period, when production volume and demand declined.

Table 3.2. Compliance with Recommended Lot Size Production Targets, 1967

Machine Type	Lot Size	Number of Firms	Firms in Compliance	Percentage Compliance
Table Boring Machine	300	7	2	28
Ordinary Lathe	50	22	6	27
Turret Lathe	50	8	1	12.5
Automatic Lathe	50	10	5	50
Standing Boring Machine	50	9	2	22
Milling Machine	30	12	3	25
Radial Boring Machine	20	13	3	23
Bed Milling Machine	20	13	3	23
Cylinder Grinder	20	8	2	25
Surface Grinder	20	14	3	21

SOURCE: Nihon Kōsaku Kikai Kōgyōkai (1982), *shiryō* sec., pp. 25–26.

Finally, targets in the field of product technology were not effective. The Recovery Plan had stipulated "efficient" lot sizes for specific types of machine tools; the optimal lot size for lathe production, for example, was set at fifty units. A survey by the *gyōkai* in 1967, two years after the plan had expired, indicated dismal compliance with recommended production goals (see Table 3.2). Only in automatic lathes did even 50 percent of total producers achieve the planned goal; overall, an average of just 24 percent of the surveyed firms were building machines in "appropriate" lot sizes. A similar study by MITI, also in 1967, showed that even among the five largest firms, just 60 percent of production (fifteen types of machines out of twenty-five surveyed) was in what the bureaucracy thought were efficient lot sizes.[25] The regulation of production technology was a manifestly ineffective tool for prompting changes in company behavior.

There is not a single instance, then, in which the objectives set forth in the first two five-year plans on the Machinery Promotion Law came close to being realized. As these planning documents were the basis for bureaucratic regulation between 1956 and 1965, it is difficult to claim that MITI effectively managed the machine tool industry. The record suggests instead that MITI's plans were inaccurate in their assessments of the market and weak in their ability to compel businesses to comply.

The failure of the plans can be partially explained by a consideration of how MITI actually generates industry goals under such legislation as the Machinery Promotion Law. Proponents of the bureaucratic regulation thesis argue that MITI staff are the "best and the brightest" of Japanese society, developing comprehensive strategies that are enforced through legislative sanctions or "administrative guidance"—the latter notion portrays Japanese firms and lending institutions as obeying the government even when not legally compelled to do so.

When MITI officials retire to large firms, a well-known process called *amakudari* (the descent from heaven), they join a cadre of former bureaucrats for regulators to contact. Through this network of former bureaucratic officials, it is argued, MITI can supplement its direct planning authority with effective, behind-the-scenes persuasion.[26]

The regulatory load placed on the Industrial Machinery Division is, however, extensive; the general machinery sector alone accounts for nearly one-tenth of all Japanese manufacturing establishments and value added, 63,000 firms in 1982. The bureau is responsible for manufacturers of large-scale equipment as well as precise, miniature machines and for firms using materials such as paper, metal, plastics, and foods. Even in 1956 there were nearly 20,500 machinery firms in Japan.[27] Managing all of these firms was even then all but impossible. The Machinery Promotion Law alone, itself only one of several industry bills, designated thirty-three different industries to receive comprehensive planning attention.

The size of the constituencies for which small bureaus in MITI are responsible raises acute problems for obtaining information, let alone actually making policy for a particular industry. Normal, non-oligopolistic sectors provide no network of former officials from whom to draw trustworthy observations, nor can MITI try to use former bureaucrats to influence company behavior. There are no *amakudari* placements in any of Japan's machine tool firms.[28] And the small-scale, fragmented nature of Japanese manufacturing also prevents the bureaucracy from guiding sectors by influencing leading companies or banks. Finance for the machinery sector, unlike for autos and oil, is dispersed among many banks and other lending institutions; single, dominant producers do not exist.[29]

Staffing problems and employment practices within MITI itself impede planning even further. Professional members of the Industrial Machinery Bureau staff number about twenty. Many are new MITI recruits, whose long work hours in support of senior directors and duties such as answering telephones are essentially those of a secretary.[30] Moreover, MITI staff are regularly scheduled to be rotated to new divisions every two years. Staff in the machinery bureau may find themselves transferred to the International Information Bureau, a public relations post, just as they begin to settle into the job of machinery regulation. Of course bureaucrats in the midst of important projects may be retained to complete their work; some will remain for a long time, providing a degree of continuity. But the two-year transfer is generally applicable and is in fact the focus of promotional politics within MITI, for individuals usually move up or down the hierarchy during the job rotation period.[31] As a consequence, staff in MITI bureaus frequently do not have personal expertise on any given industry, nor do they have a comprehensive memory of the history of policies applied to a specific case.[32]

MITI officials therefore face significant obstacles in regulating a particular industry. In the case of legislation like the Machinery Promotion Law, which mandated regular, published plans, officials had to rely on the *gyōkai* for basic information, and they were forced to apply extremely simplistic techniques to obtain figures for their planning documents.[33] One technique was simple extrapolation from periods of successful development to plan for what the future should be; if the industry had grown, for instance, during a three-year period in which investment was 5 percent of income, then the 5 percent figure was used as a baseline for preferred annual investment over the life of the five-year plan. Linear extrapolations of this type are fraught with problems, of course, as product mixes, technological change, and management capacities affect the ratio of investment to income or output. A second method was to use the performance of the largest or leading firms in the industry as a baseline.[34] Again, this technique improperly draws industry-wide targets from only a few firms. Even the definition of "leading firm" and the choice of product specifications is problematic, because different companies often have varying market strengths in different niches.

Reliance on the *gyōkai* did not ensure accurate data or intelligent planning goals. The *gyōkai,* like the prewar cartels, was always the scene of intense competition between member firms for market advantage. In a number of cases the majority of constituents ignored the surveys that the *gyōkai* used to establish baseline figures for company investment or other strategic information, because they feared that revealed information might give competitors an advantage.[35] Furthermore, the wide variance in *gyōkai* company size, links to other firms, and proportion of machine tool specialization made it extremely hard to generalize from past experience, let alone plan for the future. Compounding the problem was the fact that the *gyōkai* represented at best 75 percent of the industry; fully 25 percent was not part of the group at all.

When we consider these constraints on the formulation of industry plans, it is difficult to argue that MITI can plan effectively. The capacity to identify concrete goals and then achieve them authoritatively is central to the bureaucratic regulation thesis, but examined in detail, Japanese practices reduce to little more than guesswork. Apparently detailed industrial targets had little or no validity. And whatever the value of the numbers that eventually found their way into planning documents, MITI had no compliance powers. Industrial goals, in sum, were unrelated to industrial performance. The two elements essential to bureaucratic guidance, the creation of valid goals and the authority to implement them, were absent from the machine tool plans of 1956–1965. Machine tool and other machinery firms may have appeared to accept formal MITI authority as the price for obtaining promotional legislation; in practice, however, this authority was not exercised. One reason was MITI's reliance on the *gyōkai*; another, as we shall see, was that private firms were adept at forestalling compliance while securing material benefits. In this respect postwar industrial regulation bore a striking resemblance to prewar cartels and license schemes.

Financial Support and the Machinery Promotion Law

The Machinery Promotion Law is also an excellent test for the proposition that MITI provided effective financing for machinery manufacturers. Analysts who believe that MITI's policies shaped industrial outcomes argue that financial support had two consequences for Japanese development. First, in the 1950s and 1960s MITI directed capital to industries that could not obtain loans; by providing public support, the bureaucracy in effect nurtured firms until private lenders saw them as a better risk. Second, MITI employed indicative planning, targeting selected industries for government financing. Private lenders realized that such sectors were to be promoted and sought to lend to favored firms, because they knew state intervention would reduce risks. Thus even when the amount of MITI's support was low, the effect was to induce financial institutions to lend to preferred industries.[36]

Consider the notion that government loans produced early or consistent growth in supported industries. One way to evaluate this claim is to compare total investment with government assistance and with the record of expansion or contraction in a particular industry. If government support is a large proportion of total investment, and periods of assistance correlate with growth, then the bureaucratic regulation thesis would be confirmed. Under the Machinery Promotion Law, however, government-backed loans to machine tool firms were a small fraction of total investment, and they did not produce growth but, rather, correlated with recession. Figure 3.2 shows total investment by machine tool firms against the value of JDB loans, which accounted for over 90 percent of all government support to the industry, for the periods 1956–1965, 1970, and 1975–1983. Public loans were not a major component of investment. In 1956–1965,

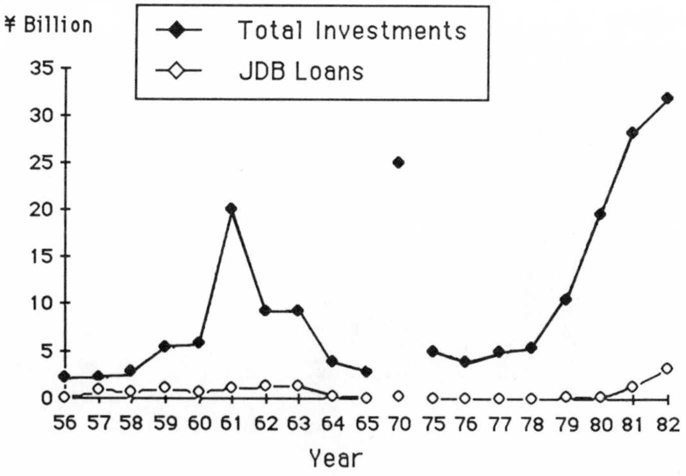

Figure 3.2. JDB Loans and Total Capital Investment in the Machine Tool Industry for 1956–1965, 1970, and 1975–1982
SOURCES: Investment data calculated from Wender, Murase, and White et al., "Investigation of Imports of Metal Cutting and Metal Forming Machine Tools under Section 232 of the Trade Expansion Act of 1962" (submitted to the International Trade Administration, U.S. Department of Commerce, Washington, D.C., 1983), p. 104; JDB loans from confidential data supplied by MITI's Industrial Machinery Bureau. Investment statistics are lacking for 1966–1969 and 1971–1974.

during the Rationalization and Recovery Plans, the total value of all government loans was just 11.51 percent of the total value of investment by machine tool firms. Then government loans fell off to practically zero, and in the early 1980s they were just 3–5 percent of industry investment.

This pattern is highlighted in Figure 3.3, which compares JDB loans to total investment. Only in 1957 did government funds rise above 20 percent of capital needs in the machine tool industry, and even in that case only 12 firms of 40 in the *gyōkai,* and 303 in the industry as a whole, were recipients.[37] The averages fell until 1965, when JDB loans were zero, and rose again only in the early 1980s. The heaviest support was in 1956–1965, but clearly JDB loan support was heaviest in the 1950s when the machine tool industry was still mired in its postwar slump.

Did this government assistance enable the industry to start its recovery, paving the way to its subsequent successes? One way to evaluate this claim is to compare annual government assistance with industrial performance. If government lending activity was effective, periods of heavy loan support should correlate with growth. Figure 3.4 illus-

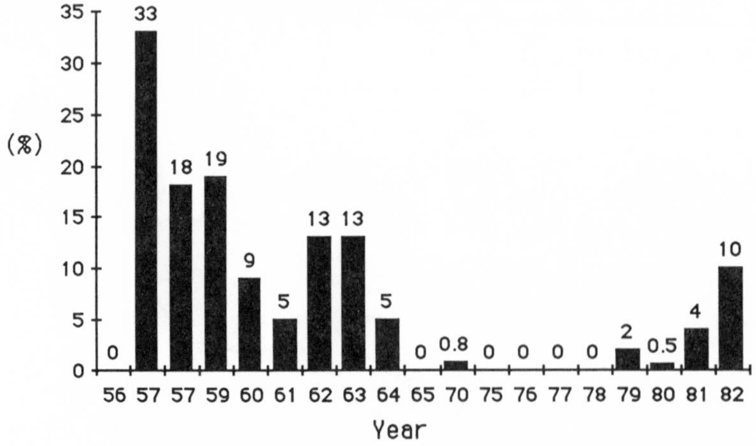

Figure 3.3. JDB Loans as a Percentage of Total Capital Investment in the Machine Tool Industry for 1956–1965, 1970, and 1975–1982
Sources: Same for as Figure 3.2.

trates the history of JDB loans to the machine tool industry relative to annual output. The patterns suggest that government loans do not associate with periods of rapid economic growth. The highest level of JDB outlays were recorded in the 1957–1963 period; output was minuscule in the same years, although it did rise slightly. But immediately following the outlays of the 1950s and 1960s the industry went into a prolonged slump from 1962–1966, quickly overshadowing this extremely modest success, if indeed a success it was. Apparently government support did not create a foundation for future expansion. In fact, machine tool recovery came only in 1966, when no JDB loans were made, and in the spectacular growth years of 1975–1980 there was almost no government support at all. Thus the financial incentives provided by the Machinery Promotion Law not only failed to induce compliance with MITI's five-year plans but also were ineffective in stimulating general economic development.[38] The machine tool case does not confirm the claim that early industrial support led to long-term growth. MITI authorized a modicum of loan assistance, but even when government activity was at its height (1957–1964), private lenders accounted for 88 percent of capital investments in the industry. And government loans failed to produce growth; during the period of sustained expansion, government loan assistance was zero.

Next let us consider the idea that when an industry is authorized to receive funds from the JDB or other government lenders, it becomes

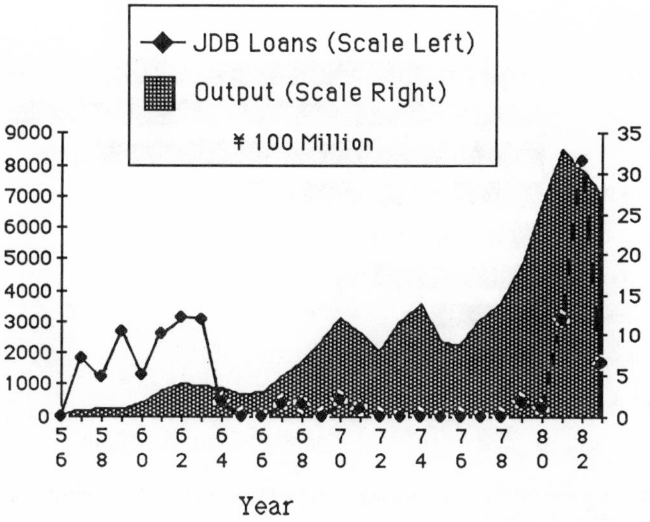

Figure 3.4. Machine Tool Industry Output and JDB Loans, 1956–1983
SOURCES: JDB loan data from confidential data supplied by MITI's Industrial Machinery Division. Output data from Nihon Kōsaku Kikai Kōgyōkai (1982), p. 121.

in the eyes of private bankers a priority, low-risk investment. If this notion were true, then government finance may have made it possible for machine tool firms to receive private funds more readily than otherwise would have been the case. Crucial evidence in support of this argument would be proof that the government directed JDB loans to special, high-growth sectors, because it would suggest that the state applied its support *selectively,* to induce private lenders to enter chosen fields.

However, no manufacturing sector did *not* receive government financing through JDB loans. More significantly, the industries most heavily dependent on government lending were generally industries in decline, those which contributed little to the postwar Japanese miracle. Figure 3.5 shows the government's percentage of total investment for major industries between 1954 and 1967. The industries that received heaviest support were agriculture, fisheries and forestry, coal mining, and water transportation. Each of these sectors experienced chronic adjustment difficulties in the postwar Japanese economy. In fact, some sectors obtained government protection even though support flew in the face of economic logic; rice subsidies, for instance, were undertaken at tremendous cost for symbolic rather than economic reasons. In contrast, iron and steel, chemicals, ma-

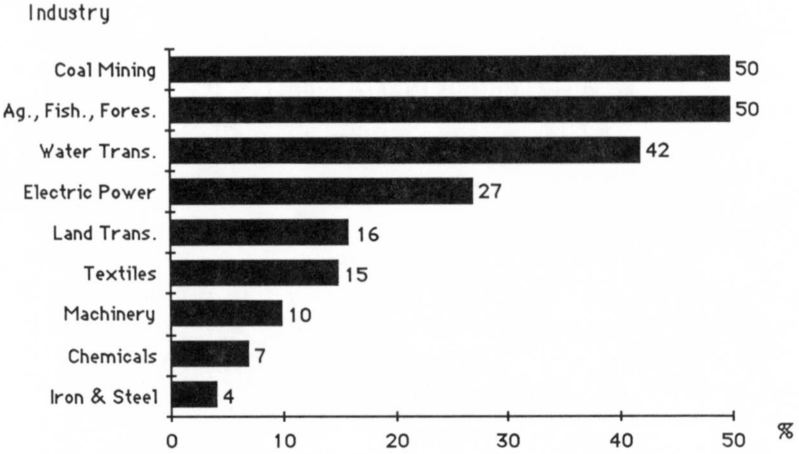

Figure 3.5. Government Financing of Investment in Selected Industries, 1954–1967 (percentages)
Source: As compiled by Horiuchi Akiyoshi, "Economic Growth and Financial Allocation in Postwar Japan" (University of Tokyo research paper 84-F-3, August 1984), p. 43.

chinery, textiles, and land transportation had the lowest levels of support, ranging between 4 percent and 16 percent. These industries were the major contributors to Japan's rapid industrialization.

If JDB and other government loans had acted as indicators of preferred investments, then private lenders would have been drawn to agriculture or extractive industries rather than to manufacturing. Government support cannot have resulted in a shift of funds to high-growth sectors, because finance was supplied to nearly every industry in Japan; private banks would not have been able to distinguish "preferred" sectors from others receiving support. The pattern of state finance does not support the view that MITI used JDB loans as rational, indicative policy tools. Rather, it suggests that private interests induced MITI to provide funds when needed; unable to resist political pressures from sagging sectors, MITI authorized huge outlays for struggling industries. In contrast, growth actors such as machinery obtained a small, marginal portion of total public outlays, a portion that fell as their economic position improved.

To conclude this evaluation of the role government finance played in the early postwar growth of the machine tool industry, consider the program of experimental subsidies. Some observers have argued that MITI's outlays on research stimulated technological and industrial development.[39] But support for company research dropped dramatically, as indicated above, after the passage of the Machinery Promotion Law. Indeed, from 1965 to 1977 only sixteen firms received subsidies totaling ¥455 million.[40] Research subsidies amounted to less than 1 percent of total capital investment. The true insignificance of this program becomes clear if we compare it to just one of several machinery research programs operated in the United States by the Department of Defense. The budget for the Manufacturing Technology Program, ManTech, for the 1977–1981 period was $745 million.[41]

In fact, although the subsidies were one of very few financial resources MITI had authority to disburse directly, the bureaucracy usually was not able to decide which firms and which proposals should receive funding. Rather, experimental subsidies were generally distributed at the request of other government institutions, such as localities, which were acting on behalf of the eventual recipient.[42] Moreover a good deal of the research undertaken by machine tool firms was accomplished by the *gyōkai* itself. Between 1956 and 1963 the *gyōkai* funded studies to develop the ability to manufacture at home various tools produced by other countries, under the auspices of a program called the Joint Research for Achieving International Standards. This research was in no way the product of MITI's guidance; indeed, MITI listed it as a goal in the five-year plans only because it was told in advance of the machine tool association's intent. The results were published in the public domain, available to *gyōkai* members as well as "outsider" firms. Because firms could use the research free of charge, the overall effect of the *gyōkai*'s studies was to increase the potential for new entrants in the market and for product shifts by member firms.[43]

MITI, despite the planning and financial support authorized by the Machinery Promotion Law, was powerless to implement its goals in the first ten years of the Temporary Measures Law. Its objectives bore no relation to the actual market circumstances of the machine tool industry. Furthermore, in its disbursement of funds MITI provided amounts that were at best marginal and did not correlate with periods of sustained growth.[44] In sum, evidence from the 1956–1965 period fails to confirm the bureaucratic regulation thesis with regard to planning or fiscal strategies.

Cartels, Production Restraints, and Machinery Promotion

After 1965 MITI's policies for the machine tool industry abruptly switched from planning and financial support to overt consolidation.

For nine of the thirteen years between 1965 and 1978 the value of government disbursements was zero, and the *total* of JDB loans to the industry in the whole period never equaled the *annual* average for 1956–1965. The third extension of the Machinery Promotion Law in 1965–1970, and the passage of a new promotional measure called the Temporary Measures Law for the Advancement of Designated Electrical and Machinery Industries (Tokutei Denshi Kōgyō Oyobi Tokutei Kikai Kōgyō Shinkō Rinji Sochi Hō), enforced during 1971–1978, coincided with efforts to change the structure of the machine tool industry. Long-dormant provisions in the Machinery Promotion Law regarding "concerted action for rationalization," and much stronger language concerning "rationalization cartels" in the later Electrical Machinery Law, were the focus of policy debate as MITI urged or threatened to force firms to centralize through mergers, cartels, and product specialization.

This phase was part of a more general strategy that saw rationalization plans or merger schemes throughout the Japanese economy, involving steel, autos, oil, and many other industries. The cause was capital liberalization in the aftermath of Japan's 1964 entry into the Organization for Economic Cooperation and Development (OECD). By the mid-1960s many OECD member countries, led by the United States, were pressuring Japan to alter its restrictions on direct foreign investment and capital ownership, limitations authorized in surviving prewar legislation such as the Emergency Capital Regulation Act. By 1967, in response, Japan began to relax restraints for selected industries.[45] Yet MITI feared that direct foreign investment would lead to increased foreign power in the economy, either by displacing domestic firms or in the purchase of Japanese companies by American-led investors (as had happened in Europe). Capital liberalization was seen as the wedge allowing an American-dominated flood of world producers into Japan, a development MITI believed would overwhelm what it perceived as smaller, vulnerable domestic firms.

The bureaucracy's response was to seek to centralize production and increase the scale of enterprises through mergers or cartels. Companies with capital links to larger firms, or enjoying price advantages conferred by mutual agreements with competitors, would be less vulnerable, the bureaucrats believed, to capital takeovers from abroad. Moreover, MITI believed that Japanese companies, to compete with huge foreign firms, particularly American enterprises, needed the same high levels of capitalization, scale, and output. Capital liberalization therefore brought about in MITI a concern to increase company scale, and the mid-1960s witnessed intense struggles between government and industries as MITI repeatedly attempted to force firms to merge and to consolidate.

Proponents of the bureaucratic regulation argument have interpreted cartelization and consolidation as part of a state-sponsored scheme to reduce production costs, by forcing firms to increase their production scale while assuring them of cartel profits to be used for additional investment. One study has contended that MITI authorized over one thousand postwar cartels and takes this as evidence of the scope of the bureaucracy's control.[46] Others see the 1960s as a time for consolidation following the nurturing of the 1950s and early 1960s.[47]

Machine tools provide an excellent case for evaluating these arguments. From 1965 members of the *gyōkai* were under direct pressure to merge, form cartels, restrict output to promote product specialization, enhance scale economies, and reduce interfirm competition. Machine tools are explicitly cited by studies that advocate the bureaucratic regulation thesis; one scholar contends, for instance, that the 1966 Nakayama Committee report, which called for "mergers or cooperation" among seven industries including machine tools as a response to liberalization, was the basis for MITI's "very successful efforts to link the electronics and machine tools industries.[48] Another has stated that seventeen cartels were authorized in the machine tool industry, which he interprets as evidence that MITI-inspired collusion was both widespread and effective in promoting Japanese high-speed growth.[49]

These claims, I believe, seriously misinterpret the nature and development of schemes to reorganize the machine tool industry. Even to apply the word *cartel* to the machine tool case is incorrect; the *gyōkai* emphatically rejected plans to impose so-called recession cartels even while its members were lobbying for state assistance in the 1960s. To satisfy the bureaucrats' conditions for receiving aid, the *gyōkai* set up "groups," but their explicit purpose was to *subvert* MITI's plans for consolidation. Both public and private production restrictions and other consolidation plans were ineffective. In particular, they had no influence at all on firm entry or competition related to NC development. The actual measures implemented by the *gyōkai* were weak, so much so that they rarely lasted for more than two or three years and did not achieve the goals that MITI sought. As before the war, and in the earlier application of the Machinery Promotion Law, politics sharply attenuated bureaucratic initiatives.

Debate over structural policy intensified when the Machinery Promotion Law was extended for a third five-year period beginning in 1965. As before, submissions from the *gyōkai* and individual firms

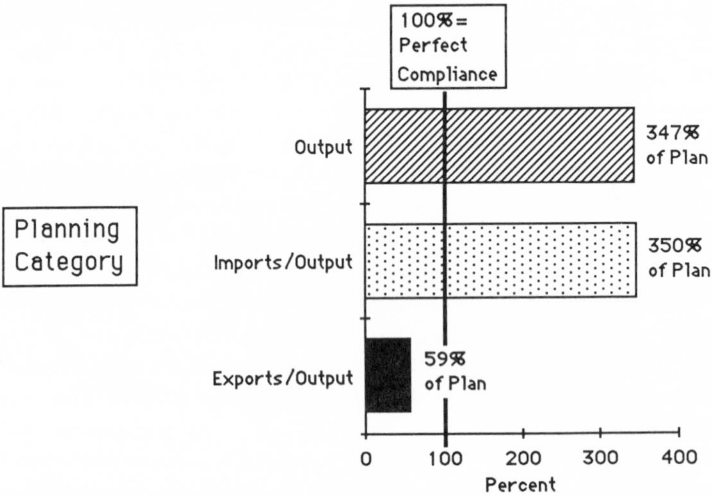

Figure 3.6. Degree of Compliance with the Third Promotional Plan, 1965–1970
Source: Same as for Table 3.1, p. 67.

were consolidated into a five-year plan, the Machine Tool Manufacturing Basic Promotional Plan. Part of this new plan set output, export, import, and investment goals and called for various technical improvements, such as low-cost NC machines and the creation of export organizations. Annual production was supposed to be ¥90 billion, exports were targeted to rise, and import dependence was to have been reduced to 22 percent of output by 1971. But as in earlier planning periods, MITI's efforts were ineffective; as Figure 3.6 illustrates, firms either fell short of the targets or exceeded them by wide margins.

The plan put unprecedented emphasis on structural consolidation (*taisei seibi*) as it attempted to use the "concerted action" clauses of the original Machinery Promotion Law. It called for cooperation among producers of similar machinery to promote greater production scale. It also suggested that "groups"—a term discussed below—should become the locus of an effort aimed at consolidating industrial production through cooperation, leading to joint ventures and mergers.[50]

The 1965 plan was updated in 1968 as pressures for capital liberalization peaked. In July of the latter year MITI published a Basic Promotional Plan for the Metal Cutting Machine Tool Manufacturing Industry (Kinzoku Kōsaku Kikai Seizōgyō Shinkō Kihon Keikaku) as part of a comprehensive response to the elimination of restrictions on foreign capital. Under the plan all companies would stop manufacturing machines for which their market share was less than 5 percent of total *gyōkai* production in the appropriate category of equipment (lathes, mills, etc.) and which amounted to less than 20 percent of their product mix. The intention of this 5 percent–20 percent rule was to force firms to specialize, enhancing their scale of production and reducing competition. In addition, the 1968 plan reiterated the earlier call for group cooperation and collaboration among individual firms to increase scale and centralization.[51]

The Machinery Promotion Law was finally allowed to lapse, but structural policies continued under the Electrical Machinery Law of April 1971. The law affected firms in electrical machinery industries. It aimed to promote the use of electrical components in machine design, to reduce pollution and costs, and to enhance the development of integrated manufacturing systems. The law resembled the Machinery Promotion Law in calling for MITI to draft industry plans for designated machinery producers. NC tools were included among the equipment receiving special status. However, the "concerted action" clauses of the Electrical Machinery Law were strengthened. A system of rationalization cartels was created to advance designated machinery sectors, and the clause reflected MITI's continuing concern about capital liberalization, as well as its ongoing search for policy tools to consolidate production.[52]

The law contained financial provisions for designated industries, but in fact there were no loans of any consequence to the machine tool sector between 1971 and 1978. The law also set up one body to advance loans to producers of integrated machine tools, in 1971, and another to provide long-term leases to purchasers of safety or energy-saving equipment, in 1972. Overall, however, financial support was negligible under the law.[53]

After consultations with and submissions from affected industries, MITI published the Machine Tool Manufacturing Advancement Plan. "Advancement" (*kōdoka*) here meant the stimulation of more sophisticated products. The plan first established various performance targets for production of NC equipment. By 1977 it wanted NC tools to amount to 50% of the value of total production, NC output to be ¥151 billion, and NC exports of ¥5 billion. These planning targets were, like previous targets, ineffective. As Figure 3.7 shows, the value of NC output and the ratio of NC production to total output were only half the target, whereas NC exports were only a quarter of the planned amount.

Finally, echoing the desire to centralize and consolidate the machine tool firms first expressed in 1965, the Advancement Plan called for further specialization to increase scale economies. It also sought

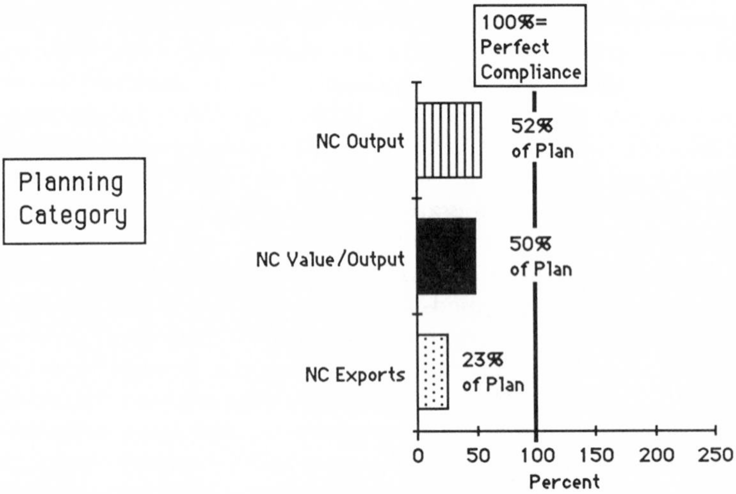

Figure 3.7. Compliance with the Machine Tool Advancement Plan, 1971–1978
SOURCE: Same as for Table 3.1, pp. 67–68.

joint activity in production, exports, and technology, again suggesting that "groups" would assist the industry in reaching these goals.[54]

The third Machinery Promotion Plan and the Advancement Plan offer an opportunity to test over the 1965–1978 period the proposition that MITI devised and imposed cartels or cartel-like activities on the industries it sought to regulate. Through them we can evaluate the policy climate and the empirical behavior of machinery producers. As I will show, manufacturing plans in both 1965–1970 and 1971–1978 were based on *gyōkai* production schemes that predated MITI's concern with reorganization by ten years; they were not the product of independent bureaucratic power. Moreover, the schemes were failures. Later, the *gyōkai* did adopt explicit cartelization strategies, but these strategies did not reflect bureaucratic guidance; rather, they were a cosmetic attempt to respond to MITI's pressures—and to obtain state support during a recession—while much stronger MITI control proposals were rejected out of hand. None of the "group" or production specialization schemes was effective, and machinery markets were extremely volatile in the period of apparent cartelization. Postwar consolidation policies, in sum, were as empty and ineffective as those of the prewar period.

The *gyōkai* first attempted to institute a production restraint program in 1957. Machine tool producers were experiencing a deep recession; demand was so depressed that even the Korean War boom, the catalyst for postwar growth in industries such as automobiles, failed to bring machinery producers out of their economic stagnation. *Gyōkai* members wanted to reduce competition by promoting specialized production and limiting entry into the market. Their first step was taken in August 1957, when a "production field discussion committee" was set up as one of the special standing bodies of the *gyōkai*. The committee's initial task was to survey current types of machines produced by member firms and develop baseline data on company market shares as well as import penetration.[55]

Gyōkai members divided over restraint measures, and three years passed without a plan. Finally, in March 1960, under a new chairman, the committee proposed a draft strategy for encouraging specialization and discouraging competition. Its central concept was to ensure that firms "not produce machinery that was not currently under production, and to concentrate production only on the main types of machines rather than subsidiary types within a firm's product mix." Each company would voluntarily give the *gyōkai* a statement of its existing machinery products, and an "agreed machine type list" would then be compiled. This list would be the basis for determining which types of tools a firm might produce.[56]

Though this draft was substantial progress toward an agreement, some *gyōkai* members balked again. A restraint system based on previous production records could either benefit or threaten future stability, depending on whether a company had already moved into growth fields or was producing outdated products. After more negotiations the proposal was watered down. Firms would "endeavor not to expand into fields for which they had no actual production records"; and this draft was adopted as a formal agreement (*mōshiawase*) in November 1960.

In no way was the 1960 agreement a product of MITI's planning or influence. Although the Machinery Promotion Law of 1956 expressly provided for concerted action and set up a system for applying to MITI for authorization, the *gyōkai* did not base its agreement on the terms of the law. It never submitted any documents to MITI for approval; indeed, as discussed below, in 1968 it tried to have its agreement retroactively authorized under the Machinery Promotion Law to ward off pressure from the Fair Trade Commission and possible foreign criticism.[57] Though MITI supported the agreement once it learned of its existence, the agreement did little to advance the bureaucracy's goals. The production restraint plan was hampered by collective action problems and competitive pressure from outsider companies.

Intercompany mistrust was the primary obstacle. As markets shifted, firms would try to move into areas that they were supposedly prohibited from entering, while companies in profitable markets would argue they were entitled to exclusive production rights. The *gyōkai* had further difficulties with new products. The terms of the agreement required a firm contemplating a new tool to notify the *gyōkai* but left undetermined whether notification gave it exclusive production rights. In fact, the definition of a new tool was problematic; when a piece of machinery was only slighty modified, did it fall into a new or an existing production category? *Gyōkai* members argued the question according to their individual interests. The fact that notification was completely voluntary deepened mistrust, because one firm might suspect another was modifying its reports to leave its market options open.[58]

Changes in *gyōkai* membership further confused matters. New members had to establish what their main and subsidiary products were and be apprised of relevant limitations. Departing members, freed from whatever constraints might have once existed on their product plans, became able to disrupt the orderly development of markets for certain classes of machine tools. The years 1957–1965 saw one of the most active periods of company activity in the *gyōkai*; membership rose from 63 to 105 firms, while fourteen firms left the group.[59] This unsettled climate precluded effective production management.

Outsiders, of course, were under no obligation to observe the restraint agreement. Theoretically MITI might have compelled all machinery producers to follow the agreement's terms, under the concerted action clauses of the Machinery Promotion Law. However, the bureaucracy did not have a basis for invoking those clauses, because the agreement was not in fact authorized by the law. Moreover, MITI was politically constrained from using its authority; in no single case were outsiders in any of the machinery industries forced to obey *gyōkai* policies by MITI's application of its regulatory power.

Consequently, outsiders could produce and price as they pleased. In some segments of the machine tool market outsider firms were the largest single manufacturers. One example is Mori Seki, which joined the *gyōkai* in 1983 only after trade friction prompted it to enter an emergency export control program in order to appease the United States. In 1981, when still an outsider, Mori Seki controlled 22 percent of the NC lathe market, the largest share of any Japanese firm, and was among the top three machine tool companies overall.[60] Clearly, such large, outsider machinery makers, not subject to the provisions of *gyōkai* agreements, frustrated attempts to regulate prices and competition in specific product niches.

The myriad difficulties involved in establishing a production agreement led the *gyōkai* to completely revamp its operation two-and-a-half years after the initial agreement. In 1964 the "production field discussion committee" was replaced by a new "enterprise structure committee." The new committee proposed to do away with voluntary report submissions and to base decisions about which firms could produce what products on prior production records. It sponsored studies of the output of member firms from 1962, compiling results that indicated machines for which a firm had prior records and whether the equipment was the firm's major product or a subsidiary interest subject to production restraints.[61]

The new proposal had considerable support because the machinery industry was in the midst of a prolonged slump. In November 1964 a new pact was approved as the Agreement Concerning Concentrated Production (Shūchū Seisan ni Kan suru Mōshiawase). It aimed to enhance the growth of member firms to the "appropriate scale" by reducing price and product competition through specialization. This scheme was called "product field regulation" (Seisan Bunya Taisei). Companies were asked to produce only those tools for which they had made prior notification of production to the *gyōkai* between 1962 and 1964. Production of machinery for which prior notice did not exist was prohibited. The agreement also called for (but did not set up any system for achieving) domestic production of imported products, cooperation in technical matters, and technical tie-ups with foreign firms.[62]

The new regulation agreement was in no way associated with MITI or the Machinery Promotion Law; *gyōkai* members conceived and directed the policy themselves. Later it would become the model for discussions about industrial reorganization between MITI and the *gyōkai*; a modified version of the agreement became part of the 1968 supplemental plan discussed above. However, the subsequent insertion of a *gyōkai* scheme into bureaucracy planning documents does not represent a triumph for MITI; indeed, the political history of regulation from 1965 shows that MITI was forced to accept what the *gyōkai* had developed, as the only form of reorganization policy acceptable to machine tool companies. From 1962 to 1965 the value of total machine tool production fell 30 percent, from ¥100 billion to ¥70 billion. Thirteen firms in the *gyōkai,* about 12 percent of its membership at that time, went bankrupt. The prolonged slump led machine tool firms to petition MITI for demand stimulation measures; in 1964, for instance, a petition was submitted calling on government to restrengthen the scrap and build policy.

For its part, MITI regarded the machine tool industry as one of the "sick men" of the Japanese economy. Growth was unremarkable and unstable; imports were, as of 1965, still at 20 percent of domestic production, one of the highest levels of import dependence in any manufacturing sector. Fears both of foreign takeovers and of increased market penetration were at their peak. Consequently, MITI's response was to make demand stimulation measures conditional on the consolidation of machine tool firms. The bureaucracy wanted to force firms to merge, to counteract the industry's structural fragmentation. It would not provide support to the slumping machinery industry, it announced, until mergers were carried out.[63]

But the *gyōkai* flatly rejected any idea of merging: as one president of a major machinery manufacturer active in the 1960s put it, "They told us to form into larger companies. We told them 'the hell with that' and refused."[64] MITI countered with a proposal for the imposition of "recession cartels." Again the *gyōkai* refused. It answered with a special White Paper, "The Current Situation and Countermeasures for the Machine Tool Industry." It reviewed industry's slump while reiterating the need for government support to stimulate demand. The document rejected recession cartels because, it argued, the broad product range and uncertain demand for machine tools would render such measures ineffective; in fact, *gyōkai* members were no more interested in recession cartels than in mergers. The document argued for loose federations of firms that would share in operations such as public relations, joint use of specialized machinery, and limited joint production of similar machine types. Eventually, the report suggested, such joint arrangements might lead to the mergers and market control the bureaucracy sought.[65]

The *gyōkai* wanted to build a basis for future consolidation, but its member firms adamantly opposed any arrangement that would reduce corporate independence. However, the continuing recession required some form of concrete action to satisfy the bureaucrats and obtain demand stimulation from the government. The *gyōkai*'s solution was to call for the formation among member firms of a series of "groups," each composed of select companies.[66] Groups and their overall purpose were defined entirely by the *gyōkai*. If companies producing the same machinery were consolidated into cooperative organizations, the notion suggested, then joint research, joint production, and coordination of sales and marketing might be achieved. These groups would thus be able to foster production controls and scale economies while building a basis for future coordination. At the same time member firms would not lose their corporate identity.[67]

So the notion of groups, even as originally contemplated, was much more modest than what MITI sought. But implementing even this modest group plan turned out to be difficult. Negotiations about

Table 3.3. Groups Formed in the Machine Tool Industry, 1965–1966

Name	Date Formed	Participant Firms
Dai-Ichi Group	December 1965	Hamai, Hitachi, Ikegai, Toyoda, Tokyo Tosemitsu, Kashifuji, Japax
Tokyo Group	February 1966	Makino Mill, Mitsui, Toshiba, Niigata
Central Group	February 1966	Enshu, Okuma, Osaka, New Japan, Nippei
Automatic Lathe Group	March 1966	Towa, Kondo, Taiyo
Standard Group	March 1966	Takizawa, Yamazaki, Yoshida, Roku Roku, Washino
Osaka Group	March 1966	Greater Japan Metals, Nomura, Osaka, Nishibeya, Kiwa, Wakayama
Kansai Group	March 1966	Anda, Ooya, Japan Grinder, Marufuku
Eastern Japan Group	April 1966	Ikegai Machinery, Okamoto, Sanjo, Shoun
Tobu Lathe Group	May 1966	Hamatsu, Ogawa, Kyoba, Tosei
Automatic Lathe Research Group	May 1966	Fuji, Bori, Nomura Seiki, Funemoto, Toyo Seiki

SOURCE: Same as for Table 3.1, p. 72.

group affiliation were complicated because companies could not readily determine which group was best for them; suspicion among firms was high, and various affiliation plans were proposed and rejected.[68] MITI pressured for group schemes subjugating a number of smaller firms behind a large leader such as Toshiba or Ikegai.[69] It wanted to use large companies as capital buffers and to focus the consolidation of small firms, a strategy it also tried to apply in such other sectors as autos, but its entreaties were ignored. Finally, on December 13, 1965, a breakthrough occurred: the Dai-Ichi [first] Group was formed. Other machine tool firms organized, and by May 17, 1966, nine more groups had formed (see Table 3.3).

The ten groups formed in 1966–1967, and two others that were organized by 1969, were the only cartel-like activities undertaken by the machine tool industry. Invented and organized by the *gyōkai*, these groups emerged only after much stronger MITI plans for mergers and cartels had failed. It is impossible to interpret the development of such groups as a victory for the bureaucracy or as an example of effective guidance. Nor did implementation of the groups meet any of MITI's objectives—indeed, in several respects their operation was problematic.

The basic difficulty was the fact that the members of each group did not, as a rule, produce sufficiently similar machinery to permit consolidation for scale economies. The plan drawn up by the *gyōkai* staff foresaw makers of lathes, mills, or other types of machines joining with one another and collaborating on research, production, and marketing. This development would limit direct competition, permitting capital accumulation and stable manufacturing. Furthermore, it would pave the path for future integration leading to mergers, which would satisfy MITI.

Instead the major groups were composed of firms that did not compete with one another or that had product lines so dissimilar as to make integration impossible. Members of the Dai-Ichi Group were for the most part very large prewar-licensed firms such as Hitachi and Toyoda or their affiliates.[70] Historically they were related, but their manufacturing operations were not complementary. For example, Hamai had long had a capital and technical tie-up with Hitachi.[71] Indeed, the overriding objective in setting up the Dai-Ichi Group was to show MITI that large firms were willing to go along with the scheme. It was hoped that later groups, composed of firms with more suitable products for consolidation, would be stimulated by the example. But the Tokyo Group, the second to be established, was composed mainly of *zaibatsu* and other larger enterprises, such as Niigata Machinery. These companies resembled one another only in their relation to outside capital (they were branches of larger manufacturing concerns), and their product mixes were utterly distinct. Added almost as an afterthought was Makino Milling, a much smaller independent specialist producer. Makino was admitted into the second group because its president, who had political ambitions, sought to be at the forefront of the reorganization effort.[72]

Paradoxically, when firms in a group actually did share machinery or technology in common, the effect of their tie-up ran counter to MITI's consolidation goals. Groups were supposed to lead to mergers and centralization. But in the Tobu, Automatic Lathe, and Osaka groups, very small firms were enabled to share technical, marketing, and research costs, thereby ensuring their individual survival. Groups, that is to say, were being used to preserve the very small firms that MITI wanted to dissolve.[73]

Group composition was not the only problem with the machine tool industry's countermeasures against capital liberalization. Another major difficulty was that a large number of firms were never involved in any group at all (see Figure 3.8). *Gyōkai* firms in groups represented about 60 percent of the value of total output, and if we consider outsider firms, then, over half the industry was unaffected by the group program. Obviously plans to consolidate production and control competition were hampered by the fact that for every unit of

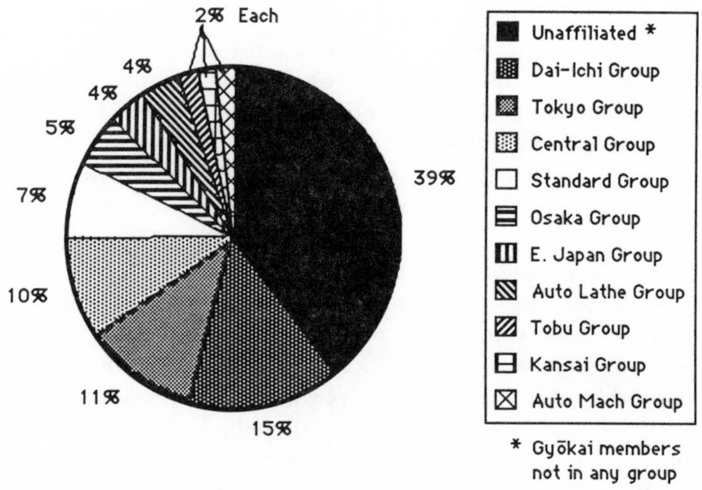

Figure 3.8. Production Shares of Machine Tool Groups, 1967
SOURCE: "Kōsaku kikai gurupu no "ayumi" to genjō" (The current condition and "development" of machine tool groups), as reprinted in Nihon Kōsaku Kikai Kōgyōkai (JMTBA), *Ni-ju nen no bijaku* (Twenty years of growth) (Tokyo: Seisanzai Marketing, 1972), p. 490.

production to be controlled in groups, another outside was not subject to control.

The industry recognized that the groups were primarily designed as a half-hearted response to MITI in exchange for market stimulation measures. The major machinery publication in Japan, *Seisanzai Marketing,* ran a special article in 1970 reviewing the activities of the groups four years after their creation. It found that instead of consolidating, firms had used groups to bolster their own competitiveness: "To anticipate our overall evaluation [of the groups], in reality the effort to promote the structural adjustment of the *gyōkai* through the use of groups was, regrettably, extremely weak. With the recovery that began in 1966, the rationale of the groups moved away from one based on structural adjustment. It shifted instead to an attempt by firms, through the groups, to try to improve their individual international competitiveness. In this respect, the overall evaluation of the groups cannot be said to be good."[74]

The article also quoted company managers to illustrate the degree of latent competitiveness and political calculation that went into the groups' creation. Some observed that the groups were "just something to put before MITI's face," "an empty shell carrying with it no real substance." Others did say that they felt group membership enhanced their companies' competitiveness. But negative observations like this one from a member of the Eastern Japan Machine Tool Group clearly suggested the degree of interfirm mistrust, which prohibited real consolidation: "I'm not sure how I should interpret the internal nature of the groups. In one respect, everyone shakes hands in the spirit of reconciliation; on the other, the hands are cold and hard. Which attitude is the real one?" A manager of an outsider firm was even more blunt in assessing the political significance of the groups and the problems of cartel-like coordination: "The purpose of the groups that have been announced is far from that of 'real' groups. Rather, they serve the purpose of achieving such things as merely creating diversion for other groups, or making a gesture to MITI." Capturing the overall state of affairs was a cartoon: on top of a pedestal, machine tool firm managers, portrayed as warriors, were loudly swearing "*kyōchō*"—cooperation or harmony—while beneath them lesser-ranking soldiers, company employees, were busily tearing the pedestal apart in pursuit of individual gain.[75]

Not only did the groups not promote centralization, but they were designed explicitly to avoid that outcome. Consequently, the planning and operation of the groups, which were the only manifestation of a "cartel" in the postwar machine tool industry, does not support the bureaucratic regulation thesis. The groups did not escape the pitfalls inherent in collective action and in any case were primarily designed not to promote coordination but to pacify MITI in exchange for government support. Indeed, that groups were a response to a temporary recession which made government market assistance seem attractive is illustrated by the fact that they were abandoned as the market recovered. Machine tool output nearly doubled in 1967, from the previous year's ¥70 billion to ¥129 billion, and the perceived need for government demand stimulation diminished rapidly; the recovery ended the political conditions that had temporarily strengthened MITI's position.[76] By 1970 the groups existed in name only. In the absence of a compelling need to negotiate with the bureaucracy, the reorganization effort died.

But MITI's fears about the damage potential in capital liberalization intensified. In February 1968 Industrial Machinery Bureau staff met representatives from each group to try to evaluate whether the consolidation objectives were likely to be met. Its findings were unequivocal: "We have lost hope that structural adjustment can be accomplished through the group program." MITI was pessimistic because individual companies used the groups for their own purposes and because overall the groups had little effect on the production and management strategies of member firms.[77] Bureaucrats pushed hard for a reorganization of the groups or for actual cartels, but with market pressure greatly reduced, machine tool firms had little incentive to negotiate. The strengthened group plan was rejected.

From 1967 to 1970 the bureaucracy pressured for alternative reorganization strategies. In 1968 MITI's efforts resulted in a supplemental Basic Promotional Plan for the Metal Cutting Machine Tool Manufacturing Industry, which focused around production restraints: it would bar the manufacture by any firm of products that amounted to less than 20 percent of its product mix or less than 5 percent of total industry output in the relevant category of products. MITI had abandoned explicit cartel measures, hoping instead through the 5 percent–20 percent rule to create larger, specialized firms with greater unit-scale operations.[78]

The promulgation of the 5 percent–20 percent rule may suggest that MITI was at last directing the industry. Indeed, the rule was the first application of the Machinery Promotion Law's concerted action powers in a plan that would guide machinery production. But, as I will show, the 5 percent–20 percent rule was established as part of a subtle, ultimately unsuccessful attempt by the *gyōkai* to protect itself from complaints filed by the Fair Trade Commission while appearing to cooperate with MITI. It was neither developed nor actually enforced by MITI. Furthermore, *gyōkai* members so limited the rule's scope that it applied only to old types of machines for which no growth was expected; NC and other tools at the core of the industry's miraculous advance were explicitly excluded.

In response to MITI's pressures after the breakdown of the group program, the *gyōkai* at first offered its still effective "concentrated production agreement" of 1964 as protection against challenges expected from overseas producers. The *gyōkai* suggested that the agreement be retroactively based on the Machinery Promotion Law as a countermeasure against capital liberalization.

This move was made with several calculations in mind. First, the production restraint agreements were not working well; they had to be continually revised, and which firms had the right to make new machines—indeed, what a "new" machine was—had yet to be resolved. The members of the *gyōkai* most comfortable with production restraints, large producers whose markets were threatened by new entrants, thought they could enlist the bureaucracy to help restrain newcomers. At the same time the firms threatened by restraints wanted a much weaker program or the maintenance of existing policies.[79]

Second, in conjunction with GATT and OECD compliance, the Fair Trade Commission (FTC) was aggressively prosecuting cartels and informal production restraint agreements. Though the FTC was certainly weaker than its model agency in the United States, it exerted significant influence. In several industries, including autos and steel, concern about FTC responses prompted MITI and the affected firms to redesign or eliminate cartelization schemes.[80] By retroactively authorizing their agreement as concerted action activity as specified in the Machinery Promotion Law, the *gyōkai* could build a legal shield against reprisals from other agencies. But MITI wanted stronger production restraints, and *gyōkai* members were badly split on what tools should be affected and which firms would retain production rights. Eventually the *gyōkai* itself developed the 5 percent–20 percent rule to satisfy MITI, but only after imposing limitations on its application. Then the 1964 agreement was modified to reflect the new rule, retroactively authorized in the 1968 supplementary plan, and administered by the *gyōkai* in a Special Structural Reform Committee from January 1969.

The revised agreement placed significant limitations on the 5 percent–20 percent rule. Member firms wanted to preserve market flexibility, particularly where new growth prospects were high. As a result, they agreed to apply the rule to only twelve types of standard machines, such as ordinary lathes, ordinary grinders, and ordinary milling machines, for which only limited future growth was expected. All NC machine tools, machine tools to which NC equipment might be attached, machining centers, and "designated machine tools"—tools that the *gyōkai* had identified as "underproduced" in Japan and thus for which growth prospects were high—were explicitly excluded from the production restraint agreement. New machines, and those being developed in joint ventures with foreign firms, were also exempt.[81]

The exceptions were thus extremely broad. NC tools, of course, accounted for most of the machine tool industry's rapid growth from 1970 onward. Tools that could be adapted to NC use included virtually all of the machines nominally covered by the restraint agreement. "Designated equipment" referred to unconventional versions of the twelve machine types subject to the 5 percent–20 percent rule; for instance, ordinary lathes with a feed of between 400 and 1000 mm were subject to the rule, but lathes with feeds above or below the basic specifications were not. And finally, more flexibility was added to the agreement because it was difficult to determine whether a tool was new or produced under license from a foreign firm.

These reservations and limitations stripped the agreement of any real power. Though the 5 percent–20 percent rule did urge *gyōkai* members to act as if the restraints applied to excluded tools as well as to the twelve target categories, this admonition had no effect on product stability, nor did it lead to an orderly market. A firm could enter a restricted market under several pretexts: future NC applications, new design features, or the "special" nature of the machinery to be built.

Even in its truncated form the 1968 Concentrated Production Agreement survived only until January 1971, an effective period of less than two years. It was repealed in March and replaced with a voluntary reporting scheme for *gyōkai* members regarding new tools. The immediate cause of abolition was pressure from the FTC, which, unimpressed by the retroactive link of the agreement to the Machinery Promotion Law, had issued a cease and desist order in 1970. In the *gyōkai* itself there was substantial pressure to either abolish or further amend the agreement; of sixty-eight firms replying to a survey, sixteen called for outright repeal of the agreement, the rest for either continuation or continuation with adjustments.[82] After consultations with MITI the *gyōkai* scrapped the whole program. It retained only the reporting clause about new machine tools, an idea that had been part of all production restraint schemes since 1960.

Thus the passage of the Electrical Machinery Law in 1971, even with its strong cartelization clauses, actually coincided with the end of the effort to reorganize machine tool firms. From a broad attempt to merge the industry, MITI had retreated to the group scheme, then to the limited 5 percent–20 percent rule, and last to the position that firms should stay away from one another's market niches as indicated in new product reports. Even this final program, the new product reporting scheme, was a *gyōkai* invention carried forward from the 1960s. Six years after the capital liberalization crisis had brought structural adjustment to the head of MITI's action list, not one of its objectives had been accomplished.

The attempt to cartelize the machine tool industry strongly contradicts the idea that MITI was able to plan, let alone implement, effective policies. The claim that machine tool cartels permitted orderly, low-risk scale expansion misinterprets the way such industry organizations operated in Japan. The machine tool cartels, the "groups," were totally ineffective and were designed to be that way; they cannot be called cartels at all. If they had any effect on the industry, it was to permit smaller producers to economize on research and marketing costs, helping them to resist further consolidation schemes.

Was the machine tool industry ever consolidated at all? It is possible, of course, that even if MITI's efforts failed, machinery advances were the result of privately organized cooperative schemes that artificially reduced Japanese production costs. Alternatively, despite the apparent ineffectiveness of the cartel schemes, real consolidation actually took place through some other means. If so, even though the

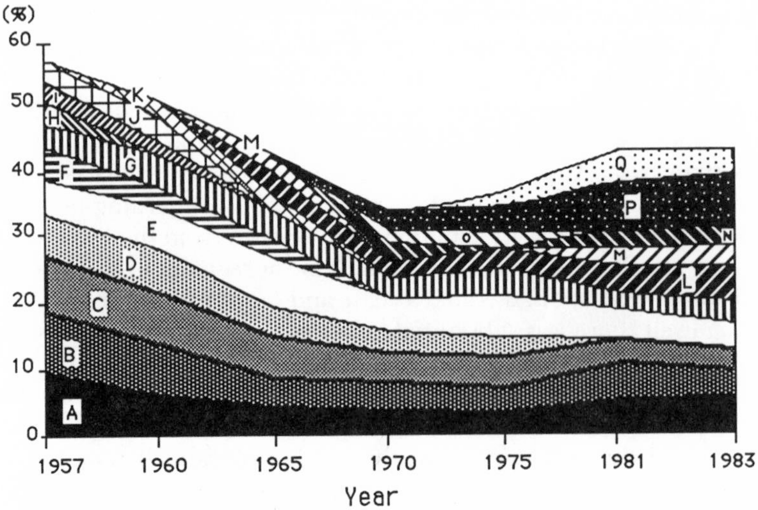

Figure 3.9. Market Shares of Top Ten Firms (A–Q) for All Machine Tools, 1957–1983

SOURCE: Market share data are reported to the FTC and to MITI under conditions of strict secrecy, to protect the industrial position of the reporting firms. The data were supplied by the Industrial Machinery Bureau in January 1984. To protect confidentiality, individual companies were not named but were identified as A, B, etc. The same letter always refers to the same firm.

bureaucratic regulation thesis fails, the basic economic theory on which that thesis is based might still be sustained: Japanese successes would still be a function of increased efficiency relative to other countries in the manufacture of standard goods.

One way to test these issues is to examine market share data by firm and by type of machine tool. If it is true that efficiency advances resulting from scale economies sustained Japanese growth, then in any given market segment the number of firms should have fallen or remained stable as companies built scale economies aided by production restrictions. Conversely, evidence of shifts by firms into new markets or of growing fragmentation in specific machinery segments would strongly contradict the idea that consolidation helped Japanese firms advance.

Market share movements of Japan's top ten producers for all machine tools from 1957 to 1983 appear in Figure 3.9. If cartels were effective, then the major firms in the 1950s and early 1960s should also be industry leaders in the 1970s and 1980s, and the market shares of each firm should remain stable. In fact, five of the top ten firms in 1956 were not in the top ten in 1983, and by the 1980s new

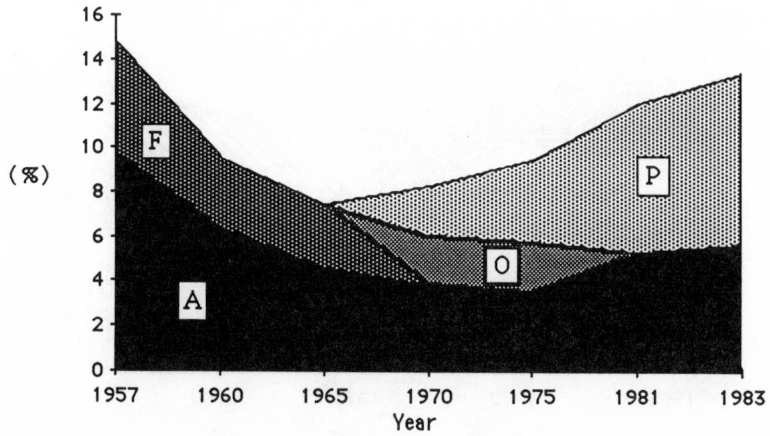

Figure 3.10. Market Share for Four Selected Cases, All Tools, 1957–1983
SOURCE: Same as for Figure 3.9.

firms had become dominant in the machine tool industry. Moreover, the market share of the top ten machine tool companies fluctuated greatly, from 57 percent in 1957 to just 33 percent in 1970 and rising again to about 42 percent by 1983. A major factor in this movement was the entry of new firms as older companies fell out. The pattern is the opposite of what a cartel should have produced.

We can see how market shares shifted in detail by isolating four companies from the aggregated data (see Figure 3.10). Company A is an established machinery firm that experienced a steady erosion of its market share until 1975, when it made a partial recovery in the NC era. Significantly, the company's greatest losses occurred in 1957–1970, when the structural consolidation schemes were at their height. Such firms are located in the lower left of Figure 3.9. Company F is an established firm completely eliminated from the top ten by 1970, again in the period of the most intensive efforts to preserve and stabilize markets. Such firms are found at the upper left of Figure 3.9. A third set of firms, represented by Company O, emerged in the top ten during the period of NC transition around 1970, then disappeared, most likely because they did not take advantage of NC markets to sustain growth. They can be observed in or around the center/right of Figure 3.9. Finally, firms like Company P made strong advances in the postwar machinery industry. They grew steadily from 1975, with the expansion of the NC market, and supplanted more established firms. These new companies are concentrated at the upper right of Figure 3.9.

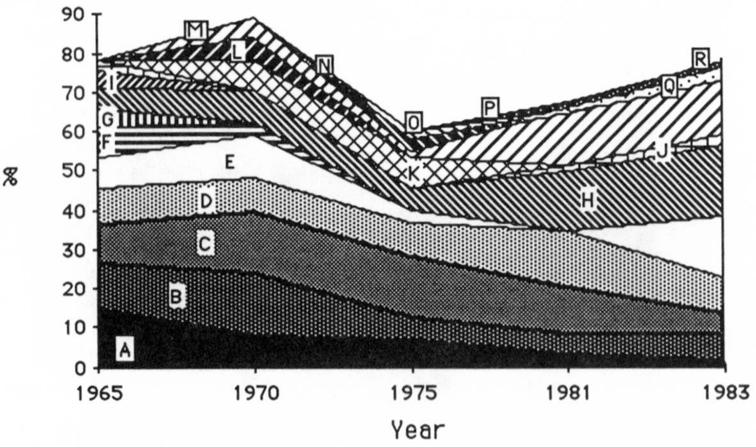

Figure 3.11. Market Shares of Top Ten Producers (A–R) of Ordinary Lathes, 1965–1983
Source: Same as for Figure 3.9.

The market share data in these figures do not support the idea that the *gyōkai* successfully operated a cartel-like production agreement. First, shares vary widely over time, whereas the purpose of the various schemes was to freeze market shares to permit stable growth. Second, companies displaced one another. Though preventing market entry was a key aim of MITI and, to some extent, *gyōkai* strategies, new entrants were crucial in the 1975–1983 period. Finally, overall market share fell for the top ten producers, from nearly 60 percent to just 33 percent in the period of restraint agreements, 1957–1970, recovering somewhat thereafter. More and more firms shared the market with the top ten producers. The intent of the production agreements, however, was not to promote relatively small advances by many firms but to spur scale economies in the largest firms.

Next I examine market share data for separate segments of the machine tool market. Figure 3.11 shows market share data for ordinary lathes for the top ten firms from 1965 to 1983. Ordinary lathes were subject to the *gyōkai*'s first restraint agreement in 1960 and to the 5 percent–20 percent rule promulgated in 1968. If cartelized market behavior is observed at all, it would be in the case of such targeted equipment. But as Figure 3.11 demonstrates, market shares varied widely despite the production agreements. The four biggest firms in 1965 (A–D) experienced a decline in their share from about 45 percent to about 22 percent by 1983. Company E experienced huge shifts in its market share, even falling out of the top ten in 1975. Only

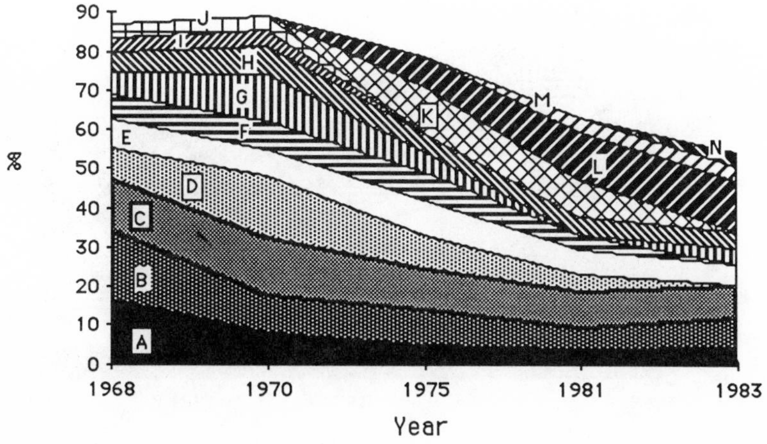

Figure 3.12. Market Shares of Top Ten Firms (A–N) for NC Tools, 1968–1983
SOURCE: Same as for Figure 3.9.

company H of the top ten firms in 1965 registered increases. Meanwhile, as for machine tools overall, new firms displaced older companies. If the consolidation schemes had worked, there would be straight, horizontal lines across the graph. Instead there is considerable fluctuation. Thus, even in a declining, low-growth market segment specifically targeted for control there is little evidence of effective cartelization and restraint.

The same is true of NC machine tools. NC tools were explicitly exempted from the production agreements, but did an informal cartel operate nevertheless? Market share data for all NC tools are shown in Figure 3.12. Once again we see enormous market variance in NC production after 1968, when the 5 percent–20 percent rule was issued. A cartel-like policy would have produced more horizontal patterns of company shares. Though the largest firms, A–E, captured 60 percent of the NC market in 1968, their share fell to just over 30 percent by 1983. Meanwhile new companies supplanted more established firms. Overall, the top ten firms took 87 percent of the market in 1968; their share was only 59 percent by 1983. With expansion came not consolidation but market diversification.

The records for individual NC machine tools confirm the degree of market volatility associated with NC development. Market shares for the top ten firms in machining centers are illustrated in Figure 3.13, and shares for NC lathes in Figure 3.14. Both graphs give evidence considerably at odds with the view that the machine tool industry was successfully consolidated. As in previous examples, older leading

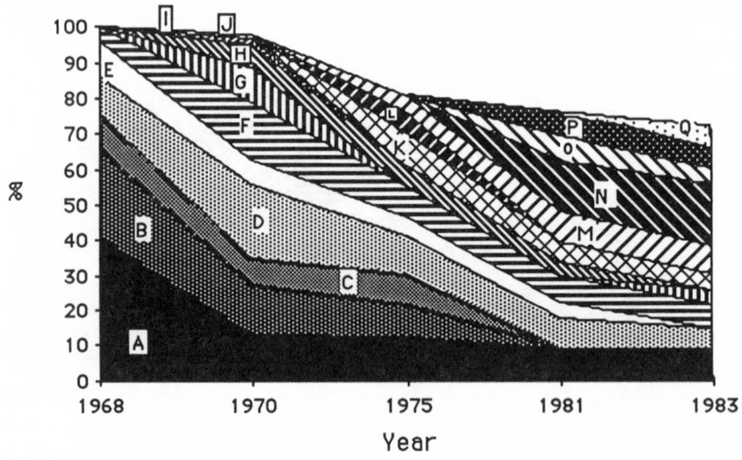

Figure 3.13. Market Shares of Top Ten Firms (A–Q) for Machining Center, 1968–1983
SOURCE: Same as for Figure 3.9.

firms experienced dramatic drops in their shares of overall production between 1968 and 1983. New firms—independently and without the assistance of older companies—entered the market and began to displace previous leaders. Total concentration fell overall, though less for NC lathes. Nowhere do we observe the horizontal, static market shares that would be characteristic of effective restraints on production.

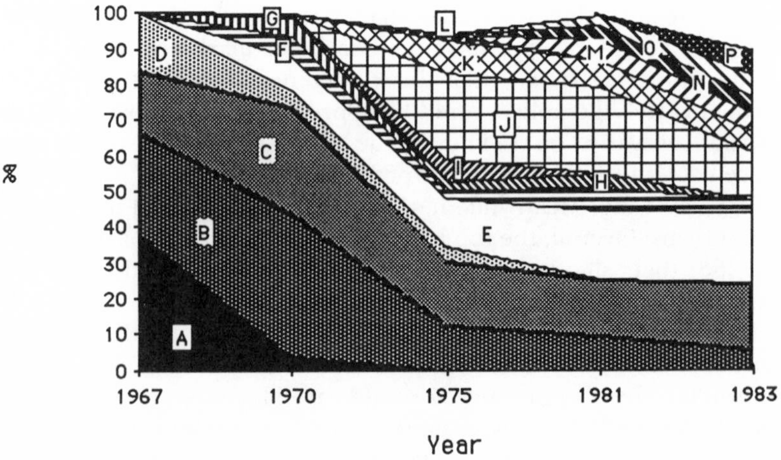

Figure 3.14. Market Shares of Top Ten Firms (A-P) for NC Lathes, 1968–1983
SOURCE: Same as for Figure 3.9.

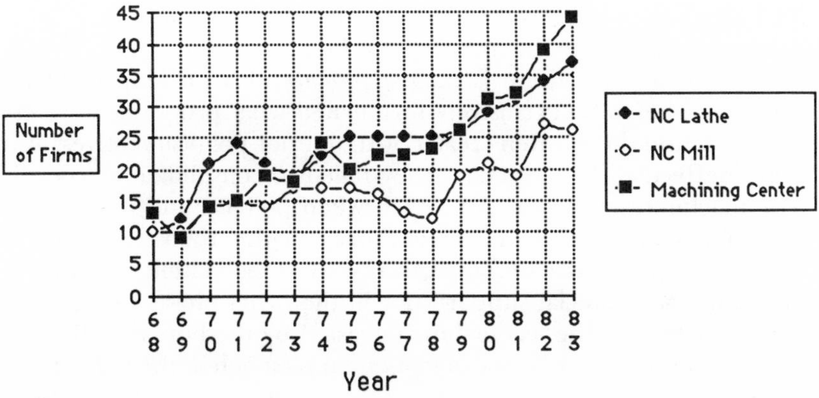

Figure 3.15. Increases in Number of Firms Producing Selected NC Tools, 1968–1983
SOURCES: NC output data same as for Figure 3.1, p. 133; NC firm and machine type data collected from annual "Suchi seigyo kōsaku kikai sangyō jisseki nado chōsa" (Surveys of aspects of the current NC machine tool industry), in *Kōsaku Kikai News* (Tokyo: JMTBA, July 1975, 1979, 1984).

Figure 3.15 records growth in the number of firms producing NC lathes, machining centers, and NC mills. In each case study increases are shown. When markets became profitable, Japanese firms rapidly retooled to enter them, unimpeded by formal or informal restraints. The number of NC lathe producers rose from 10 to 37 firms, the number of NC mill makers from 10 to 25, and the number of machining center specialists from 14 to 45 companies. There is no evidence of cartel-like regulation in this pattern of NC development.

Statistical measures confirm the relationship between firm entry and NC output. If consolidation strategies had been successful, the correlation between firm entry and product growth should be random (as NC output rose with no corresponding firm entry) or negative (as companies increased scale production). Instead, the relationship is strongly positive, $R = .855$ and $\rho = .0001$, a very high index of probability. Furthermore, the relationship between the number of machine types built and expansion was very strong, $R = .843$ and $\rho = .0001$. NC gains were not achieved by restricting designs to a limited range of products in an effort to consolidate manufacturing; again, increases in output associate very strongly with increases in the different types of machine tools produced. These data support the argument that consolidation did not take place; unit-scale increases were not achieved by sacrificing market entry or machinery diversity.[83]

In 1978, as the Electrical Machinery Law expired, explicit cartelization efforts ended in failure. For close to two decades the *gyōkai* and the bureaucracy struggled with each other and with machinery producers to consolidate the industry. In the history of the postwar machine tool industry there is *not one instance* of a MITI plan being adopted. The *gyōkai* exclusively formulated what programs were established, and these, often created with ulterior political motives, also were ineffective. In particular, they failed to consolidate or coordinate machine tool production. Even when political and market circumstances maximized MITI's authority in the 1960s, the *gyōkai*'s "group" response was designed to thwart consolidation. Neither in planning and financial support, nor in the cartel phase, did the bureaucracy exhibit the leadership suggested by the bureaucratic regulation thesis, nor was consolidation implemented through other means.

Exports, Imports, and Centralized Authority

Finally, let us consider the possibility that public or private coordination of machinery production and marketing led to Japanese export successes in the late 1970s. It has frequently been suggested that Japanese exports were targeted and subsidized through government programs, which artificially reduced Japanese costs.[84] As a result U.S. firms, unable to compete, suffered economic reversals.

Japanese export growth in machine tools, I will argue, was due to the development of a new product—small, general-purpose NC tools—that U.S. firms for the most part ignored. Government strategies for export promotion actually did little more than recognize efforts planned and conducted by the *gyōkai*. These promotional efforts were largely unsuccessful until NC tools were developed, and in any case they never amounted to more than a market survey and a public relations campaign. In turn, the advance into U.S. markets occurred because of a gap in American tooling supply; Japanese machinery makers, like those in electronics and autos, filled unexploited market niches and thereby earned substantial profits.

New products also help explain the decline in imports into Japan. Excessive restrictions, it is sometimes claimed, blocked foreign competitors from entering the Japanese market, permitting the rapid attainment of scale economies. In fact, imports were quite high until the NC era. Then as demand shifted, in Japan as in the United States, to smaller NC tools, the ratio of imports to total output fell, though the actual level of imports stayed steady or even grew. The level of imports was also affected as Japanese manufacturers increasingly licensed products or technology from overseas firms. The reduced

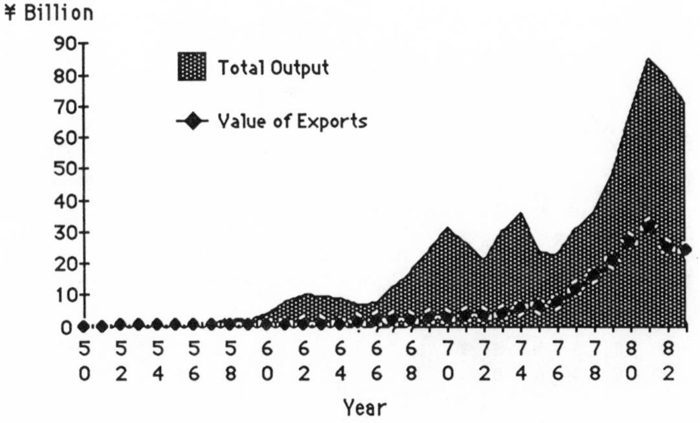

Figure 3.16. Exports and Total Output. 1950–1983
SOURCE: Same as for Table 3.1, p. 121.

foreign presence resulted from the strategic calculations of foreign producers who evidently felt they could earn more in fees than in direct sales.

The postwar history of Japanese machine tool exports as compared with total production is summarized in Figure 3.16. Exports did not become important in the industry's growth until about 1975; as late as 1973 they were only 11 percent of production. Then overseas sales rose steadily, peaking at 44 percent of production in 1978. Figure 3.17 depicts the record on imports during the same period. Unlike in

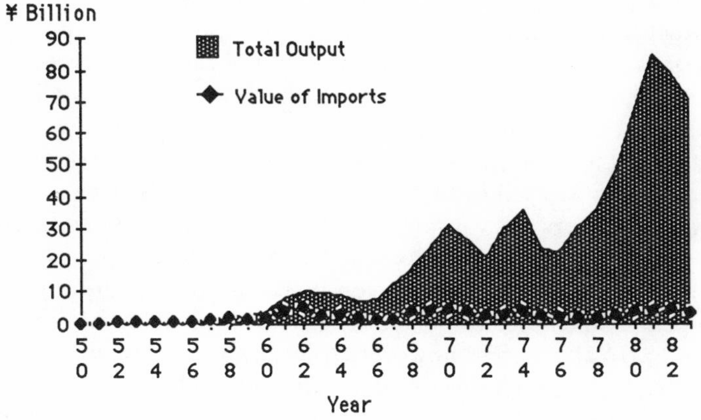

Figure 3.17. Imports and Total Output, 1950–1983
SOURCE: Same as for Table 3.1, p. 121.

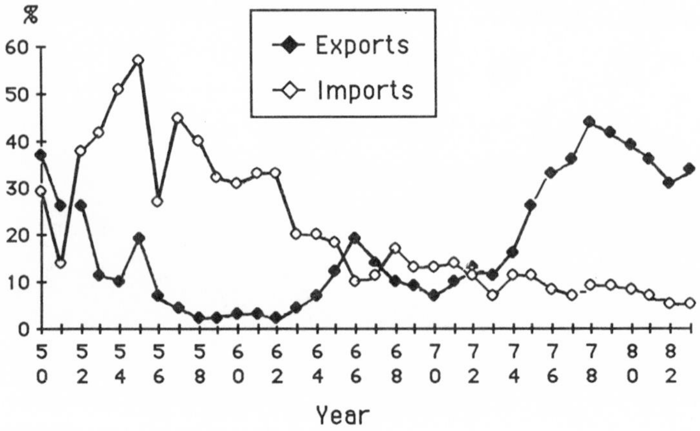

Figure 3.18. Imports and Exports as Percentage of Total Production, 1950–1983
Source: Same as for Table 3.1, p. 121.

other industries, the level of imports in machine tools was historically quite high. Throughout the 1950s foreign firms accounted for between 30 percent and 50 percent of the market, and well into the 1960s their market share was running at 20 percent. By the 1970s, however, imports were 11 percent of total production and fell to a low of 5 percent by 1983. However, the absolute level of imports remained more or less steady and even increased in 1978–1982.

The percentage of imports to total output fell and exports advanced dramatically at the same time. It is tempting to suggest that once foreign firms were driven out of the domestic market, Japanese manufacturers then had a base from which they could export safely. Indeed, as Figure 3.18 shows, declines in the rate of import penetration are associated with export growth. But there would be some grounds for believing that import restraints coupled with overseas targeting led to Japanese successes only if the initial growth in domestic production was achieved in market segments formerly occupied by foreign producers. As we shall see, it was a market shift, to small NC tools, that explains Japanese export successes. The absolute volume of imports remained steady and even increased in the late 1970s, and the types of machines imported by Japan were stable between 1950 and 1980. In the 1970s, however, NC output and exports rose dramatically, driving up both overall production and the volume of overseas sales. Imports, measured against traditional market segments, fell slightly in the postwar period to about 15 percent; measured

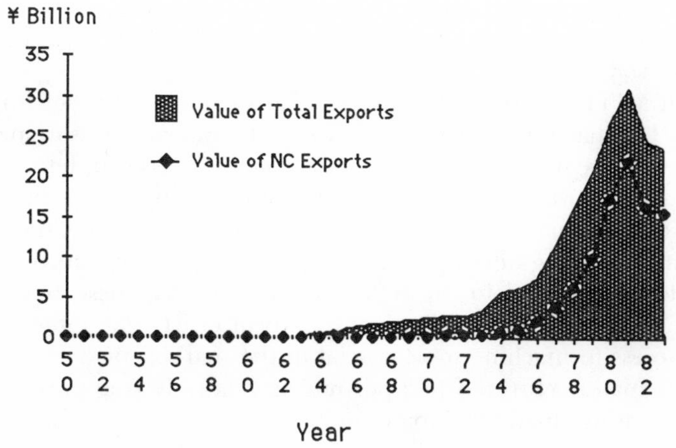

Figure 3.19. NC Exports Compared to Total Exports, 1950–1983
SOURCE: Same as for Table 3.1, p. 121.

against NC output, however, the volume of imports was insignificant.[85]

The importance of NC tools in export advances is shown in Figure 3.19. Up until 1974 the machine tool industry had experienced extremely cyclical growth in which, on average, overall production and export volume increased slightly, but at rates far below those in other sectors in the Japanese economy. As late as 1977 exports to the United States and Europe were just 37 percent of Japan's total; Eastern Europe (20 percent), the Far East (26 percent), and South America were the crucial markets for standard machines. It was only as NC machinery reshaped the industry that rapid export advances began; after 1974 NC machine tools accounted for nearly all of the changes in export volume for machine tools. By the 1980s the American and European market for high-quality products amounted to over 70 percent of Japanese exports.[86] To understand the growth of Japanese exports, therefore, we must evaluate the degree to which the government, or the *gyōkai* acting with government authorization, planned and targeted increases in *NC exports.* As we shall see, there is little evidence of a concerted export drive by either public or private authorities.

Trade restraint and export promotion policies were at their height between 1956 and 1977. Very early trade policies were, we have already seen, actually import subsidies. Machinery firms were provided with matching funds and write-offs to buy the foreign tools necessary to rebuild their manufacturing operations. This policy, effective from 1952 to 1955, helped drive imports to 57 percent of domestic production by 1955.[87]

Both MITI and the *gyōkai* pushed hard for import relief through tariffs, but machinery-using firms scuttled initial attempts to increase the cost of the machines they needed from overseas suppliers. By the late 1950s, however, a series of tariffs was approved. Machines not produced in Japan at all were subject to a 10 percent rate, those that were just entering development received a 15 percent rate, and tools considered essential to the industry's and the Japanese producers' future growth were subject to a 25 percent tariff. The intent was to limit access to machine tools crucial to the markets of domestic machinery manufacturers while permitting relatively free purchases of equipment not made in Japan.[88]

No sooner had the tariffs gone into effect than pressures began from the OECD for capital liberalization. Planned tariffs were rolled back on 96 of 99 machine tool categories in 1964, and by 1970 all tools were "liberalized." Actual tariff rates varied widely, but by the mid-1970s they ranged from 4 percent to 7.5 percent. These levels were not particularly high; comparable tariffs in the United States were 5 percent to 6 percent. In 1983 all tariffs were removed.[89]

The relation between imports and tariffs contradicts the idea that the government affected foreign machinery sales in Japan and hence bolstered the domestic industry. Between 1955 and 1960, when tariffs were rigorously imposed on imported machinery, import sales actually rose, from ¥4 billion to ¥38 billion. From 1960, as tariff rates were progressively lowered, import volume sharply fell to just ¥7 billion by 1966. When rates were liberalized in 1970, import volume recovered to ¥44 billion. With constant tariff rates in the 1970s, however, imports showed a very erratic pattern; they fell to ¥13 billion in 1976 and rose again to ¥43 billion by 1981. Imports then dropped after 1983 as all tariffs were completely removed.[90] Tariff increases therefore are associated with import volume increases, and tariff decreases occur with import volume decreases—the opposite of what we should observe. In periods of stable tariffs, moreover, imports showed huge swings. It is highly improbable that the government's tariff policies were a major factor in determining import demand.

Other MITI strategies were even less effective. The bureaucracy's basic strategy was to set export volume targets, undifferentiated by country or machine type, for the duration of various five-year plans. But as we have already seen, Japanese firms never came close to achieving the export targets established in each of the three plans under the Machinery Promotion Law and the basic plan of the Electrical Machinery Law. At best those targets represented guesswork on the part of the bureaucracy. Nor were subsidies or other programs ever offered to assure the realization of MITI's goals.

Throughout the 1960s and 1970s the only export promotion program for machine tools was conceived and directed by the *gyōkai* itself. In May 1962 the *gyōkai* set up a "sister" Japan Machine Tool Export Production Association (Nihon Kōsaku Kikai Yūshutsu Shinkō Kai), and in August this Export Association opened offices in Chicago and in Düsseldorf. Its major tasks were to affiliate with trade shows in Europe and the United States so that Japanese machines would be represented, conduct surveys of foreign markets, and develop general public relations handouts for distribution to overseas customers. The Export Association never actually sold tools itself, nor did it arrange financing. It was abolished in June 1978 as machine tool firms pursued their own marketing strategies, and only in the late 1970s did its activity coincide with export increases. The percentage of exports to total production actually fell from 1965 to 1972 after the organization was established, while absolute volume was increasing only slowly. NC export gains occurred only after the association was disbanded. This evidence makes it hard to link concerted action with export gains.[91]

Two other facts undercut the notion that machinery exports were planned and targeted. The more important was the strength of outsider firms. Mori Seki, an outsider that was Japan's second-largest NC producer by 1981, was exporting over 60 percent of its products, 10 percent of the *total* value of Japanese machine tool exports.[92] But the firm was neither a member of the *gyōkai* nor a party to the Export Association. Rather, Mori Seki had formed a technical link with an American entrepreneur that then served as a conduit for exports to the United States.

The other fact is that, in general, machinery exports were accomplished in an extremely eclectic manner. Japanese firms typically sold overseas to individual companies or affiliates with which they had long-term links. Shizuoka Machinery, for example, had an arrangement with a small U.S. shop to provide knock-down standard milling equipment to be assembled abroad. The U.S. partner noted that the equipment was suitable for NC retrofitting, which led Shizuoka to try to design a full NC mill for export. It first copied a German NC mill and then designed its own. The American affiliate liked the design, bought the rights to market it in the United States, and expanded output. As a result Shizuoka became a major exporter of NC mills.[93] Other companies, such as Hamai, built license links with overseas firms and used them as distributors. Hamai was licensed to build a machining center by Pratt and Whitney, which it sold in Europe under the Japanese name. In exports to the United States, Pratt and Whitney had the right to use its own name on the tool even though the tool was made in Japan.[94] Finally, most firms, in the absence of direct contacts with overseas dealers, sold their machines through a commercial broker. One with a long-term relationship with smaller tool makers was Yamazen, around which a short-lived "group" had been founded in 1967. Other firms associated themselves with different commercial houses; Mitsubishi and Mitsui, for example, tended to market through their old *zaibatsu* affiliates.

The limited nature of *gyōkai* promotional efforts, the diversity of both exporting companies and their access to overseas markets, and the absence of a coherent, effective import-export policy by the government—these points do not support the idea that machinery exports were planned. Furthermore, in the 1960s and the 1970s American and European manufacturers increasingly chose to license technology rather than sell products directly in Japan. As a result, import penetration decreased as machinery demand grew. Between 1952 and 1981 there were over 160 foreign tie-ups in the machine tool industry, more than one for every company in the *gyōkai*. In addition, Japanese firms set up close to seventy related technology licenses, including those for NC controllers. Figure 3.20 breaks down foreign licenses for machine tool technology by country of origin. Historically Europe, especially France, first licensed technology to Japanese manufacturers in the

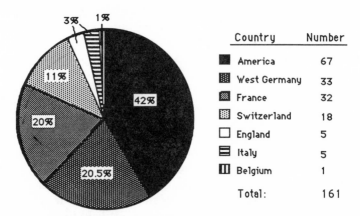

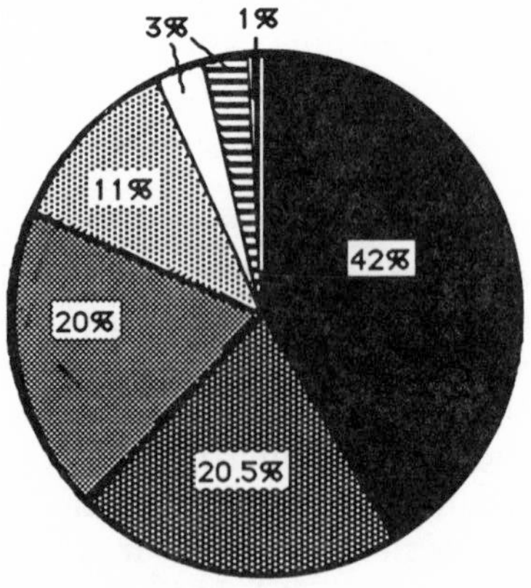

Country	Number
America	67
West Germany	33
France	32
Switzerland	18
England	5
Italy	5
Belgium	1
Total:	161

Figure 3.20. Machine Tool Technical Licenses Issued in Seven Countries and Number of Firms Involved, Cumulative Records for 1952–1981
SOURCE: Same as for Table 3.1, pp. 86–90.

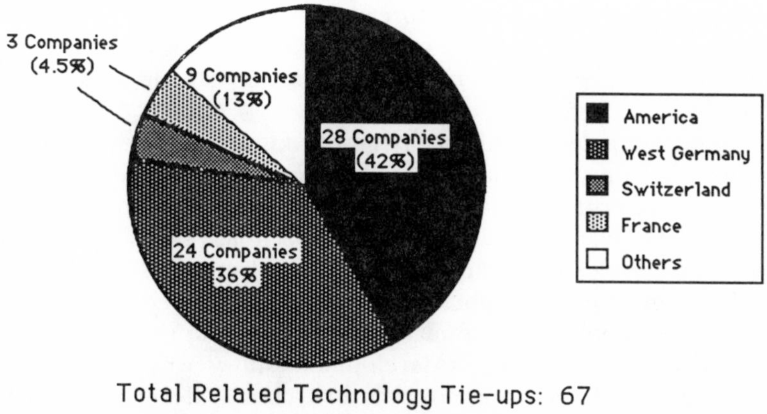

Figure 3.21. Related Technology Contracts by Country of Origin and Number of Firms. Cumulative Records for 1970–1981
SOURCE: Same as for Table 3.1, p. 91.

1950s. Gradually, with advances in electrical controllers, the United States became the largest single source of technical tie-ups. These tie-ups usually involved a license arrangement; the Japanese firm either made the licensed equipment to the specifications provided and paid a fee on sales, or it incorporated the foreign technology into its product and provided remuneration on some predetermined basis. After the expiration of the agreement the Japanese firm would usually retain all rights to the technology in a specific market—the Far East, say, or Africa.

Related technology tie-ups included those for NC controllers, for specialty steels used for cutting tools, and for servomotors used to move NC machine components according to computerized instructions. Such high-tech licenses were particularly prevalent between 1970 and 1981 when Japanese firms were eagerly seeking the expertise necessary to build NC equipment. America was the source of most of this technology; Figure 3.21 displays related technology contracts by country of origin.

Even though MITI had viewed the promotion of the machinery industry as a major objective in its overall effort to enhance the competitiveness of Japanese manufacturing, bureaucratic influence on technical tie-ups was marginal. Yet it is sometimes argued that MITI's right to review all foreign contracts in the postwar era, a power based on the Foreign Capital Laws of the 1930s, helped allow MITI to regulate market access in Japan.[95] But machine tools, one of 33 industrial groups in the "general machinery" classification, alone had over 220 tie-ups. It would have been impossible for the bureaucracy, and the Industrial Machinery Bureau, to have controlled the terms of all of these agreements. No plan existed for technology imports; individual companies decided how and when they should seek foreign contracts.[96]

A good example is Fanuc, the largest producer of NC equipment in the world. Fanuc's dominance of the Japanese controller market is sometimes interpreted as the result of conscious policy. In fact, Fanuc is one of the few companies in high-cost technical fields that has not once made use of JDB loans or experimental subsidies.[97] Instead, it used foreign licenses to obtain the technology it needed, then supplied this technology to the machinery industry in the form of customized controllers. Fanuc's development shows why experimental subsidies played such a minor role in technical development after 1955 and why imports stagnated while licenses flourished. Instead of carrying out their own basic research, Japanese machine tool firms found willing foreign partners who sold them the technology they needed.

Japan's first NC controller was produced after the electronics giant Fujitsu and Makino Milling created a joint venture to build an NC milling machine.[98] They copied NC mill specifications developed by the MIT Servo Labs in conjunction with a military project. Eventually the venture succeeded, and Fujitsu, impressed with the market potential of the NC controllers, spun off an independent company called Fujitsu Fanuc. Fanuc obtained several technology licenses. In 1974 Fanuc became a license of the American firm Geddys, a specialist in DC servomotors. Then, to produce smaller NC equipment, Fanuc imported technology from the German giant Siemans. Another American company was approached in 1976 to assist in stop placement switches.[99] Later the ties to Geddys and Siemans were renewed.

Fanuc's early reliance on foreign technology, which overseas firms supplied willingly, was typical for the industry. For instance, Fanuc's main competitors, Yasukawa Electrics, Okuma, and Toshiba, all had technical license agreements with an American NC controller manufacturer, Bendix. MITI had little or no influence on these contracts; foreign firms were eager to license Japanese manufacturers, thereby gaining a stake in a difficult market at little cost. Furthermore, the availability of foreign contacts may actually have prevented the consolidation that the bureaucracy sought; as we have noted, tie-ups with foreign firms were excluded from the production restraint agreements, and in part it was such ties that made possible the rapid entry of firms into machining center, NC lathe, and NC mill markets. Thus even in the case of controllers Fanuc's early market dominance was short-lived. By 1983–1984, Yasukawa and other producers had gained a growing share of the NC controller segment by means of foreign technology applications; Fanuc's share fell to under 50 percent.[100] Thus, technology licenses help explain the fall in import activity; foreign firms opted for an indirect market presence.

In fact, the only export scheme ever enforced by MITI was intended to *restrain* trade. As trade friction with the United States grew, Japanese producers feared for their access to the American market. The machine tool industry was especially vulnerable because of its rapid export gains in the late 1970s and early 1980s. In response, the government began to urge a number of industries, including machinery, to cut back on sales. It wanted to establish a quota system so as to set up an orderly export arrangement.

In December 1977 MITI issued a preliminary draft of a program to control exports of machine tools to the United States, and in March 1978 it established a North American Trade Requirements Rule under the Export/Import Commercial Law. Then it extended the rule to cover outsider firms, the first time in Japanese history that machinery laws had been enforced across all classes of producers. This extension resulted from several factors. Machine tool firms believed that some form of response to U.S. criticism was necessary, or their most lucrative market might be lost; consequently, even outsiders like Mori Seki joined the *gyōkai* explicitly to support a generalized restraint scheme.[101] Pressure had mounted from other business sectors and political and industrial leaders as well, strengthening MITI in its bid for control.

MITI's export restraint strategies were no more effective than its other policy efforts. Even those companies which had supported a response in principle failed to agree on how to proceed; no system of compliance or penalty was enacted. From 1978 to 1981 exports doubled, and the proportion of exports going to the United States rose from 25 percent to over 51 percent of the Japanese total.[102] MITI extended the rule for 1981, but again to little effect. The rule's main utility was as evidence that Japan was attempting to respond to U.S. objections.

Why did the U.S. market prove so lucrative? Part of the answer lies in the technical and marketing relationships between Japanese and U.S. firms, market positioning, and global economic conditions. First, Japanese licensing patterns had shifted from Europe to the United States because NC technology was more advanced in America. Most overseas NC users with which Japanese firms had direct contact were located in the United States. These license contacts were often the basis for marketing agreements, and so it was natural for Japanese firms to concentrate on U.S. users first. Next, the fact that American manufacturers ignored the small, job-shop NC market was crucial; Japanese firms were selling in a niche distinct from the U.S. norm, just as they had pioneered in smaller, economical cars. In Europe, Italian and German machinery producers had long experience selling to small-scale users, though their lagging NC development still made them vulnerable to Japanese product competition. But in the United States, Japanese manufacturers were selling to firms that had no other source for small-scale equipment, as American NC production was concentrated on larger, specialty markets. Finally, American users could afford the equipment. The only customers with the ability to pay for NC machinery were in Europe and the United States, but Europe had been in a long-term slump whereas the United States was headed for recovery. Moreover, U.S. macroeconomic policies in the early 1980s fostered capital investment and—by increasing the strength of the dollar—imports. The production of Japanese NC tools coincided with favorable conditions in the United States, producing an export boom.

However, there is little evidence of concerted, coordinated export activity. *Gyōkai* endeavors were not associated with export expansion. MITI policies were ineffective; they neither fostered nor hindered overseas sales. Import declines were associated with vast increases in technology licensing, which gave Japanese firms the ability to make new NC products. It is the development of NC tools and their subsequent popularity which explains Japanese successes.

CONCLUSIONS

The prewar and wartime history of policies for the machine tool industry does not support the bureaucratic regulation thesis regarding the Japanese economy. We should have observed a government building economies of scale in prewar machinery industries, nurturing firms immediately after the war, consolidating production to permit enhanced scale economies in the 1960s, and then directing the industry's movement into NC technology. To do so, Japan, guided by its economic bureaucracy, should have built a more efficient, consolidated industry than the United States, a development that would have accounted for its competitive success. Instead, we observed policy and planning efforts that were ineffective, a decentralized machine tool industry, and in particular government initiatives that had no apparent relation to NC breakthroughs. Indeed, even among "private" consolidation efforts the record of new entrants and diversity in the industry belies the notion that *gyōkai* direction was any more effective than MITI guidance.

Though the bureaucratic regulation thesis contends that Japanese industry was guided by a "strong state," the machine tool industry exhibits an unbroken record of policy failures dating from the late 1920s. From the Depression to the present there is not one example of the adoption, let alone the success, of a MITI or an MCI initiative. If we think of a strong state as one that sets goals and then manipulates financial and other incentives to achieve them, Japan appears to be extremely *weak:* the government was forced to provide resources but could not insist that its goals be met in exchange.

The restraint of bureaucratic power by the machine tool industry was symptomatic of a general policy struggle in Japan, a struggle whose resolution enhanced the spread of flexible production. If the MCI had succeeded in fostering machinery production in larger firms, it might have greatly reduced the number of small-scale producers. Then MITI's continual efforts to increase scale economies might well have consolidated Japanese manufacturing further. But the politics between regulated firms and the bureaucracy pointed elsewhere. As we shall see in the next chapter, the government, despite its industrial policy goals, was induced to support smaller manufacturers.

Political conflict between member firms in industry groups, and between *gyōkai* members and outsider companies, also counteracted trends toward consolidation. Privately organized cartel schemes broke down, both before and after the war, because of ineffective enforcement and mistrust. As a result, production restraints and attempts to stop new firms from entering segments of the machinery market were ineffective. Thus politics forestalled the emergence of policies that might have reduced opportunities for flexible manufacturing in Japan.

Finally, Japanese machinery advances, we have seen, were predicated on rapid market entry by new producers, new product developments, and new applications of technologies frequently pioneered abroad. To assess the reasons for Japanese success, we need to know why Japan took advantage of latent design opportunities that were apparently ignored elsewhere. Why were Japanese machinery producers able to enter the market with new product applications? And why should Japan have had an apparently stronger demand for very small NC machinery than other countries? If the bureaucratic regulation thesis can tell us little about the nature and sources of Japanese machinery developments, the market regulation thesis, as I show in the next chapter, is also of little use in answering these questions. Instead, we must look to the political events surrounding the expansion of flexible manufacturing enterprises in Japan.

Chapter Four

Flexible Production and Small-Scale Manufacturing

Several features of the Japanese machinery industry were associated with rapid growth. They included continuous firm entry into promising segments of the machine tool market, extensive market volatility, and unique demand for small NC equipment. If we discount the effects of purposive coordination efforts by the state or the *gyōkai,* do we thereby confirm the market regulation thesis? Were Japanese industrial achievements simply the result of companies pursuing their economic advantage in the most efficient way?

The capacities of Japanese firms to meet market demands, and indeed the structure of the market itself, cannot be understood apart from the political events that created them. Japanese small-scale manufacturers modified the overall character of the country's manufacturing enterprises. Many small firms, especially in advanced sectors, became highly sophisticated producers of parts or key components used in assembling finished goods. They were able to do so because of a number of politically contingent events, among them the transformation of worker career perceptions in small and large firms, the development of independent relations between contractor and subcontracting producers, and the restructuring of capital markets to support investment in small manufacturing enterprises. These events, I will argue, are among the background conditions that enhanced flexible manufacturing opportunities in Japan.

The market regulation thesis cannot address the reasons for the widespread adoption of flexible operations in small-scale factories, because these reasons are ultimately political in character. It can provide explanations for industrial outcomes when material or market constraints are fairly rigid: when technologies are fixed, business practices well entrenched, and the character of competition long established, then the analysis of producer behavior as a function of the rational pursuit of economic advantage is valuable. But when such competitive constraints have yet to be fully formed, they exert a much weaker influence on industrial choices. Industrial actors then have to base their decisions about how to organize production on other grounds, including ideologies, the balance of power between competing interests, and the like. In roughly similar circumstances, equally "valid" industrial outcomes are possible, and we cannot explain the shape and nature of particular industrial organizations without reference to the background politics that formed them.

To demonstrate this proposition, I examine the development of small-scale manufacturing in Japan. First, the widespread perception of Japan's smaller firms as technically inferior, using cheap labor, and subject to cyclical shocks to the benefit of large factories—the so-called dual structure argument—is substantially mistaken. Adjustment patterns, wage rates, and worker career expectations in small and large firms fail to conform to the theory. Second, political events ultimately led many small manufacturers to flexible production strategies. This outcome could well have been different; in the 1950s a dual structure–like industrial order was generated and might quite easily have been institutionalized. But the manufacturing strategies of large firms unintentionally cut against dual structure practices, and a complementary transformation of financial markets provided additional incentives for small firms to avoid subservience to larger producers. In part because of these political events, in part because of others (including the growth of industrial regionalism, discussed in chapter 5), many small-scale manufacturers were able to become flexible, high-tech specialists. Machine tool developments in particular and Japanese high growth in general can be explained with reference to this development.

In this chapter I begin to identify the politically contingent industrial events that permitted Japanese firms to adopt flexible production. Once we see how politics made it possible for small producers to escape from dual structure arrangements, then we can understand flexible manufacturing as a "rational" response to market imperatives. But in the absence of the political basis for such responses, contemporary Japanese industrial practices could have been, and indeed very nearly were, completely different. Recognition of the political roots of the Japanese industrial order makes possible a more comprehensive and more accurate explanation for the nation's remarkable growth.

The Dual Structure Revisited

The "dual structure" (*ni-jū kōzō*) theory of smaller firms in Japan has enjoyed widespread acceptance there and has been adopted more or less uncritically in foreign studies as well.[1] According to this argument, small producers in Japan survive by producing cheap, labor-intensive parts at the behest of larger firms, and they serve as an economic buffer for more modern, larger enterprises by absorbing the costs and dislocations of Japanese economic reversals. Large firms expand their capacity to the minimum level of demand in any market and then try to stabilize their operations and increase efficiency. They pay comparatively high wages to pacify their work force and offer permanent employment to obtain long-term labor peace. Because worker recalcitrance is reduced and market demand easily estimated, large firms are able to make especially effective machinery investments. Small firms, in contrast, cluster about the larger companies and get subcontracting work in accordance with business cycles; they meet excess demand in boom times and retrench during slack periods. Their labor force is impermanent and poorly paid, which makes the small firms attractive to large firms as a source for parts.[2] And because of their instability, the small firms cannot obtain financial support; financial markets are stratified, with rich capital resources available for larger firms and a tight money market for smaller ones. As Nakamura Takafusa explains, such a system has transferred the burdens of economic adjustment onto small manufacturers:

> When business was poor, parent firms would drop their subcontractors and postpone payment on their accounts, while in good times they would increase subcontracting. Then, citing the need for rationalization among subcontractors, they would beat prices down to low levels. . . . The large firms got away with this sort of thing because the small companies were at a great relative disadvantage. For example, in the 1950s, the small firms could not entrust their survival to the expectation of loans from monetary institutions. During periods of monetary ease when funds were abundant banks went ahead and made loans to small businesses, but when money became tight they would hurriedly call in these loans. Needless to say, subcontracting firms were also at a disadvantage in terms of competitive ability in the marketplace.[3]

Thus small firms are subservient to larger companies, they cannot develop technical skills, and they are forced to depend on cheap labor for their existence. They are, as one scholar has suggested, a "shock absorber," insulating the largest manufacturers from economic stress.[4]

If the notion were true, small Japanese firms would hardly warrant attention; their plight would be comprehensible as an example of the normal, if regrettable, stratification of skills and opportunities present in all economies. Yet as I will show, except for a brief period in the 1950s the dual structure theory does not accurately describe the nature and role of small manufacturers in Japan. Small firms did *not* insulate larger companies from adjustment costs; wage differentials were much *less* than supposed, and improved greatly in the 1960s and 1970s; and the skills of small manufacturers frequently *surpassed* those of larger firms in specialized areas. It is not my purpose to deny that smaller firms were exploited or that they did not face hardship; the dual structure thesis was founded on real exploitation and hardship in the Japanese economy and elsewhere. Long working hours, low pay, and desperate dependence on uncertain subcontracting orders are the dark side of all industries. But even if such disturbing economic problems exist in Japan—as they do in all countries—the dual structure argument nevertheless has numerous problems. In sum, a large number of Japanese small firms have escaped permanent dependence and technological inferiority by adopting flexible production strategies.

Let us begin by examining the argument that in Japan large firms, frequently called "parent firms," forced smaller ones to absorb the costs of demand shifts. We can test this hypothesis by examining the adjustment patterns of small, medium, and large firms during periods of recession. If the dual structure argument is correct, then as the economy contracts, employment should be stable in large firms while small firms trim their work force through layoffs. In addition, the number of large firms should be more or less fixed, while the number of small firms should drop as markets, financing, and orders evaporate.

Excluding the period when Japan's defeat affected adjustment patterns, since 1920 the Japanese economy has undergone four severe economic contractions: the Great Depression (1929–1932), the "mini-recessions" of the 1950s (1957–1959), the first oil shock caused by the Arab oil embargo (1975–1977), and the second oil shock brought about by the Iranian crisis (1978–1980). For each sector and type of economic undertaking, service industries, banking, extraction, energy, and manufacturing, the periods of contractions were different. The dates I have highlighted may not correspond exactly to conventional delineations of each period, but they represent the peak and the trough of the retrenchment in *manufacturing* alone for the four recessions. I concentrate on the moment of greatest stress in the economy for manufacturing enterprises, to determine which classes of firms suffered the most.

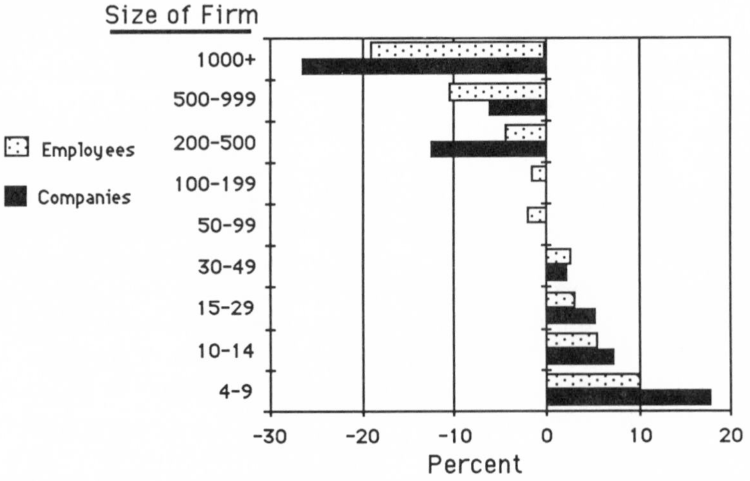

Figure 4.1. Employment and Number of Firms by Size Class, 1929–1932
Source: Compiled from Tsūsanshō (Ministry of International Trade and Industry), *Nihon no kōgyō tōkei* (Industrial statistics of Japan) (Tokyo, 1930–1933).

The pattern of change in the Japanese economy during the Great Depression was precisely the opposite of what the dual structure hypothesis would predict (see Figure 4.1). The largest decreases in both employment and number of firms occurred among the largest firms; for example, the number of companies with more than a thousand employees fell 27 percent and employment dropped 19 percent. These reductions are comparable to those in the United States during the Depression. But unlike in the United States, as company size decreased, so did the effects of the Depression, until at the 30–49 employee level, gains were recorded in both the number of companies and employment. These gains peaked with the smallest class of firms, those with four to nine employees.

The adjustment pattern during the Depression clearly shows that large firms did not respond to demand shortfalls by cutting back on subcontractors while stabilizing internal operations. Instead, large firms were profoundly affected by the Depression. This finding challenges one of the basic hypotheses of the dual structure theory, that large firms maintained a stable work force at the expense of smaller enterprises. Depression-era evidence indicates that large firms adjusted by making wholesale cutbacks in their work force when demand was reduced.

The mini-recessions of the fifties were most severe in manufacturing between 1957 and 1959. Figure 4.2 illustrates changes by firm size

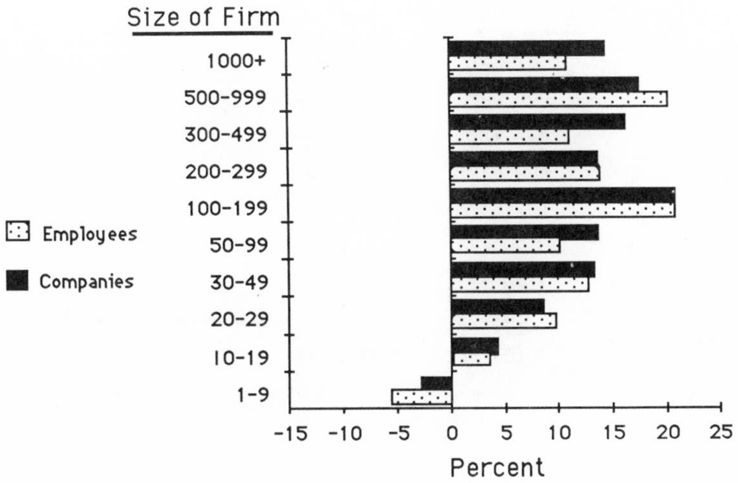

Figure 4.2. Employment and Number of Firms by Size Class, 1957–1959
SOURCE: Same as for Figure 4.1, for 1957–1959.

during the contraction. In this case we do see adjustment patterns consistent with dual structure theory. Increases in employment and number of firms are greater for larger firms. Indeed, almost all reductions in total employment and numbers of companies during this period were accounted for by the smallest class of companies, those with fewer than ten employees. As we shall see, it was in the fifties that the emergence of a Japanese "dual economy" was most likely. It is understandable that the dual structure thesis was widely accepted in this period. But adjustment data from later recessions and developments in the relations between large and small firms reversed these trends as smaller firms adopted flexible manufacturing strategies.

The 1975–1977 recession was the worst manufacturing slump in Japanese postwar economic history. In contrast to the pattern exhibited in the 1957–1959 slump, adjustment was negative for all size classes (with the notable exception of firms with 20–29 employees), and the magnitude is similar independent of size (see Figure 4.3). The data indicate considerable inconsistencies within the dual structure view. Firms with more than a thousand workers show the second-highest rate of company and employment declines, though the size class should have been the most stable. Indeed, if we exclude the 10–19 class, employment and firm reductions are either of equal magnitude or slightly less for small firms as for large firms. Even the 10–19 size class declines are offset by massive increases in the 20–29 employee category. The figures do not indicate that small firms were

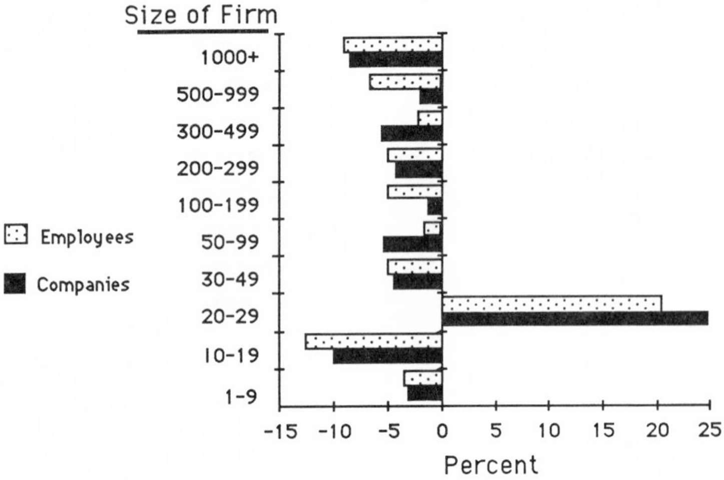

Figure 4.3. Employment and Number of Firms by Size Class, 1975–1977
Sources: Same as for Figure 4.1, for 1975–1977.

sacrificed to maintain stability in large companies. Instead, large firms had as much trouble with the recession as small ones, and the greater burden of adjustment fell on the top size classes.

The adjustment pattern for 1978–1980, during the second oil shock, shows a mixture of declines and growth, some consistent with the dual structure argument, others contradicting it (see Figure 4.4). Firms in the upper range of the "small or medium" category, those with 100–299 employees, and companies in the lower range of the "large" category, with 300–999 employees, show considerable growth in the number of both employees and firms. The very largest and the very smallest firms registered declines. And apart from the 30–49 size group, other categories experienced little change. The eclecticism of the 1978–1980 adjustment pattern once again fails to support the dual structure notion that small firms are the Japanese economy's shock absorber. Both very large and very small firms experienced comparable declines. Medium-sized firms expanded, as did companies at the lower end of the large-firm spectrum. Adjustment is not a function of firm size.

Aggregate data comparing employment and company changes by size classes for each period are presented in Figure 4.5. In the Depression, small firms, those with fewer than two hundred employees, expanded their overall work force and grew in numbers, whereas large firms registered massive declines on both scores. During 1957–1959 smaller firms suffered more than larger ones, but in the 1975–1977

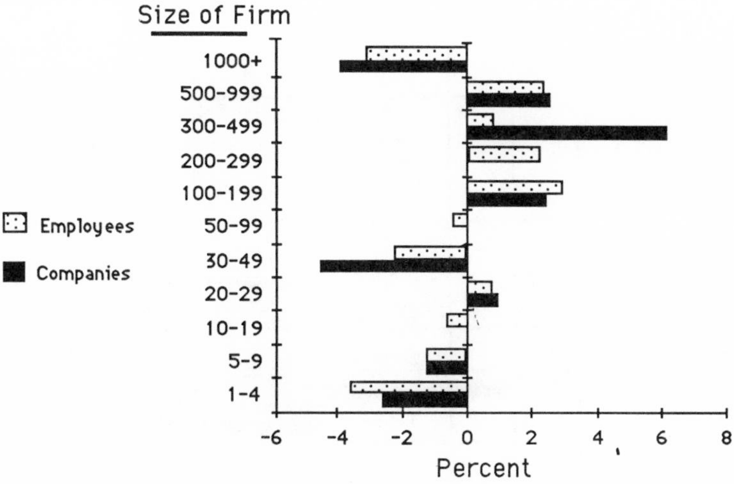

Figure 4.4. Employment and Number of Firms by Size Class, 1978–1980
SOURCES: Same as for Figure 4.1, for 1978–1980.

recession both small and large firms registered numerical and employment declines, and the shifts were greater for the large class. Finally, in the 1978–1980 recession, adjustment burdens appear to have been evenly distributed between large and small firms. Employment decreased for large firms and increased for small companies; the number of enterprises increased for large firms and decreased for small firms. Only in the 1957–1959 period does adjustment correspond with what dual structure theory would predict.

It is difficult to reconcile these findings with the dual structure argument without abandoning the assumptions that make the argument compelling in the first place. One possible explanation, for instance, is that during contractions, large firms force small firms to accept their surplus workers, increasing the total employment accounted for by, and the number of, smaller-scale producers as large firms reduce their operations. This idea has problems, however. The main rationale of the dual structure is that it *insulates* large Japanese firms from internal disruptions, maintaining economies of scale up to the minimum level of stable demand. If large companies foisted surplus labor onto small firms, they would sacrifice both economies of scale and company harmony. Production during recessions would be increasingly fragmented among small firms, and the factory work force of large firms would be in turmoil, contradicting our basic understanding of the dual economy—that employment is permanent in large firms, which preserve stable economies of scale, and cyclical in

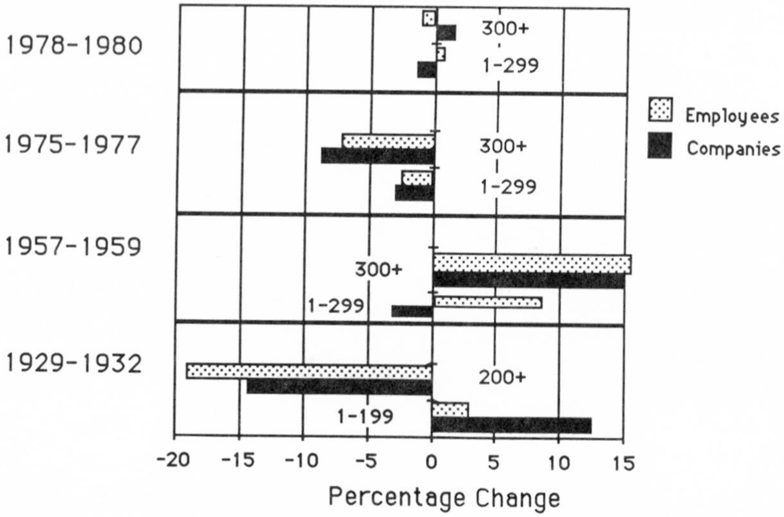

Figure 4.5. Employment and Number of Firms by Size Class, 1929–1932, 1957–1959, 1975–1977, and 1978–1980
SOURCES: Based on Figures 4.1–4.4.

small ones. Even if the explanation were true, then the nature of the Japanese economy would be quite different from what dual structure theory suggests. In fact, as I show in the next section, quite different relations between large and small firms account for these adjustment patterns.

In the dual structure view, low wages in Japanese small businesses are symptomatic of the subjugation of smaller producers to larger firms. Low wages developed as contractors pressured subcontractors to cut costs. Managers of small and medium-sized businesses had to push their workers' pay far below that of the secure, "permanent" laborers in large businesses. They could do so at first because of a weak labor market. Meanwhile, large firms were willing to pay higher wages to secure a stable, skilled work force, while outside sourcing for low-wage, cheap parts reduced the overall cost of their products.

We can test this hypothesis with two kinds of data. One concerns historical emergence of wage differentials according to firm size. If the dual structure argument is right, large firms should force small ones to pay lower wages in return for cyclical contract work. The other is the pattern of Japanese and comparative wage differentials. If the stratified labor market suggested by dual structure analysis compensated for high wages in large Japanese firms, then wage differentials should be particularly wide in Japan and especially apparent during the nation's economic "miracle" of the 1960s and 1970s, as

Japanese manufacturers exploited price advantages in world markets. But an entirely different process led, as I will show, to the emergence of wage differentials in Japan, and remuneration differentials had fallen to levels consistent with those in the United States by the start of Japan's postwar resurgence. This does not mean, of course, that there was no inequality in Japanese industry, but it does mean the belief that wage differentials comprised a system of exploitation integral to Japanese industrial achievement must be rejected.

How did differentials emerge in Japan? Though there are a variety of cultural and other collateral explanations in the Japanese literature, the conventional view, consistent with the dual structure argument, is that large firms stabilized their wage rates to secure internal harmony while forcing small companies to cut costs by squeezing their workers.[5] So powerful were large industrialists that they could force labor in their own factories to accept minimal but slightly favorable payoffs in return for stability while creating a huge pool of suppliers of cheap parts to support the concessions. It was the power of large-scale capitalists, their ability to reorganize the economy, which accounted for the dual structure in Japan.

The history of the prewar emergence of wage gaps in small and large firms belies this account. Labor unrest in large firms forced industrialists to offer real increases in wages relative to small firms. It created a pluralistic pattern of labor careers. Workers in large firms fought for high wages because opportunities for independence were reduced in the giant factories, whereas in small firms workers accepted lower wages as the price for training that might lead them to become independent factory operators.

Turn-of-the-century labor strife led to concessionary labor payoffs, and a crucial period was the immediate aftermath of the Russo-Japanese War as large manufacturing concerns in steel and armaments first expanded in the economy. From traditional relationships with employers workers were thrust into new roles as blue-collar laborers in large companies—something novel in the Japanese setting. Until the turn of the century, production workers had endured low wages to get the training that would subsequently permit them to become independent.[6] This, the *deshi* system, resembled the way apprentices were trained in craft guilds in Europe. Late nineteenth-century factory recruits accepted low pay in the expectation that they would develop manufacturing skills and soon become self-employed. But as large-scale factories grew, the older rules governing factory relations came under increasing strain. Intensely personal training and subsequent financial support were impossible in the large factories, where workers agitated for both higher wages and job security in compensation.

Consequently, as Yasuba Yasukichi argues, work in large firms was reorganized to reflect new demands, whereas small firms preserved the *deshi* system:

> [Traditional] human relations continued into the modern period in small businesses where, with the system of apprenticeship, paternalistic care of the workers and hope for future independence could compensate for low wages. In larger businesses, however, it was becoming increasingly more difficult for employers to keep close informal contact with workers. The hope for future independence was also diminishing. As a result, the old *deshi* (apprentice) system was becoming unpopular in larger businesses even in the Meiji period, as exemplified in a most dramatic way by the strike of workers at Harimaya ([later] Sogo Department Store) demanding the modern salary wage system. Thus, it was natural that larger firms should institutionalize paternalism into seniority-oriented, higher wages and richer fringe benefits.[7]

High-wage, stable employment grew in large firms because of labor militancy. The labor force was split between blue-collar workers earning high wages in large firms and low-paid workers in small factories who understood they had different rights in the workplace. (This plurality of career paths characterizes much of the Japanese labor market to the present day.) In contrast to the dual structure argument that differentials emerged because large firms had the power to create them, the wage gap grew because workers forced industrialists to pay a premium for work in large factories.

These developments did not begin to affect the relative position of small and large firms until late in the prewar period. Wage surveys taken during World War I show that Japanese differentials based on firm size had yet to appear; wages in all factories, independent of size, were uniform and low. There is some evidence that from 1914 to the Depression a considerable wage gap developed, one that more or less endured until the end of World War II.[8] One reason was that high wages spread as large firms copied the permanent employment strategy of leading firms in response to labor militancy. Just as the GM Basic Agreement in postwar America affected pay and benefits for other industries, so the high wage–stable employment solutions offered by influential Japanese firms such as Yokosuka Shipbuilding became models for other large companies.[9]

The fact that wages were driven higher in large firms contradicts the idea that small firms were forced to reduce pay scales to become attractive subcontracting sources. To be sure, wartime dislocations and government policies that favored large firms required smaller enterprises to operate in an often difficult environment. Many small firms did try to compete by reducing wages. But in general historical terms the wage gap appears to have developed because of the way workers responded to large factories and the resultant payoffs they forced large firms to make. Two career paths were created: workers in large firms enjoyed the promise of security with higher wages; employees in small firms sought independence and higher eventual incomes through their training in manufacturing.

Although there were huge, size-related wage differentials in the Japan of the 1950s, these were gradually reduced by the early 1960s. During the high-growth decades of the sixties and seventies size-based differentials were brought into line with, and were sometimes even smaller than, those in the United States. Indeed, small factories in Japan had to pay a premium for new recruits, and younger workers received higher pay in small companies than their counterparts in large firms.

Figure 4.6 illustrates the postwar development of manufacturing wage differentials for males in firms of 500 or more employees as compared to those in companies of 5–29 and 30–100 employees.[10] Wage differentials were very wide in the 1950s, when manufacturing firms of 5–29 employees paid wages just 42 percent of those in larger firms. But as the Japanese economy entered its high-growth phase in the 1960s, wage differentials rapidly closed. By 1965 wage disparities had narrowed by close to 20 points for all size classes. Even in the smallest firms wages were over 65 percent of what large companies were paying, and firms with 30–100 employees were paying close to

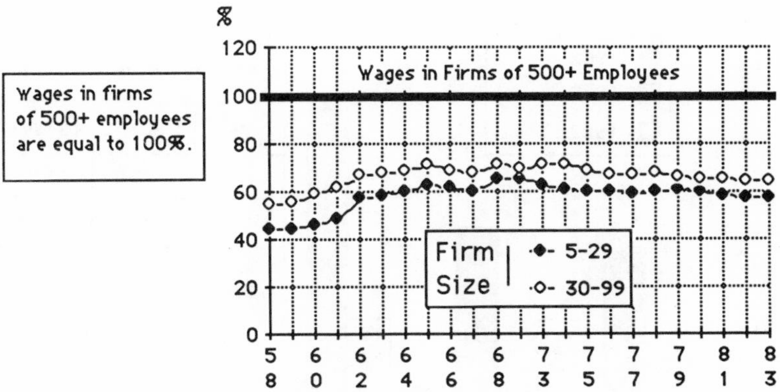

Figure 4.6. Wage Differentials in Manufacturing, 1958–1982
SOURCE: Rōdōshō (Ministry of Labor), *Maigestu tsurō tōkei chōsa,* (Monthly wage statistics) (Tokyo, published monthly).

75 percent of salaries in large firms. These differentials then remained steady until a small decline in the 1980s. The huge wage gaps of the 1950s had been greatly reduced.

The disparities of the 1950s were produced by the effects of the wartime recovery. Until the late 1950s Japan's sagging economy, coupled with a huge labor surplus caused by the return of former soldiers to civilian status, created an extremely weak labor market. Wages were depressed throughout Japanese industry, but especially for small firms where workers were not organized.[11] In contrast, large firms experienced considerable labor unrest, prompted in part by SCAP's support for unionization. Large firms tried to secure corporate harmony by paying higher wages, leading to wide differentials. High-speed growth subsequently reduced size-based differentials by reducing the size of the available labor force. As labor surplus gave way to labor shortage, small firms had to try to match the wages in larger companies.

The pattern of wage increases paid to employees in various sizes of factories confirms this interpretation. Labor pressure prompted huge increases in the larger firms, as Figure 4.7 shows. These gains are particularly noteworthy because from 1960 onward inflation in Japan was the lowest of any industrial notion. Even more impressive, wage levels in small firms in 1962–1972 outstripped gains in large companies and stayed close in 1972–1982. The 1962–1972 increases for the two categories of small firms averaged 268 percent and 250 per-

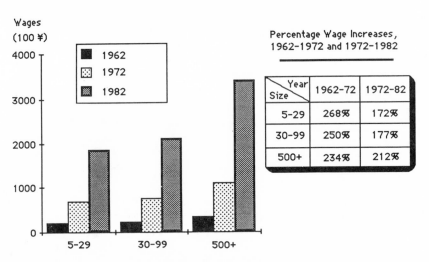

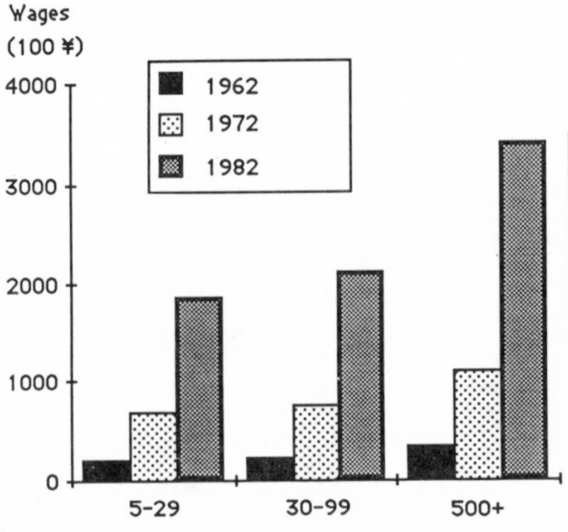

Percentage Wage Increases, 1962-1972 and 1972-1982

Size \ Year	1962-72	1972-82
5-29	268%	172%
30-99	250%	177%
500+	234%	212%

Figure 4.7. Wage Increases by Firm Size, 1962–1972 and 1972–1982
Source: Same as for Figure 4.6.

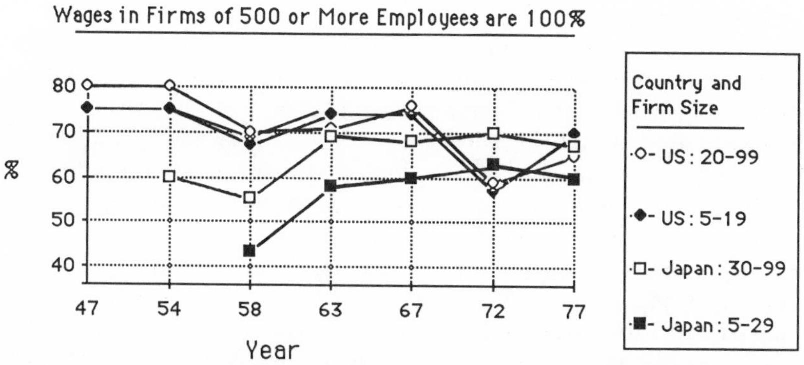

Figure 4.8. Wage Differentials in the United States and Japan, Selected Years, 1948–1977
SOURCES: For Japanese data, same as for Figure 4.6; for American data, Census of Manufactures for the years cited.

cent respectively. Then, between 1972 and 1982, the pace of increases in small firms fell off to around 170 percent, although it was still high. Meanwhile, labor payments in large firms were increasing over 200 percent for both decades. Small firms had to match the wage increases offered by large companies as the labor market tightened.

Figure 4.8 illustrates American and Japanese postwar wages in small, medium, and large firms. Japanese differentials improved during the high-growth period to the point where they were narrower than in the United States. American wages were essentially stable in the 1940s and 1950s: firms with both 5–19 and 20–99 employees paid 80 percent of the wages of large firms. Then, as wage differentials in the Japanese economy started to close, American differentials began to widen. By 1972 the wage gap in Japan was smaller than in the United States, where wages in small firms had eroded to less than 70 percent of what large firms paid. Thereafter Japanese and American differentials remained about the same.

That wage differentials in the Japanese economy were about the same as in the United States and declined throughout the postwar period cuts against the view that small and medium-sized Japanese firms paid particularly low wages relative to large companies. It contradicts the notion that cheaper labor in small firms was a structural feature unique to the Japanese dual economy. Furthermore, the historical development of the wage gap did not occur as the dual structure argument predicts. Labor unrest drove up wages in large firms, but these gains were gradually matched by small enterprises as labor markets tightened.

If it is true that there are distinctive career paths for workers in small and large firms, moreover, wage disparities would be further reduced in significance. In the dual structure argument, small-firm, blue-collar workers are forced to accept low wages as they spend their working lives in highly cyclical firms for which low-cost production is the basis of survival. But do employees in small firms accept low pay early in their careers because they aspire toward a subsequent independence as self-employed owner-operators or expect eventually to be appointed to managerial positions? If, in fact, the majority of employees of Japanese small firms leave their factories to open their own manufacturing enterprises, or are promoted to white-collar work in the course of their employment, their career paths would be more complex than previously assumed.

Workers entering the labor market face a choice between comparatively stable employment as a life-long, blue-collar worker in a large firm or a short stint in a small firm followed by the high possibility of self-employment or managerial promotion. The lifetime wage payments made to such workers are more or less equal. Only small-firm employees who fail to open a firm or be promoted suffer substantial wage losses as compared with blue-collar workers in large firms.

Attitudinal data showing that manufacturing recruits actually perceive their employment choices in this way do not yet exist. But statistically, as I will show, most Japanese small-firm, blue-collar workers will actually have the opportunity to operate their own enterprises or to be promoted. What can be demonstrated, therefore, is that the career path of small-firm, blue-collar laborers is structured *as if* the desire for future independence or promotion was the predominant goal. It can further be demonstrated that as employee careers develop in small firms, so Japanese wage differentials are reduced. This finding contradicts the dual structure argument. If the careers of small-factory workers are positively influenced by opportunities that moderate wage differentials, then the notion that small firms survive solely through exploitation is incorrect. Rather, small firms and large firms in Japan represent two distinct, equally remunerative choices.

First, I disaggregate wage differentials between small and large firms in Japan by the age of the employee. Figure 4.9 illustrates the pattern of age-related wage differentials for firms of 10–99 employees and firms of over a thousand workers. It shows that from about the mid-1960s young workers (17–29 years old) in small firms earned 90 percent to 100 percent of the wages paid in large firms. Furthermore, from about 1975 onward, competition for school leavers and employees in their twenties became so great that salaries in

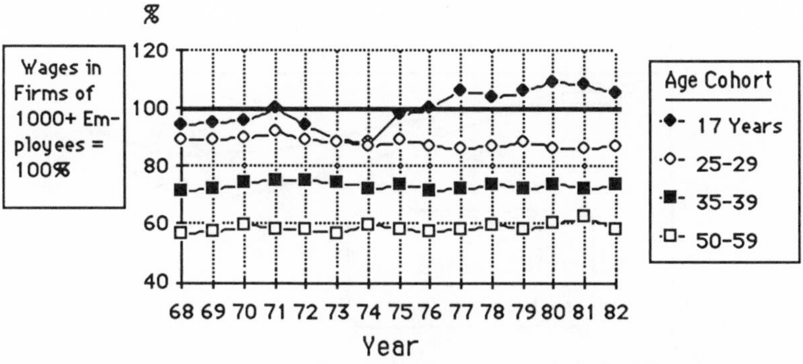

Figure 4.9. Wage Differentials by Age in Firms of 10–99 Employees, 1968–1982
SOURCE: Same as for Figure 4.6.

small firms actually exceeded those in large firms. By 1979 high school leavers were receiving 110 percent of the wages available in large firms. But the longer small-firm employees remained as production employees, the greater the gap became between their pay and that in large firms; workers between 35–39 years old were paid just 60 percent of what a similar age cohort received in large firms, and workers in the 50–59 age category were paid just 70 percent.

Wage differentials are less severe or nonexistant early in the career of a worker in a small firm. Among blue-collar workers on the shop floor, younger employees will be earning about the same as large-firm workers, but older workers will do poorly in the same comparison. As Figure 4.10 demonstrates for 1982, until the age of about twenty-nine small-scale factory workers receive 85 percent to 90 percent of the pay in large firms, but workers in their late forties earn less than 60 percent of what large factory employees make.

The longer blue-collar workers remain production workers in small firms, especially after their mid-thirties, the more they suffer in comparison with workers in large firms. These laborers may or may not view their position in these terms, but they act as if they do. In particular, there are two methods of overcoming age-based differentials available to Japanese blue-collar workers: opening their own manufacturing enterprise, and promotion. The more rewarding solution, as we shall see, is to start one's own firm. But even promotion can be lucrative; if employees advance even to the level of a foreman, the lowest white-collar job in Japan, they can earn wages equal to those of blue-collar workers in the largest firms.

Consider the potential income of a worker who opens a new, small-scale factory. A good indicator is the change in earnings over time for

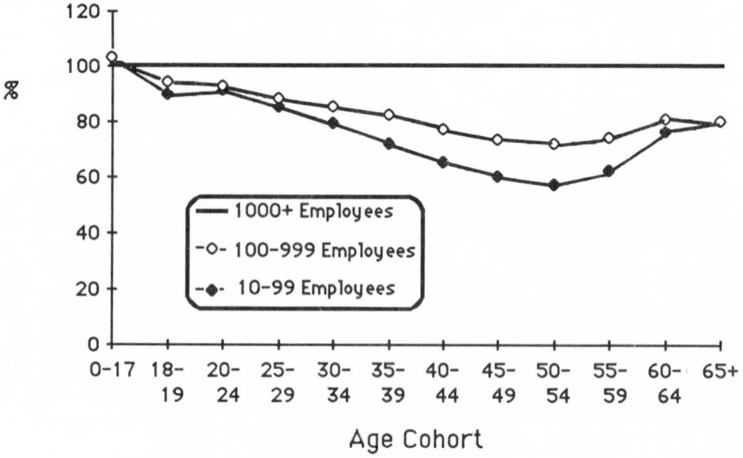

Figure 4.10. Age-Based Wage Differentials, 1982
Source: Same as for Figure 4.6.

very small manufacturing enterprises, those with one to three employees. The majority of such firms are family enterprises, and remuneration there is lower than in any other class of firm. The results, summarized in Figure 4.11, show a dramatic rise in earnings in small-scale firms across the 1960s and 1970s. The level of earnings exceeds the wages that might be earned as a large-firm, blue-collar worker; in 1975, for instance, operators of family firms earned 150 percent of pay in factories of five hundred or more workers, even though factory wages had risen precipitously.[12] Moreover, small-factory income rose over 600 percent from 1960 to 1975, slightly exceeding the pace of wage increases in large firms. For workers in small firms, independent operations, even on a petty scale, were highly profitable.

The profitability of small firms raises an additional point that contradicts the dual structure argument. If large firms were exploiting small ones, earnings in small-scale factories should have been much lower than those in the biggest enterprises. In fact, small firms in Japan were markedly more profitable than large ones, and the rate of profitability actually increased as the size of the enterprise fell. In 1970, for instance, after-tax rates of return were only 15–17 percent for large enterprises but 24 percent for firms capitalized at between ¥2 million and ¥5 million.[13] These "inverse" differentials, in which small firms are better off than large ones, have persisted since before the war.[14] Historically, employees of small business could look to the possibility of independence for a risky but often rewarding answer to the problem of age-based wage differentials. Such inverse differen-

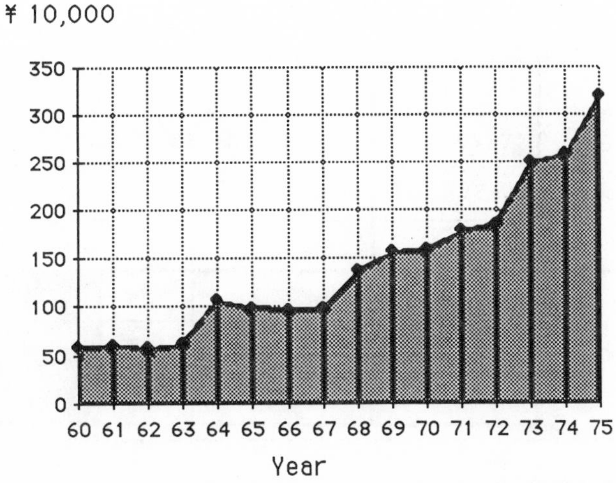

Figure 4.11. Actual Earnings in Manufacturing Firms of 1–3 Employees, 1960–1975
SOURCE: Kiyonari Tadao, *Chūshōkigyō dokuhon* (An introduction to small and medium enterprises), (Tokyo: Toyo Keizai, 1984), p. 88.

tials stand in marked contrast to what the dual structure argument suggests should have been the case.

To what extent do workers in small firms actually open their own firms in Japan? Kiyonari Tadao has demonstrated that close to 70 percent of all small and medium-sized manufacturing enterprises were run by former blue-collar employees of small firms.[15] Estimating the number of workers in a similar age cohort who might attempt to open a firm, and controlling for closures, he also argued that as many as 50 percent of Japanese small-firm, blue-collar workers would become independent during their careers.[16] Kiyonari's work was strongly criticized by other Japanese scholars, because he did not determine whether the separation rate was uniform for minute as well as medium-sized companies. Koike Kazus contended, for example, that the estimated rate was too high for medium-sized manufacturing firms and thus overstated the probability that small-firm workers would operate a factory.[17] To refine the statistics, Koike carefully controlled for firm size and other factors that might influence rates of independence. His results, though conceived as an explicit critique of Kiyonari, still show very high independence rates (see Figure 4.12). The movement toward self-employment in manufacturing is highest in firms of 1–9 employees, where the rate increased from about 30 percent in the early 1960s to 45–50 percent by the 1970s. Though the

<table>
<tr><th></th><th>Scale</th><th>Year: 1971</th><th>1968</th><th>1965</th><th>1962</th><th>1959</th></tr>
<tr><td rowspan="4">Non-agricultural Industries</td><td>1-9</td><td colspan="3">50%</td><td colspan="2">33%</td></tr>
<tr><td>10-29</td><td colspan="5">30-33%</td></tr>
<tr><td>30-99</td><td colspan="2">30%</td><td colspan="3">20%</td></tr>
<tr><td>100-299</td><td colspan="2">25%</td><td colspan="3">18%</td></tr>
<tr><td rowspan="3">Manufacturing</td><td>1-9</td><td colspan="2">45%</td><td>30%</td><td colspan="2" rowspan="3">Not Available</td></tr>
<tr><td>10-29</td><td>20%</td><td>33%</td><td>10%</td></tr>
<tr><td>30-99</td><td colspan="2">20%</td><td>6%</td></tr>
</table>

Figure 4.12. Percentage of Work Force Becoming Self-Employed in Manufacturing, Selected Years and Size Classes
Source: Koike Kazuo, *Chūshōkigyō no jukuren* (Training in small and medium enterprises) (Tokyo: Dōbunkan, 1981), p. 89.

rate of independence drops as the size of the firm in which workers begin employment increases, about 20–30 percent of workers in firms of 30–99 employees and 25 percent in the 100–299 size class apparently left their jobs to open their own factories.

A significant movement toward self-employment was most marked in the very smallest firms; the work force in firms with more than ten employees was more or less stable. But employees in firms with fewer than ten employees made up about 25 percent of total small and medium-sized firm employment in Japan.[18] Consequently, from the 1–9 employee class alone about 12.5 percent of the total small-firm manufacturing work force became self-employed each year, and the annual move toward independence by all employees in small and medium-sized firms approached 22–23 percent. Indeed, the startups for new manufacturing firms are so high in Japan that in any given year the number of new, small-scale, startup factories is equal to more than half the *total* number of manufacturing factories. New openings are infrequent in the United States—the distinguishing mark of the Japanese economy is that manufacturing startup opportunities are much higher. In fact, during the 1960–1980 period there was a net drop in the total number of small manufacturing firms in America.[19]

The career path of small-firm workers who open their own enterprises further reduces the impact of blue-collar age-based wage differentials. The peak age at which small-firm employees open their own enterprises is in the 24–30 age bracket, precisely when wage

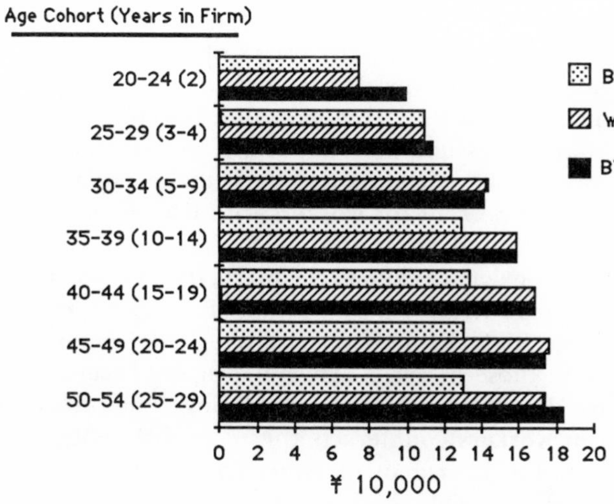

Figure 4.13. White- and Blue-Collar Wages by Age and Firm Size, 1974
SOURCE: Same as for Figure 4.12, p. 83.

differentials begin to appear in small factories. Workers who obtain training for five to ten years and then become self-employed can make much more money than is possible in large firms. Of course, higher income is contingent on success, and there is a high failure rate among these new enterprises, but a single employee may attempt to open his own firm several times.[20] As the large number of small firms in Japanese manufacturing suggests, self-employment is an important career option for blue-collar workers in small businesses.

Of course, it would be impossible for all small-firm, blue-collar workers to open their own plants. But workers who do not become independent operators are not doomed to work for poor wages; promotion to white-collar status is another solution. Wages for white-collar workers of all ages in small firms (10–99 employees) are virtually identical to blue-collar pay in large firms of a thousand or more employees (see Figure 4.13). Wages are about the same for all groups until workers reach their mid-thirties, when small-firm, blue-collar workers begin to experience a wage gap relative to blue-collar workers in large firms. This gap widens steadily as age increases. For white-collar workers in small enterprises, however, the career wage pattern is the same as that for production workers in large firms. If blue-collar employees are promoted to white-collar status in their thirties, their career earnings will be very similar to those of blue-collar workers in large firms.

What percentage of small-firm manufacturing workers are promoted to white-collar jobs? Koike argues that, as a conservative estimate, 33 percent of those with five years or more continuous experience in 1968 and 1969 were promoted to white-collar positions. He also contends that the promotion rate rose to 45 percent by 1974. Furthermore, if assumptions about the rate of firm leavers were relaxed slightly, Koike concludes that the actual promotion rate may have been over 60 percent for workers with five years or more experience in the 1960s and 1970s.[21]

If these figures are anywhere close to the mark, the probability that blue-collar staff in small firms will be promoted after five years of employment is quite high. Promoted employees then enjoy wage scales comparable to those in large firms, and again, because most promotions are for those in the thirty-year-old range, the career pattern for small-firm workers counteracts the wage differentials. Indeed, the potential for management experience may even make small-firm work more desirable than a career of blue-collar work in large firms.

The pattern of career shifts to white-collar promotion or self-employment further undercuts the dual structure argument. Well over 60 percent of Japanese blue-collar employees in the 1960s and 1970s either opened their own firms or were promoted to jobs that equalized pay differentials with blue-collar staff in large firms. The career structure of small-firm, blue-collar employees is therefore not consistent with the idea that such workers were unskilled providers of cheap labor. Rather, they appear to be highly skilled and thus capable of managing or operating their own industrial enterprise.

Evidence regarding the degree of small-firm dependence on large companies further rebuts the notion of dual structure. According to the argument, small firms provide cheaper parts to large contractors. High-skilled operations are the province of the larger firms, whereas low-skilled, low-wage work characterizes production by subcontractors. To enable small firms to meet even limited production goals, the contractors have to provide technical guidance and support personnel. Thus we should expect small firms to receive a considerable degree of aid from larger companies.[22]

In general, subcontracting in Japan is extensive; about 70 percent of all companies with more than thirty employees subcontract for a portion of their production needs. The percentage of firms that do subcontracting work varies with the nature of the industries involved. In some cases small firms do not primarily accept subcontract work at all; rather, as before the war, they transform raw goods into final goods. Examples are furniture, food, and clothing. In such sectors as general machinery, which includes machine tools, the proportion is

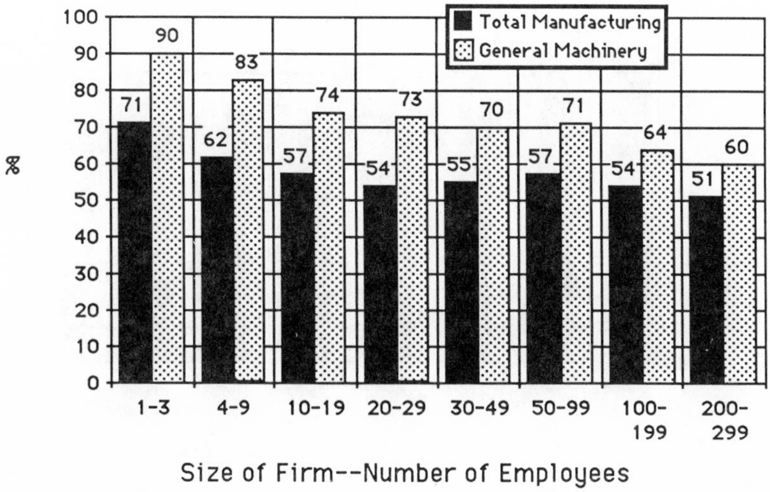

Figure 4.14. Subcontract Work as a Percentage of All Income in Manufacturing and General Machinery, by Firm Size, 1982
SOURCE: Small Business Survey (1983). See footnote 22.

very high, about 90 percent. Producing complex electronic machinery requires a greater number of highly specialized parts, and in such fields subcontract acceptance rates are high. As Figure 4.14 illustrates, the degree of subcontracting work as a percentage of total income in the machinery sector increases as the size of firm decreases, from a low of just 60 percent in the 200–299 class to a high of 90 percent in the 1–3 class. However, even in subcontracting sectors such as general machinery, as many as 30 percent of firms with as few as ten employees accept no subcontracting whatsoever. Subcontracting is not the universal experience of small firms. Those firms that do subcontracting work, however, tend to earn most of their income from it (see Figure 4.15). Again, the rate of subcontracting reliance is highest for small firms and falls as firm size increases.

These figures tend to obscure the fact that large numbers of Japanese small firms depend little on subcontract orders; firms that either do no subcontracting, or rely on subcontracting for less than 60 percent of their income amount to 44 percent of all firms and about 30 percent in general machinery.[23] Subcontracting work is clearly a major part of the activity of small and medium-sized enterprise, but clearly it is also much less important than conventional wisdom suggests. Yet the usual perception is that small firms are pressured by larger ones to cut costs and depend on them for technical and financial guidance. This picture is unlikely in the case of firms that accept

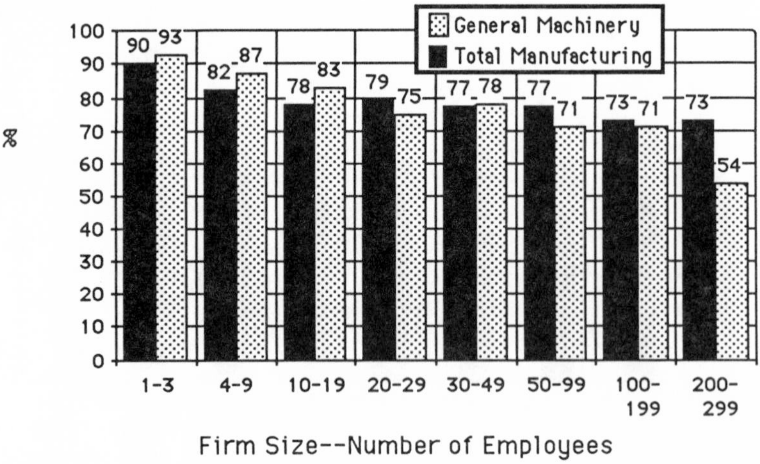

Figure 4.15. Subcontracting Firms Earning at Least 60 Percent of Their Income from Subcontracting, 1982
SOURCE: Small Business Survey (1983).

little or no subcontract work. Is it true that the small factories that rely on subcontracting depend on their large clients?

One measure of the pressure exerted by large firms is the number of contracting firms with which subcontractors do business. The smaller the number, the more the assumption is warranted that large firms exert powerful price or cost pressures. A firm that relied entirely on a single buyer would naturally be in a much weaker position than a company with many customers. As Figure 4.16 shows, even the smallest firms accept subcontract work from at least four firms; larger companies sell to as many as twelve buyers. Moreover, the number of clients per company in each size class is generally higher in the machinery sector than for manufacturing as a whole. High-subcontract sectors are typically such fields as machinery, electronics, and autos, and so in the case of complex products, demand for small-firm skills is spread out among more buyers.

This pattern cuts against the view that the contracting company dominates small subcontract firms, because firms avoid relying on a single contractor for most of their income. Of course, hidden in Figure 4.16 are cases in which subcontractors do work for only one firm; several studies indicate that about 20 percent of subcontractors fall into this category.[24] But many firms spread orders out among several clients, reducing pressure from large firms. Indeed, as I show in the next chapter, small firms not only try to increase the number of

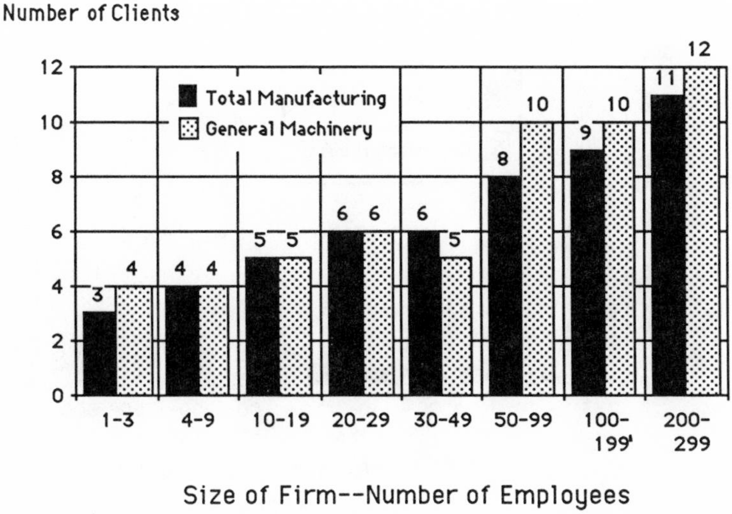

Figure 4.16. Number of Clients per Subcontractor among Smaller Manufacturers, 1982
SOURCE: Small Business Survey (1983).

buyers but also try to move into different fields to reduce dependence on any one firm or sector.

Price pressures, technical assistance, or financial support from large firms would be most effective if the firm that accepted parts orders also made the equipment. The number of firms to which small subcontractors resubmit orders is extremely high, however, as Figure 4.17 illustrates: even family firms with 1–3 employees subcontract to an average of three additional firms. The number rises to forty-seven for machinery firms in the 200–299 employee class. Of course, large firms with over a thousand employees subcontract extensively; in general machinery they place orders with an average of 291 firms.

The dual structure argument portrays large firms as passing on orders to a set of "captured" manufacturers who then are forced to produce goods to a specified price. Instead of working within vertically organized subcontracting networks, however, small firms subcontract on their own as much as they accept orders. There is a *horizontally* organized network of subcontracting work. This structure reduces the cost pressures assumed to exist in the vertical system. Even the smallest firms both order from and subcontract to a large number of other companies, which argues strongly against domination by certain large firms. Indeed, as the actual manufacture of a

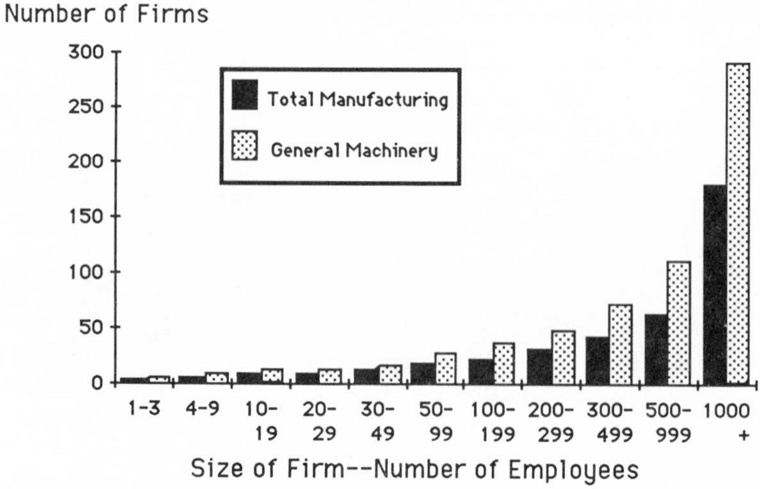

Figure 4.17. Number of Firms to Which Outside Orders Are Placed, by Size Class, 1982
SOURCE: Small Business Survey (1983).

part ordered from one firm might mean several stages of subcontracting, it is very unlikely, except in special cases, that the originating firm could effectively pressure the responsible companies to cut costs.

Finally, in the dual structure view, small firms are technically inferior to large ones, they depend on larger firms for assistance, and we should see a high degree of capital or personnel flow from large clients to their vendors. Japanese small business surveys actually indicate that the degree of small-firm reliance on capital or personnel assistance is quite low. Figure 4.18 exhibits the results of an influential survey conducted in 1982 by the People's Finance Corporation, an organization dedicated to making loans to small manufacturers. It shows that as firm size dropped, the percentage of vendors receiving capital or personnel assistance from their clients fell. Just 5 percent of smaller vendors (those with 1–20 employees) received capital assistance from their clients, and under 3 percent received personnel assistance. The percentages rose as firm size increased, but even at the 101–300 employee level over 65 percent of all subcontractors received no form of capital or personnel assistance from their clients. For the most part small firms apparently do *not* rely on large ones for management or capital assistance. Nor is this pattern restricted to the 1980s. In the 1960s, Kiyonari demonstrates, over 60 percent of all subcontractors had no links to their clients other than their contractual relationships.[25]

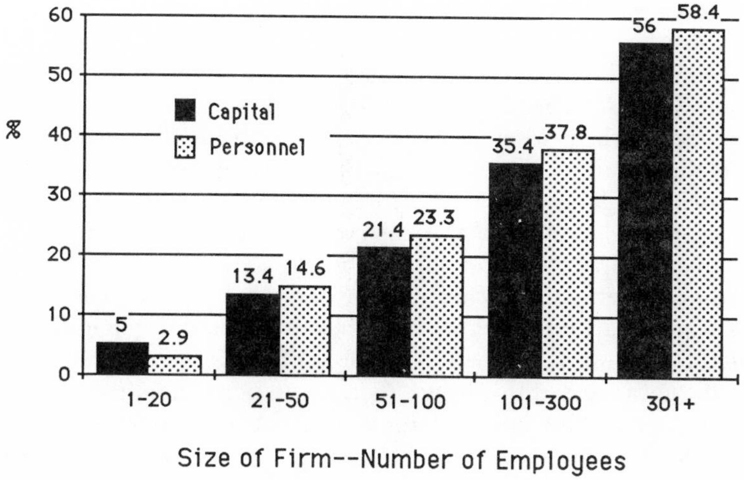

Figure 4.18. Percentage of Vendors Receiving Capital or Personnel Assistance from Clients, by Firm Size, 1982
SOURCE: Kokumin Kinyū Kōkō (People's Finance Corp.), *Shita uke torihiki kankai no jittai* (Subcontracting relationships) (Tokyo, 1983), p. 25.

The adjustment patterns, wage structure, and subcontracting relationships of small and medium-sized enterprises make clear the deficiencies of the dual structure argument. Adjustment during recessions, with the exception of 1957–1959, was not compatible with the idea that small companies acted as shock absorbers for the large ones in manufacturing. The wage structure shows that differentials by firm size shrank during the high-growth period and were about the same in Japan as elsewhere. Different career opportunities emerged for blue-collar workers in different sizes of firms: an employee could choose between stable employment as a lifetime production worker in a large firm or seek independence or a managerial position in a small firm. Finally, subcontracting relationships suggest that small firms were not dominated by the large ones.

How can one account for these findings? The relationship between Japanese large and small firms has shifted, I shall show, from the Depression to the present. Interfirm politics regarding the organization of production between contractors and small firms led industrialists to adopt flexible production techniques. This change required that smaller subcontractors become more independent, and large firms promoted manufacturing autonomy internally by spinning off separate production divisions. The shaping of relations between large and small firms was one of the political events that transformed industrial opportunities in Japan.

The Relationship between Large and Small Firms

Until the mid-1930s large and small firms had little direct contact in Japan. Small-scale manufacturers made finished goods for domestic or export markets, whereas large companies engaged in extraction or the manufacture of commodity goods. By the end of the war, however, small and large firms were forced to rely on each other in subcontracting relationships, particularly in the machinery industries, as we saw in chapter 2. After Japan's defeat a chronic capital shortage and an overt attempt, orchestrated by large producers, to enter mass production markets with low-cost goods threatened to generate a dual structure economy in Japan. A number of convergent developments halted then reversed this trend. One was experimentation with manufacturing assembly lines in large firms, which made internal operations, albeit somewhat ironically, more flexible. At the same time the coordination of subcontractors became too costly, and large firms began to *encourage* small firms to acquire capital and technical support independently. Though initially these strategies were undertaken to reduce management overhead, they had the effect of pushing smaller firms to become independent purveyors of high-tech, rapidly changing product lines. This development was part of a general movement of the economy away from a commitment to mass production; it was political in the sense that market and material conditions could have caused the adoption of either flexible production strategies or the dual structure.

Up to the mid-1930s, prewar relations between large and small manufacturing firms were very different from what the dual structure argument suggests. The argument assumes that large firms and small firms both produced the same goods; small companies manufactured inferior versions of the products of large firms, to supplement the internal operations of large companies. As the economy retrenched, so large firms would meet the remaining demand internally, and small firms would contract as outside orders were reduced. In fact, this cyclical adjustment pattern *has* obtained in Japan where products have been standardized and in extraction industries. In the coal industry, for instance, small miners met demand in boom times and then were forced out of business during recessions.[26]

The situation in prewar manufacturing was different. There, as Nakamura Takafusa has argued persuasively, large firms, especially *zaibatsu* interests, produced commodities such as raw steel stock or thread, which small firms made into specialty items.[27] Smaller companies and larger firms were thus complementary. The bigger manufacturers produced raw or semifinished materials that they sold to small firms for assembly into final products. The market for the larger firms' products was the small-scale manufacturing sector, which more or less independently transformed raw goods for end users in export or domestic markets.

The classic example of this system was silk. Silk thread spinning was concentrated in large firms, which tried to mass produce raw materials. The thread stock was then sold to wholesalers, the *toiya*, who contracted with and frequently gave financial support to a retinue of small final-goods assemblers, who made specialty Western and traditional clothes. In some cases the *toiya* financed larger thread makers as well. In this system, small and large firms complemented each other; the large firm needed the diversified expertise of the final goods assemblers to increase overall demand for its raw stock, whereas the small producer sought cheap, basic materials. If in fact small firms failed, product demand would also be reduced for larger companies, because the smaller assemblers were the main consumers of large factory output. In much the same way, in such industries as ceramics, metalworking, and weaving, small-scale factories grew into increasingly sophisticated producers for domestic and international markets. Large firms concentrated on supplying raw or semifinished goods.[28]

These relationships were thrown into disarray by the military buildup in the late 1930s. Large firms that the bureaucracy had hoped would increase economies of scale were encouraged throughout the engineering industries, as described in chapter 2, but real production gains were not achieved. Small firms actually grew in importance, because large firms had to compensate for their lack of capacity through subcontracting. Export markets closed and domestic demand collapsed; consequently, small producers entered the *tōseikai*, and by the war's end their relations with large firms had shifted. Instead of transforming the commodity products of large firms into final goods, they were now producing parts for final assembly by favored larger firms that were unable to keep pace with demand. Gradually many small firms came to supplement the production operations of large manufacturers, just as the dual structure argument supposes. Though small firms were not eliminated, as prewar policies had originally intended, the price of their survival was acceptance of a subservient role in the manufacturing economy.

Conditions immediately after the war might well have led to the institutionalization of the dual structure. In the late 1940s and early 1950s small firms faced perhaps their stiffest challenges. There was a chronic capital shortage, and banks and other lenders preferred to concentrate on what they perceived to be safer, larger enterprises; small producers had to rely on their contractors for support, and bank loans were also conditioned on cosignature by their larger clients.[29] Small firms were compelled to become dependent on large producers to obtain business and financing.

Moreover, Japanese manufacturing leaders and MCI/MITI officials were seeking to build an integrated production network that could compete on price grounds against America and Europe. They wanted to copy the American system and then surpass the United States in manufacturing efficiency. Government and private resources were concentrated on large firms, and in keeping with this strategy, large firms pressured small ones to cut costs, in order to reduce the prices of Japanese products in overseas markets. This pressure, led in turn to the wage disparities (noted above) of the 1950s. Finally, a massive labor surplus after the war made it possible for small firms to pass on price pressures from larger clients to laborers in the form of reduced wages.[30] Workers who could not find employment in large firms, where labor strife kept wages comparatively high, had to accept poorly paid employment in small firms. There was little countervailing labor pressure to sustain small-firm wages.

The wage gap and the adjustment patterns we saw for the 1957–1959 recession indicate that a dual structure had indeed developed in Japan by the mid-1950s. But several events stopped the dual economy from becoming permanent. Among the most important were the internal production strategies of large firms, the resultant transformation of smaller firms' practices, Japanese failures in the international marketplace, and the provision of finance to smaller firms to reduce large-firm influence. I concentrate here on how large firms undermined their own search for more efficient mass production techniques, which led to their adoption of flexible strategies, and how market reversals increased the need for flexibility, thus changing the relationship between large and small manufacturers.

Japanese large industrialists deliberately copied and then enhanced an American-style mass production system in the auto and other machinery sectors. The strategy involved constant experimentation. To facilitate constant changes in the workplace to promote efficiency, larger producers ultimately had to organize production in consonance more with flexible than with mass manufacturing principles.[31] And as in the United States, the experiences of leading manufacturers spread to other sectors as well. Thus early efforts to improve rapidly on U.S. mass production actually led to the growth of flexible production in the early postwar economy.

One example was Nissan, the second-largest auto producer in Japan. Nissan initially attempted to mimic the factory practices of General Motors as closely as possible.[32] The firm wanted to create a network of suppliers that would produce auto parts at low cost while it improved on the U.S. model. In practice this aim involved the continual revision of assembly lines and constant meetings with subcontractors to coordinate changing production requirements. To discover the "perfect" manufacturing system, Nissan had to modify its operations continually and then compel subcontracting firms to adjust as well.

Continual experimentation undermined both the search for stable mass production inside Nissan and its control over its suppliers. Rapid change of the workplace is, as I argued in chapter 1, antithetical to what mass producers seek; they want to stabilize the assembly line and then reduce the skill necessary for each task along the production system. Rapid transformations of the factory, even if *intended* to lead to a more efficient mass production system, make it impossible to rationalize the workplace for stable economies of scale. Instead, high-skill workers employing general-purpose machines—the hallmark of the flexible firm—have to be used to permit the very experimentation necessary to enhance efficiency or, as Nissan conceived it, to improve on American mass production techniques. In rapidly instituting and then perfecting imported manufacturing practices, large Japanese firms like Nissan were forced to make continual modifications and changes in their assembly line setups. The result was a more flexible orientation toward manufacturing.

At the same time close control over subcontractors became more expensive. Though initially Nissan was able directly to supervise the responses of its suppliers to recurrent mass production modifications, it soon realized that continuous, intimate regulation was too costly. Subcontractors had to become more independent and develop their own expertise in meeting shifting production demands. By the late 1950s Nissan was encouraging its suppliers to become more autonomous. It drafted a new code of conduct for subcontractor relations, requiring that the presidents of supplier firms be treated as independent businessmen and referring to supplier firms not as *shitauke* (subcontractor) but *gaichū* (outside order) firms. Smaller subcontractors were encouraged to become independent specialists to meet the ever-changing needs of the larger firms.[33]

Market developments enhanced these trends. The Japanese had initially sought to make their mark in international markets and at home with cheap, standard goods. Japan's early export attempts in the 1950s were for the most part failures or involved low value added items earning small or no profits. "Made in Japan" was an epithet, not an accolade. Early efforts to penetrate the American car market were completely routed; by the mid-1960s Japanese auto exports to the United States and Europe were zero.[34] Such experiences were forcing firms in the engineering and machinery sectors to rethink competition based on standard goods and to consider the need to differentiate their products from those of foreign competitors. Thus market reversals stimulated new thinking about production, undermining the attempt to put together a stable, mass production economy.

Finally, domestic competition within Japan was severe; Japanese competitors frequently bid down the price of goods to below cost, accepting losses to create potential market advances. This type of competition gave Japanese firms incentives to try continually to differentiate their products. Differentiation temporarily insulated them from direct price challenges and created replacement demand as with each year companies promoted a slightly enhanced good.

In sum, large-firm export strategies, domestic marketing, and experiments with mass production all induced a movement toward flexible production. These pressures led to changes in the way large firms organized manufacturing and to greater freedom for small companies to control their own production. As large firms created internal mechanisms to promote flexibility, they began to fragment. Rodney Clark has shown that for the most part, large Japanese manufacturers did not vertically integrate their operations like their counterparts in the United States. Rather, they specialized in a particular technique or component in any given sector and purchased the rest of the parts they needed outside the company. Furthermore, he argued, frequently the operating divisions of large firms are set up as autonomous units with the expectation that over time they will become increasingly independent, until the parent firm may hold only a small share of the new company's stock. As the result of this production strategy, large firms gradually began to take shape as collections of smaller, autonomous, specialized units.[35]

The subcontracting small producers implemented similar strategies. They started to rotate workers on the assembly lines and to give them a large degree of autonomy, in order to make it possible for the firm to make new products or to meet changing demands for existing goods. Subcontractors had to encourage high skill and worker autonomy to meet the changes that contractors sought as they began to modify their own production systems. For example, Koike describes the predicament of a small bearing manufacturer that made only three kinds of products. Even this firm had to train workers extensively because demand was unpredictable; it might need to make one kind of bearing on one day and the other two the next, or all three on the same day. This uncertainty in production scheduling forced the firm to use high-skill workers on general machines so as to meet demand for its products as rapidly as possible.[36] To respond to changing needs—even if limited to small sets of related goods—subcontractors had to employ workers and train them according to flexible principles.

As large firms decentralized and specialized, and as small firms began building their own production niches and using the same labor techniques employed in the big factories, the flexible component of the Japanese economy was strengthened. This development, coupled with trends in the politics of small-firm finance discussed below, made the subcontractors increasingly independent from large firms, and even large firms had to fragment internally and concentrate on select processes or products in any given market.

Indeed, by the late 1960s small manufacturers were becoming noted as specialist producers of unique products by virtue of skills or machines that they alone possessed. The large assembly firms—Nissan or Toyota in autos, for instance, Toshiba or Matsushita in electronics, Mitsubishi in machinery—increasingly relied on small specialist producers because they could not achieve vertical integration or mass production without sacrificing flexibility. During the 1960s one of the most pressing problems for large manufacturers was to decide which segments of the market to give up and which to retain. Large firms feared that as they relied more and more on specialist subcontractors, so they would themselves become vulnerable to price pressures.

Responses varied from company to company. Some firms attempted to retain the ability to make any component used by the company. In that way, at least in theory, they could once again shift to internal production should subcontractors prove too expensive.[37] Others chose to specialize in product design and development, functioning essentially as a research organization and subcontracting the production of mass or specialized components to Japanese and overseas producers.[38] Still another strategy was to mass produce the basic, structural items of a product and then to attach an assortment of subcontracted parts.[39] The growing complexity of the electronic and mechanical components of Japanese products made a reliance on subcontractors unavoidable. Whereas the subcontracted work on a standard lathe was about 30 percent of the value of the item, for instance, the ratio rose to 75 percent for an NC lathe; manufacturers could not internalize the production of air pressure motors, electrical controllers, and computer readers.[40] The increasing complexity of automobiles and electrical goods similarly forced firms to subcontract to an ever greater degree.

Small firms thus escaped subjugation in the 1950s and flourished

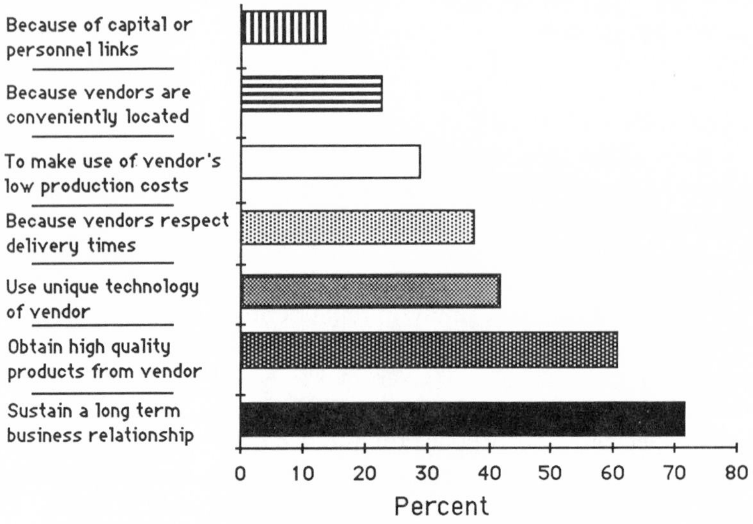

Figure 4.19. Reasons for Subcontracting in Manufacturing, 1982
SOURCE: Same as for Figure 4.18, p. 31.

with the adoption of flexible production principles. Several surveys show that large firms placed outside orders for reasons that had less to do with costs than with the superior technology and quality offered by small producers. For the most part contractors indicated that specialized technical skills or specialized equipment were much more important to their decision to subcontract than were low wage rates or cheap parts.

One 1982 survey of all manufacturing industries asked contracting firms why they subcontracted; multiple answers were permitted (see Figure 4.19). Responses such as "low cost" (29.8 percent) and "good delivery times" (38.7 percent) cluster at the top of the graph, where percentages are lower. The "unique technology" (42 percent) and "high-quality products" (61.3 percent) of the vendors were much more frequently given as reasons for subcontracting. The largest category, "to sustain a long-term relationship" (72.7 percent), is ambiguous, because it is impossible to tell why parent firms started subcontracting in the first place; was it for reasons of cost or technology? Nevertheless, the survey indicates that skill and technique were much more important than price in the decision to subcontract.

Even in the 1960s, as the dual structure was receding, surveys showed that technology (60 percent) and equipment and labor skill (72 percent) were much more important reasons for subcontracting

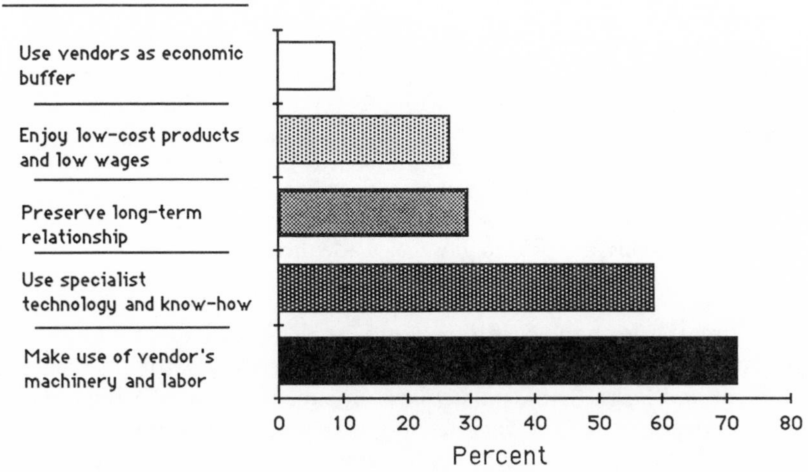

Figure 4.20. Reasons for Subcontracting in General Machinery, 1968
SOURCE: Kiyonari (1970), p. 177. See footnote 15.

than low wages (30 percent) and using subcontractors as an economic buffer (8 percent). In 1968, as in 1982, subcontractors were for the most part high-skill producers possessing unique, specialized technical abilities that large firms needed to make quality products (see Figure 4.20).

The emergence of flexible, specialized small firms in Japan helps explain the adjustment and career data presented above. There was, as Kiyonari has suggested, a marked movement away from the dual structure–like arrangements that had developed briefly after the war. Conditions of rapid expansion increased the opportunities to open or operate independent factories; workers attracted by higher incomes as enterprise operators made use of their small-firm training and developed specialist production techniques as the basis for their competitive edge. Older, low-wage small firms gave way to high-tech enterprises that transformed the entire manufacturing sector:

> As enterprise-operator income increased faster than wage growth, and as opportunities for forming new enterprises expanded, the number of new firms increased. People opening new firms were primarily in the 20–30-year-old range, and there were fewer cases in which chronically unemployed individuals were forced by poverty to become independent operators. Full employment and mild inflation preserved good conditions both for becoming self-employed and for high earnings. Consequently, individuals who had accumulated a variety of management resources and basic skills became independent. In contrast, for the unskilled, chronically

> unemployed, the period was not auspicious for learning how to manage or master manufacturing techniques. Consequently, at its root, the expansion of self-employment after 1965 did not represent a recurrence or strengthening of the dual structure but rather its elimination. The number of small and medium-sized enterprises that relied on cheap labor, or sought to counteract their low productivity by increasing work hours, fell. Instead, the dual structure continued to recede as large numbers of small businesses that achieved high productivity through sophisticated, specialized skills and paid high wages made their appearance.[41]

By the 1960s changes in large and small firms had converged to generate a new flexibility in the economy and reshape the interaction of small and large firms, particularly in subcontracting. Adjustments described above reflect various stages in the development of relationships among large and small firms. In the prewar period the difference between markets for large and small firms led to a sharp disjunction in adjustment. In the 1957–1959 period the brief emergence of a dual structure–like relationship brought increased adjustment burdens for small firms. Then, as strategic and market factors helped push large and small firms alike to seek increased flexibility, a new form of interdependence was created. Many small subcontractors became specialized, highly proficient, flexible manufacturers. Their products were then assembled by large companies, many of which had themselves diversified internally. Other large firms mass produced a limited range of standard components that were eventually assembled along with subcontracted parts. As specialist vendors, small firms increased their profitability. In turn, small-firm wages rose as price pressures became less pervasive; moreover, as the economy expanded and the labor pool shrank, small firms could no longer cut wages as easily as they had in the 1950s. Workers sought to reap the rewards of independent operation and entered manufacturing markets with new, specialist firms.

However, we cannot account for the emergence of flexible small firms as simply the consequence of market transformations or as the by-product of experiments with mass production conducted by large firms. In other countries, too, market uncertainty forced subcontractors to adjust, and large firms have elsewhere faced an inability to stabilize production. Yet flexible production was promoted in Japan to an extent not always duplicated elsewhere. Other factors must have been present to allow latent opportunities to be realized.

How were small firms able to survive in Japan after their large patrons reduced support and sought flexibility in the late 1950s? How could firms seeking technically sophisticated production niches afford the necessary investment in new machinery? How did the tight labor markets of the 1950s give way to a flourishing small-firm economy by the mid-1960s, an economy where blue-collar workers were able to open new factories whose number almost doubled between 1960 and 1980? To explain these developments, we need to understand how political struggles led to the creation of financial support mechanisms for small and medium-sized manufacturers. These mechanisms also promoted the realization of flexible production strategies in Japan.

Financial Support for Small and Medium Manufacturers

To this point I have explained the structure and function of Japanese small manufacturers by reference to the politics between producers themselves. The development of divergent career paths for production workers and the transformation of subcontractor relations enhanced flexible manufacturing in Japan. Each of these outcomes was political in the sense that neither material nor market imperatives made them inevitable; the results could have been, and nearly were, quite different. Workers came to interpret industrial options and producers to adopt strategies to promote economic recovery in ways ultimately rooted in ideologies and power struggles that affected industrial actors. Because the resultant opportunities for flexible manufacturing cannot be explained as a function of the market—indeed, they changed the market capacities of Japanese firms—they expose the limits of the market regulation thesis.

To account more fully for the diffusion of flexible manufacturing in Japan, however, it is necessary to understand how special financial institutions were established for the support of small-scale producers. The creation of specialized banks, credit associations, and government lending agencies underlines the point that market factors alone cannot explain Japanese industrial practices; rather, these institutions arose from political pressures. Financial support for small business is more overtly political than relations between enterprises; the state restructured capital markets to promote certain groups of manufacturers. This claim may appear to be a resort to the bureaucratic regulation thesis, but for two reasons it is distinct.

First, the provision of finance to small firms was the result of bureaucratic *failure*. Policies for the provision of capital to small firms began in the 1920s when the MCI tried to merge small producers by offering subsidies to promote cartels called "industrial unions" (*kōgyō kumiai*). The bureaucracy was unable to secure the market changes it sought. Gradually its subsidy programs were institutionalized into banks or trusts for the benefit of small producers. After the war pressure for financial relief for small firms led to a massive strengthening of these institutions. By the 1970s financial organs that were the direct descendants of the prewar *kōgyō kumiai* program accounted for close to 80 percent of all investment capital in small firms. Loan capital from such sources made small firms more independent and able to afford the equipment they needed for specialist operations.

It cannot be claimed that bureaucratic guidance led to the adoption of flexible manufacturing in Japanese small firms. If the MCI, and later MITI, had realized their objectives, small producers would have been consolidated and flexible production attenuated in postwar Japan. In practice, bureaucratic policies were blocked and then transformed into programs that achieved different purposes.

Second, it is highly unlikely that institutions for small-firm finance were by themselves responsible for the emergence of flexible, independent manufacturers in Japan. Strong interfirm pressures for more flexible operations and the growth of a huge capital surplus in the late 1960s make it possible that small firms would have found necessary capital even without special sources of finance. Moreover, other countries have implemented small business loan policies without generating comparable industrial outcomes, so supplementary factors must have induced the transformation that occurred in Japan. Though small-scale companies *did* rely on new sources of capital for most of their investment needs, additional political events promoted the adoption of flexible production. Consequently, the restructuring of Japanese capital markets for the benefit of small producers must be viewed as only a part of the context that generated high rates of industrial growth.

Small manufacturer policies first emerged in Japan in 1925; indeed, the very first efforts by the MCI to regulate the structure of Japanese industry—the birth of "industrial policy" in Japan—were a response to the widespread existence of small-scale producers.[42] The initial legislation was aimed at consolidating manufacturers, providing financial support for that purpose. Prewar small firms, as we have seen, concentrated on the conversion of basic commodities into finished goods for domestic and overseas consumption. They had little or no access to bank capital for investment, because the *zaibatsu* shunned manufacturing in general and small firms in particular. To obtain financing, small producers had to resort to a variety of measures. Some formed or joined special financial organizations called *mujin* companies, which were like building societies. Members paid a specified fee into a central pool, and loans were determined by lot or by a predetermined schedule.[43] Others depended on purchase agreements with merchant suppliers of raw goods.[44] This paucity of capital resources preoccupied government and manufacturers alike. The MCI attempted to provide relief from financial scarcity with the passage of two acts in 1925, the Export Union Law (Yūshutsu Kumiai Hō) and the Major Export Industries Union Law (Jūyō Yūshutsu Kumiai Hō). The former created central trade organizations (Yū shutsu Kumiai) for small and medium-sized producers, accepting goods on consignment and inspecting them to assure quality. A central trade acceptance organization, it was hoped, would provide short-term capital support through the consignment sale of products from small firms. The Major Export Industries Law provided for cartels (*kōgyō kumiai*) in designated product lines. Designated cartels would receive subsidies and access to loans from the Postal Deposit Bureau of the Ministry of Finance, and the government was authorized to enforce cartel terms against nonmember firms. The intent of the legislation was to consolidate industries, by financial inducements and, where these failed, by direct state action.

At first, the creation of small business unions moved forward, and by 1933, 111 separate *kōgyō kumiai* were reported. But these unions fell short of the goals of the legislation. The basic problem was that the unions did little or nothing to restrain the activities of their members. Rather, they existed mainly to extract subsidies from the state. Furthermore, the bureaucracy was explicitly prohibited from enforcing the union scheme. Industrial opposition made it impossible for the MCI to invoke the compulsory terms of the legislation; indeed, the passage of the export and union laws was conditioned on union membership being made nonvoluntary.[45] Not once between 1925 and 1933 was the compliance power invoked. Just as large companies affected by the Important Industries Law accepted subsidies without complying with bureaucratic objectives, so the *kōgyō kumiai* of the small firms were little more than cynical attempts to satisfy the surface requirements of state policy to receive support.

The *kōgyō kumiai* underwent considerable modification during the 1930s. In 1931 the export laws were amended, giving the MCI an explicit mandate to centralize the economy for war. The unions were expanded to cover all industries, not just export sectors. Real structural changes did not result, however, until the mid-1930s and when materials were rationed. The *kōgyō kumiai* were used to control the distribution of scarce materials much as the ticket system was employed in the Materials Allocation Council of the machinery industry and the *tōseikai*. Membership soared; there were 662 *kōgyō kumiai* by 1935, 896 in 1937, and 1,301 by 1938, affecting almost 54,000 firms.

Formal membership in the unions masked the fact that manufacturing was not being consolidated as intended. The unions were receiving funds, but the affected firms were not merging. Nor was the bureaucracy able to reform the program. Subsidies persisted because of the political sensitivity of small business support. The *kōgyō kumiai* degenerated, as Elizabeth Schumpeter and G. C. Allen argued, into an attempt by the right wing to enlist small firms in the struggle against the *zaibatsu:*

> We can conclude, then, that the *kōgyō kumiai* have been molded by various influences, and that their organization and functions carry traces of various policies by no means mutually consistent. In the beginning, they were designed to raise the quality of export goods and to improve the organization of small scale producers for export. In 1931 they became part of the government's scheme for rationalizing industry; and after 1933, while they were charged with certain duties of control [materials allocation] . . . their development was also affected by considerations of social policy. For they came to be used as a piece of administrative machinery by which the policy of supporting small producers against the larger commercial and financial interests might be carried out.[46]

The MCI was caught between the political objective of sustaining anti-*zaibatsu* policies and the consolidation of production to increase efficiency. Furthermore, the *kōgyō kumiai* were only part of the tendency in prewar government policy to favor small business. Throughout the 1930s rural areas received subsidies as part of a cooperative agricultural movement (*sangyō kumiai*) supporting farming and related industries such as warehousing, farming equipment, construction, and fertilizers. At the same time the MCI was compelled to protect small retailers from department stores and other large business concerns. Small retail firms were encouraged to form unions (*shōgyō kumiai*) to economize on certain functions in competition with large stores. Department stores were prohibited from promotional efforts aimed at luring business from traditional retailers.

The bureaucracy's solicitude was caused by the military's strong interest in small firms. Indeed, small-scale operators became one of the military's greatest supporters and to the present day are the backbone of Japanese conservative political support. The link between the military and small companies was initially forged in the Depression. Japan's first response to the dislocations of the late 1920s was a radical deflationary policy, lifting a gold embargo in effect earlier in the deade. The government's major concern was with Japan's balance of payments; Finance Minister Inoue Junosuke wanted to pay for the country's imports by exporting gold, which would also increase the value of Japanese currency while decreasing the money supply. The export of gold would thus reduce inflation and, by restricting capital available for marginal producers, consolidate production. After bitter debate in 1927–1929, Inoue, newly appointed as finance minister in the Wakatsuki cabinet, lifted the gold embargo.[47]

Both the military and small firms opposed this action. They saw deflation as a strongly pro-*zaibatsu* initiative because it would strengthen the country's financial institutions (which were dominated by the *zaibatsu*) but hurt domestic producers. (Indeed, Inoue was publicly reviled as a supporter of Mitsui; he was assassinated with Dan Takuma, Mitusi's general manager, in 1932 by enraged conservatives.)[48]

The militarists wanted to increase the budget to build up armaments, and the tight money policy made this impossible. They had other ideological incentives for supporting small firms as well. Many military economists expressed an almost romantic attachment to small producers, seeing small firms, in contrast to the *zaibatsu*, as producers compatible with rigid, traditional class distinctions. In the mid-1930s they tried to gain acceptance for a vision in which surplus or seasonal agricultural labor—workers untainted by urban manners or morals—would be employed in decentralized workshops to make small parts for shipment to central locations for assembly. Traditional hierarchies would be preserved in these workshop arrangements, and traditional life could continue amid industrialization.[49]

The anti-*zaibatsu* instinct of the military, coupled with small-firm support, generated a political reaction to deflationary policies. Tight money was an extremely unpopular measure in the Depression; popular anti-*zaibatsu* sentiment also ran high. Military opposition and popular protest led to the fall of the Wakatsuki cabinet and Inoue in 1931. The new cabinet, with Takahashi Korekiyo installed as finance minister, promptly abolished the gold standard; government outlays soared. In effect, Japan put into place the first Keynesian relief system among the major economies.[50] Outlays were provided to the military, small firms, and for local and village relief.

In this climate there was considerable support for the creation of financial institutions dedicated to the special use of small firms. In 1936 a central bank for commercial and industrial cooperatives (Shōkō kumiai Chuō Ginkō) was established to fund the union program directly. Its main role was to specialize in unsecured loans to the small industrial unions, consolidating the haphazard funding provided by the Postal Deposits Bureau and other subsidy sources. Half of its capital was supplied by the government and the rest by the unions themselves.[51] In 1938 two related institutions were established, the

People's Bank (Shomin Kinkō) and the Pension Bank (Onkyō Kinkō). The People's Bank was a 100 percent government-financed institution that made unsecured loans to small enterprises and began to support the independent *mujin* companies by accepting their deposits and providing them with loans. The Pension Bank was partially funded by the government and could make loans to holders of pensions (which secured the loans). As many pensioners were small-business operators, the Pension Bank was conceived of as an institution for small enterprises.

The operation of the new banks was affected by strict currency and materials shortages in Japan after the opening of the war with China in 1936. As companies were forced out of nonmilitary production fields, such as textiles, they sought loans for converting to war-related production and entered *kōgyō kumiai* to do so. As a result, the new banks financed munitions production as World War II drew near. When materials shortages became acute in 1941, an umbrella National Rehabilitation Bank (Kokumin Kōsei Kinkō) was set up to coordinate the financing of the liquidation or conversion to munitions of small firms.[52]

These prewar financial policies provided an institutional basis for postwar capital reconstruction schemes. The conservative leaders who dominated Japan in the 1950s remained committed to small business financing and rural support; indeed, in the early 1950s they enhanced the link between rural producers and right-wing political power. In the wake of SCAP election and trade unionization reforms, urban districts began to elect socialists or communists regularly to national and local office. In response, conservatives actively sought the support of their prewar constituency. Small businesses became the core of the Liberal Democratic Party's postwar coalition, increasing their ability to obtain government support.

The leverage of small manufacturers was enhanced by the creation of national coalitions of small enterprises, such as the Small and Medium Business Federation (Chūseiren), headed by powerful industrialists possessing "old school" links to the LDP leadership. During the 1950s the Chūseiren was headed by Ayukawa, who, as we have seen, was deeply involved with the prewar anti-*zaibatsu* militarist faction. The Chūseiren hired influential conservative spokesmen to plead their case with the government. At the same time obstacles to small business support were waning. The *zaibatsu* were weakened by SCAP policy, and by the late 1950s the tight money conditions that had followed the war also eased. Popular sentiment for the support of small firms was high; the abuse by large firms of their subcontractors was one of the most significant political issues of the 1950s.[53]

The result was an avalanche of legislation, and MITI created a special Small and Medium Enterprise Bureau (Chūshō Kigyō Chō) in 1957 to administer the programs. Other laws attempted to correct such business practices as withholding payments to subcontractors. In 1963, as the capital liberalization panic warmed up, a package of "rationalization" measures, designed to push small firms to consolidate and improve their equipment, was passed as the Basic Small Industry Law.[54] But the focus of postwar legislation was a complete overhaul of the financial system for small business funding. Successive legislative efforts created a vast array of private and government institutions committed to making loans for small-scale enterprises. In effect, the Japanese created an industrial equivalent of the American savings and loan system for the U.S. housing market. In Japan, however, the thrift institutions funded not home ownership but independent factories. This redirection of capital markets toward small firms nurtured the independent expansion of small companies during the high-growth period.

How did these initiatives affect the survival of small businesses? Consider the structure and lending orientation of Japanese financial institutions. Public and private lenders may be ranked by their degree of alignment toward small business. Figure 4.21 displays what percentage of the total loans made by various institutions went to small and medium-sized enterprises in 1966.[55]

Most of the private banks were established in the late nineteenth or early twentieth century. The *zaibatsu*-affiliated City Banks (Tōshi Ginkō) were predominant in urban centers such as Tokyo, whereas Regional Banks (Chihō Ginkō) were established in secondary cities, often with local support. Historically, the City Banks were the loan source of choice for big business, especially in the prewar years when many of the largest firms were part of combines centered on a specific lender. The Regional Banks funded whatever large concerns remained after the City Banks had allocated their funds. As a consequence, City Banks have historically focused on loans to large firms; only 9 percent of their outlays went to small or medium-sized firms in 1966. Regional Banks also concentrated on large firms, but because City Banks frequently preempted this market, they were forced to supply funds to smaller firms as well. Regional banks directed only 42 percent of their business at smaller firms.[56]

In the middle of the figure are what Japanese financial surveys call Private Small-Firm Financial Institutions (Minkan Chūshō Kigyō Kinyū Kikan). Included in this group of institutions are the Mutual Banks (Sōgō Ginkō), the Credit Associations (Shinyō Kinkō), and the Credit Unions (Shinyō Kumiai). In 1966 the Mutual Banks directed

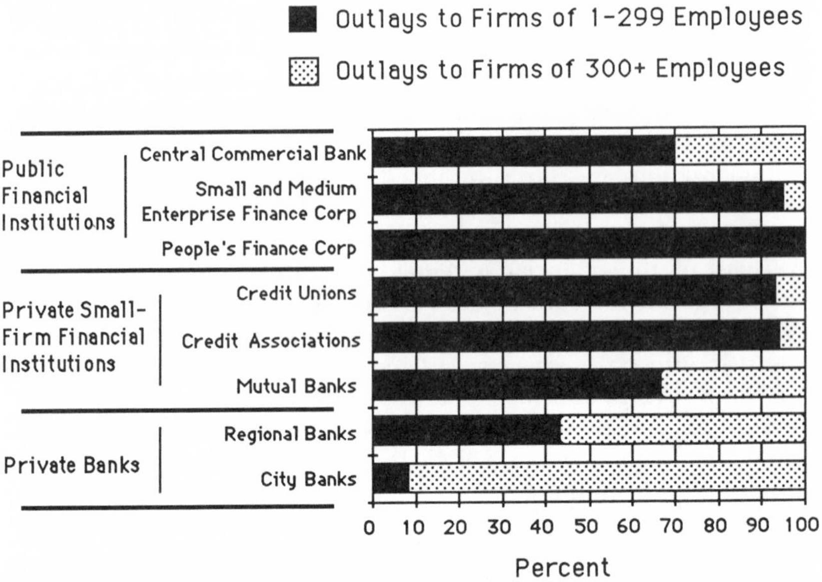

Figure 4.21. Outlays by Financial Institutions to Small and Large Firms, 1966
SOURCE: Kokumin Kinyū Kōkō, *Nihon no shō reisai kigyō* (Japanese small and very small enterprises) (Tokyo: Toyo Keizai, 1968), p. 124.

66 percent of their total outlays to small enterprises, and the Credit Associations and Credit Unions both focused over 90 percent of their business on small firms.

Mutual Banks were created in 1951 with the passage of the Mutual Bank Law (Sōgō Ginkō Hō), which transformed the prewar *mujin* companies into proper lending institutions. The *mujin* had operated as building societies, but they involved a high element of chance: a firm might pay in and then never receive a loan. In 1949 the *mujin* companies were required to provide a fixed remuneration based on deposits. The 1951 law abolished them altogether and created regional mutual banks by combining the assets of various *mujin* companies. The new Mutual Banks faced lending limits and were required to maintain reserve balances as a proportion of their deposits or loans. They were restricted geographically by the control of license to open branches, which the Ministry of Finance administered. The limitation of Mutual Banks to certain regions—typically peripheral areas—created local economies in which deposits were collected and then let out as small-business loans.[57]

The Credit Unions and Credit Associations were also created in 1951 in an amalgamation of the finance cooperatives set up under the old *kōgyō kumiai*. After the war it was initially thought that the cooperatives could simply be relicensed. Many cooperatives, however, were accepting deposits from and loaning to nonmember clients: they were operating as banks. Cooperatives of this sort were organized into institutions that closely resembled banks, called Credit Associations. Responsible to a central credit bank, they were organized as nonprofit institutions. They could accept deposits or make loans within tightly restricted geographical areas and performed much the same functions as the Mutual Banks.[58]

The Credit Unions were formed from those *kōgyō kumiai* institutions which had restricted loans to members. They were less regulated than the Credit Associations, but their lending and financial terms were prescribed by law. Their operation was also restricted to select regions; a credit union in Nagano, for instance, could not lend to clients in Aomori. In return, private banks could not enter the regions that the Credit Unions served.

All of the financial institutions serving private small and medium-sized business were sustained by the licensing strategies of the Ministry of Finance. Branch offices were crucial to the growth of a lender's deposits and loans; in a cash-and-carry society like Japan, the ability to open branches ia a major determinant of survival. Between 1951 and 1965 the Mutual Banks and Credit Unions were permitted to expand their branch networks at a rate five to eight times that of the City Banks, and between 1965 and 1980 they grew three times as fast. Eventually in number of branches they dwarfed the City Banks. Furthermore, City Banks were prevented from opening any branches in some areas, leaving large regional blocks to the small-business institutions. This policy, as one scholar has argued, was explicitly conceived as a way to give financial support to small enterprises:

> Since branch offices were quite essential to banking [in the era of rapid economic growth], branch office administration was one of the most powerful regulatory weapons available to the monetary authorities. It is noteworthy, however, that this weapon was not used for the purpose of stimulating economic growth. In actual administration, the Ministry of Finance gave preferential treatment to thrift institutions, i.e. the various financial institutions for medium and smaller businesses. Owing to this preferential treatment, the thrift institutions were able to expand their branch networks faster than could the city banks. . . . [This] was one of the reasons why the thrifts could continue to maintain a stable share of the financial markets.
>
> Thus, branch office administration and control were used to directly support the thrift institutions and indirectly to support their customers, i.e., medium and smaller businesses. . . . This suggests that it is an exag-

> geration to say that the Japanese financial policy tended to favor both big banks and big businesses to the end of promoting economic growth. For political reasons, policy makers had to pay a great deal of attention to the economic and financial environment in which medium and smaller businesses operated. The Ministry of Finance's policies on branch banking reflected this reality.[59]

Private institutions for small and medium-sized enterprises, then, survived because of explicit strategies to support small firms.

The top group in Figure 4.21 is made up of government institutions that provide small-business finance. The Central Commercial and Industrial Bank (Shō-kōgyō Chuō Ginkō) makes 70 percent of its loans to small enterprises; the Small and Medium Enterprise Finance Corporation (Chūshō Kigyō Kinyū Kōkō) lends 95 percent of its funds to small firms; and the People's Finance Corporation (Kokumin Kinyū Kōkō) is 100 percent involved with small-scale enterprises.

The Central Commercial and Industrial Bank was a restructured version of the bank chartered in 1936 to serve the *kōgyō kumiai.* Even though the bank ended up financing munitions reconversion, and thus aided the war effort, it was not a SCAP target and was rechartered in 1949. The government put up half its capital, and localities and other government-affiliated institutions put up the rest. In 1951 the Central Bank was made the coordinating institution for the Credit Unions, providing additional indirect government support for these private financial organizations.[60] Its loan authorization was also extended to include unaffiliated credit organizations.

The Small and Medium Enterprise Finance Corporation was established in 1953 with a government appropriation of ¥13 billion. The new institution also took over prewar Reconversion Finance Bank loans. The corporation was limited to lending to firms with three hundred employees or fewer, and it gradually developed into the primary means of government support for firms in the medium range of small businesses. Originally, it was supposed to act merely as guarantor of small-business loans made by City Banks and Regional Banks. In 1955, however, the corporation was empowered to make loans directly.[61]

The People's Finance Corporation was established in 1949 and specialized in government funding to very small firms, complementing the lending of the Small and Medium Enterprise Finance Corporation. The People's Finance Corporation was wholly supported by the government, although its operations were in part controlled by a private board of directors. One of its most important duties was to serve as a clearinghouse for data on small business, which were then used in public policy debate.[62]

The financial reforms of the 1950s thus created a large body of organizations dedicated to small-business finance. These institutions enhanced the capital independence of small firms. Before their establishment the 1950s had been characterized by the domination of the economy by private banks, and small firms were squeezed out of capital markets. But since 1960, as the Japanese economy has registered its most impressive gains, the new financial organs have helped generate extremely rapid expansion in the small manufacturing sector.

The importance of government and government-supported private institutions to the spectacular emergence of high-tech manufacturers in Japan is clear in the extent to which small enterprises made use of them. The newly created loan sources provided opportunities to invest in the new equipment necessary to sustain flexible operations. First, let us consider the role of private banks in lending to various size classes of manufacturing firms between 1964 and 1982 (see Figure 4.22). As the size of enterprise decreases, so degree of reliance on banks for capital also falls. Bank loans accounted for about 40 percent of all loans received by firms with one to three employees in 1964; in the same year bank loans accounted for 82 percent of borrowing by the largest firms. Though small-business loans were but a minuscule fraction of total outlays by private banks in

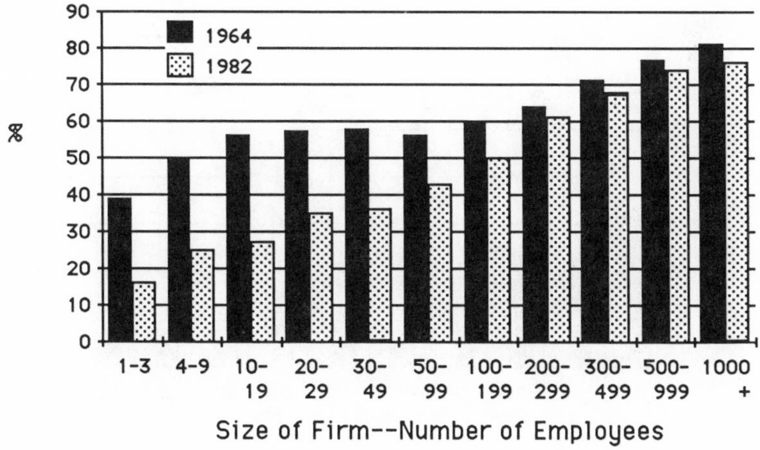

Figure 4.22. Bank Loans as a Proportion of Total Loans Received, 1964 and 1982
SOURCE: Small Business Survey (1968, 1983). See footnote 22.

the early 1960s, small enterprises relied on banks for a large part of their capital. Dependence rates for the 1–100 employee class ranged from 40 percent to 60 percent. (The proportion was almost certainly higher in the 1950s, before financial institutions for small businesses were reestablished.) In contrast, firms with more than three hundred employees depended on private banks for between 70 percent and 80 percent of their needs.

As the Japanese economy and small manufacturers registered extremely rapid growth, a dramatic transformation took place. By 1982 private bank funding for firms with 1–3 employees had declined to just 18 percent of total capital needs; companies in the 4–9 and 10–19 size ranges registered declines of close to 200 percent as the ratio fell to under 25 percent of total loans. For all small businesses the importance of private bank loans significantly declined. For firms above the 200 employee level, however, the percentage of bank lending remained very close to the 1964 levels. Private bank capital was sufficient for large companies. At the other end of the spectrum, entrepreneurs who were starting or expanding small-scale manufacturing operations did so with less and less help from banks as the high-growth period progressed.

Where did these small firms secure loans? They relied on funding provided by private, small-firm institutions and their government counterparts. We can see the development of this alternative financial system in the changes recorded between 1964 and 1982 for each type of institution. Figure 4.23 illustrates loan reliance by firms in various

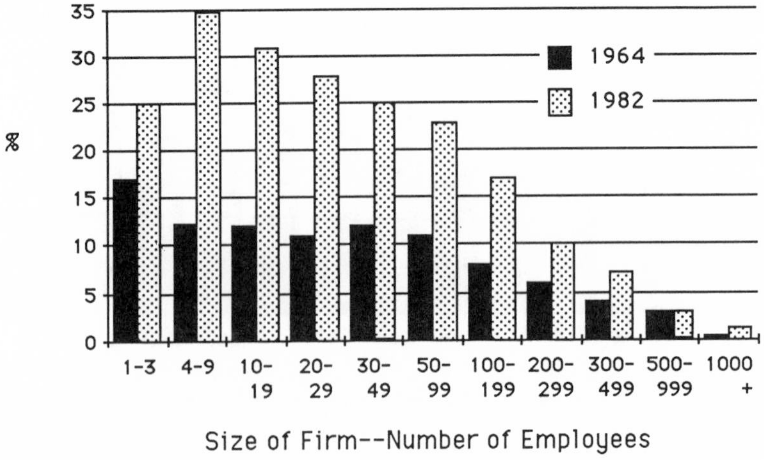

Figure 4.23. Private Loans from Small-Business Financial Institutions as a Percentage of All Loans, 1964 and 1982
SOURCE: Same as for Figure 4.22.

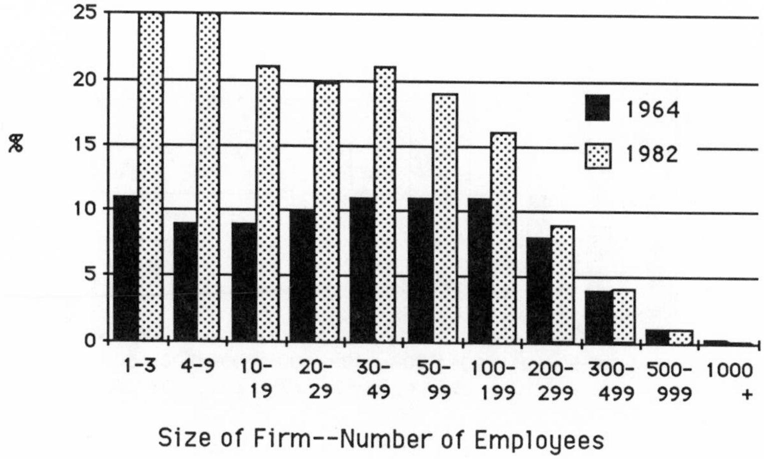

Figure 4.24. Government Loans from Small Enterprise Finance Institutions as a Percentage of All Loans, 1964 and 1982
SOURCE: Same as for Figure 4.22.

size classes on private, small-business institutions, including the Mutual Banks, the Credit Associations, and the Credit Unions. As firm size decreased, reliance on such institutions increased dramatically. For firms with 4–9 and 10–19 employees, this dependence grew from just 12 percent in 1964 to about 35 percent and 32 percent, respectively, in 1982. The new financial institutions supplanted banks in the provision of funds to small businesses, and the low level of support they gave large businesses confirms the specialized nature of their lending.

The rapid growth of the private financial institutions for small business was matched in the performance of government lenders to small enterprises. The percentage of total loans received from the Central Commercial and Industrial Banks, the Small and Medium Enterprise Finance Corporation, and the People's Finance Corporation by firms in various size classes is shown in Figure 4.24. For firms with 1–3, 4–9, and 10–19 employees, specialized government assistance doubled from about 8–11 percent to 22–25 percent between 1964 and 1982. Medium-sized enterprises also grew increasingly reliant on public loan sources. The role of government support falls precipitously as company size goes up.

The combined share taken by public and private financial institutions for small business in the total loan position of all smaller companies was extremely large. Figure 4.25 presents the percentage of total loans secured in 1964 and 1982 by firms in various size classes from public, small-firm lenders; private, small-firm institutions; and nonspecialized government sources. These loans were the major com-

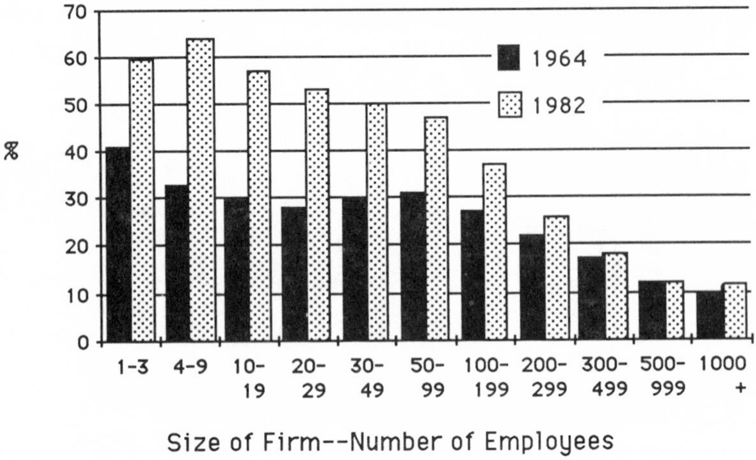

Figure 4.25. Combined Nonbank, Government Loans as a Percentage of All Loans, 1964 and 1982
Source: Same as for Figure 4.22.

ponent of small-firm financing in the high-growth period, and their importance grew from 1964 to 1982. For firms in the 1–3 employee class, government or small enterprise institutional loans accounted for 60 percent of total resources in 1982, an increase from 40 percent in 1964. Firms in the 4–9 employee class exhibited a 65 percent reliance by 1982, up from 32 percent; the 10–19 employee class depended on government or specialized small-firm finance for 58 percent of its loans as compared with 30 percent in 1964; and 52 percent of the capital supplied to the 20–29 employee class was of government or private, specialized institutional origin in 1982, up from just 28 percent in 1964. During the high-growth period dedicated public and private support nearly doubled for the smallest classes of firms and came to account for the majority of their capital needs.

This pattern of loan support shows that specialized small-firm capital assistance varied enormously with the size of the firms involved. The smaller the company, the larger was the role of the state in funding entry into the market. Then, as (or if) the company succeeded, it turned to larger, banking lenders. Consequently we may divide Japanese firms into three classes corresponding to their involvement with government or government-backed lenders. The first is the startup firm, where risks are high. Here, the manufacturer depends on public or specialized private loan institutions. The second type, which begins to emerge with one hundred or two hundred employees, is transitional; the firm is now a proven organization, and larger banks begin to supplant institutions committed to small and medium-sized enterprises. Finally, as a firm moves into the larger size classes, specialized support becomes very slight; the bulk of financial commitments are by the city banks or through equity issues. This pattern covers firms with more than five hundred employees.

The redirection of financial support toward small business was a contributing factor in the set of circumstances leading to the emergence of high-tech flexible manufacturing in postwar Japan. Whether it was a *necessary* factor is something that cannot be determined. It is possible to argue, however, that the politics of small-firm support made it more likely that trends toward flexibility generated elsewhere in the economy would ultimately succeed. Companies that had previously had limited access to capital could find a wide range of sources for industrial funding in the postwar period. Firms trapped by the business conditions of the 1940s and 1950s and thus mired in subordinate production agreements could make investments permitting them to move into independent, specialist markets. Blue-collar workers who wanted their own factories could take the first steps toward establishing their own firm with state support. Thus was the survival of small manufacturers as independent, flexible, specialist enterprises enhanced by financial politics before and after the war.

Conclusions

Several political events enhanced opportunities in Japan for the adoption of flexible manufacturing. These political factors shaped the background conditions against which industrial successes such as those in the machine tool sector were achieved. They help explain why Japanese firms could enter the market so rapidly, and why there was a particularly strong demand for unique machinery such as small-scale NC equipment. More generally, Japanese manufacturing practices cannot be understood as the natural outcome of market pressures. Neither the retreat from the dual structure nor the development of flexible, small-scale subcontractors was inevitable; political events transformed the perceptions and strategies of industrialists and workers and made possible the widespread diffusion of flexible manufacturing techniques.

In the following chapter I link the emergence of flexible manufacturing to the development of the NC machinery industry by considering another political element in the growth of small-scale firms: industrial regionalism. State financing of small enterprises, the strategic calculations of large and small firms, the transformation of worker careers, and the existence of comparatively plentiful capital might not have led to the emergence of flexible manufacturing—an even more extensive network of subordinated producers could have resulted. Industrial regionalism was a crucial ingredient, and regional regulatory systems constrained debilitating competition among small firms. The case of a manufacturing hamlet in rural Japan shows how the economy-wide developments discussed in this chapter produced one of the most highly concentrated groups of small NC-using firms in the world.

Chapter Five

Industrial Regionalism: Sakaki Township

Sakaki Township, in rural central Nagano Prefecture, is an extremely unlikely site for a high-tech manufacturing hamlet. Its growth illustrates how the national political events I have already examined produced remarkable industrial changes, even in unpromising regions. The case also shows how flexible production strategies in small firms were tied to the emergence of demand for new, general-purpose NC tools.

Regional associations of small-scale, flexible factories have figured prominently in studies of flexible manufacturing in Europe.[1] They do so because some degree of collective identity and action is necessary for flexible specialist firms to survive. In particular, regional groups are important to resist price pressures from larger companies. Should some firms in a given area begin to compete by reducing wages or profits, then all the region's manufacturers are more likely to adopt similar strategies to attract business. In a regional price war, factory practices that permit flexibility would be sacrificed, because subcontractors cannot make deep price cuts without undermining the system of high-skill labor, general-purpose machinery, and trust within the factory that is essential to flexible manufacturing. Regional coordination is one way that firms enforce what they regard as legitimate dealings upon larger companies. As I shall show, firms in Sakaki have joined together to build defenses against wage and profit pressures.

Regions also foster cooperation for the purpose of developing new product markets. The decision to move into a new market or sell a new technique involves substantial risk. Yet the main advantage of flexible production is that it permits production or manufacturing innovations, giving smaller factories their competitive edge. Regions help alleviate risks. In Italy, for instance, flexible firms collaborate to find new, joint applications for their skills, collectively defining new products to which each firm contributes a part or a process. In Japan, small manufacturers in a region borrow machinery from one another as production schedules require; the sharing of machinery allows a subcontractor to bid for new work secure in the knowledge that back-up manufacturing capacity is available. Over time, in fact, large contracting firms have come to recognize that regions provide additional production security and become more disposed to place new orders with an untried vendor. Regional cooperation has enhanced the development of new technology and markets for small firms in Japan.

Finally, regionalism reduces business overhead for small factories. In Europe, for instance, regional groups have provided plant space or infrastructural improvements to collections of flexible producers. In Japan, regions facilitate funding; regional authorities—local bureaucrats and manufacturers—make the crucial decisions about whether a certain firm should receive financial support or not. The distribution of funds from private and public small business banks and trusts takes place at the local level.

Industrial regions, in sum, give small manufacturers the ability to resist downward wage and price pressures, reduce innovation costs, and coordinate small-firm financing. But their growth and expansion in Japan was not a foregone conclusion; firms in a region had to learn to trust each other and reach an accommodation with local political authorities regarding overall industrial objectives. The balancing of individual, local, and government and private interests was *political;* it required compromise and vision among the various actors involved. The regional institutions that have grown up in Sakaki and elsewhere comprise another political event that, in concert with developments discussed earlier, have promoted flexible production in Japan.

The industrial history of Sakaki Township, a community located in Nagano Prefecture in the mountains of central Honshu, mirrors perfectly the broad trends in Japanese industrial practices that I discussed in chapter 4. Furthermore, the township's remarkable growth is closely tied to the development of advanced NC computer machinery. In 1983 Sakaki's population was only 16,000, and 321 manufacturing enterprises operated within its borders—about 0.013 percent of Japan's total population and just 0.04 percent of the country's manufacturing enterprises. Yet the township's manufacturers owned close to six hundred NC machine tools, 1 percent of the total deployed in Japan. Indeed, Sakaki could boast of one of the world's highest concentrations of sophisticated production machinery.[2]

Sakaki's geography and history make such development extremely surprising; it is as if U.S. technological leadership had passed suddenly from urban centers such as New York City to a farming village in rural North Dakota. Japan is traditionally divided into a dispersed periphery and a well-defined industrial center along the Tokyo-Nagoya-Osaka/Kyoto axis. The eastern half of this metropolitan conglomeration, including Tokyo, is the Kantō. It is separated by a range of coastal mountains from the Kansai region in the west, which includes Osaka and Kyoto. The periphery is itself highly dispersed. The most advanced regions are usually thought to be such urban centers as Sendai in northern Honshu or Sapporo in Hokkaido. These sizable cities are often known for particular industrial processes or markets. Next in line are more isolated metropolitan areas, including cities located on the Sea of Japan side of Honshu; Niigata, Toyama, and Kanazawa are three examples. Finally, at the base of this conventional Japanese industrial hierarchy are large but sparsely populated districts in the mountainous terrain that comprises 70 percent of the country's land mass. Included in this group are Nagano Prefecture and Sakaki Township. Such communities are comparatively remote and historically have experienced a population drain to the cities along the coast. The central mountain regions are the last place one would expect to find evidence of an industrial renaissance.

Even within Nagano Prefecture, Sakaki itself is particularly unpromising. It does not lie on the express train route from Tokyo; a local train, often a two-car vehicle, serves the town. Historically, Sakaki's inhabitants have lived close to the subsistence level. Its climate being unsuitable for growing rice, it was forced to trade for commodities by producing silk and fruit, but the small size of the town's plots made it difficult to compete; local growers had to accept lower profits. The silkworm industry collapsed in the late 1930s. Until the 1940s there had been a steady emigration to urban centers in the Kantō plain.

Sakaki's postwar manufacturing growth was phenomenal, however. The township had just five factories in 1945, but it had attracted 321 firms by 1983. The most rapid expansion came after the late 1950s when specialized finance institutions for small business were established nationwide. The pace of value added growth and the expansion of the value of shipments recorded by Sakaki's enterprises matched the rate at which new enterprises were created: value added rose over 1,200 percent between 1966 and 1982, shipments increased 1,000 percent (see Figure 5.1). By the mid-1960s Sakaki had entered a golden age in which, on average, one manufacturing firm was opened per month.[3] Indeed, growth slowed only in the 1980s, after all of the

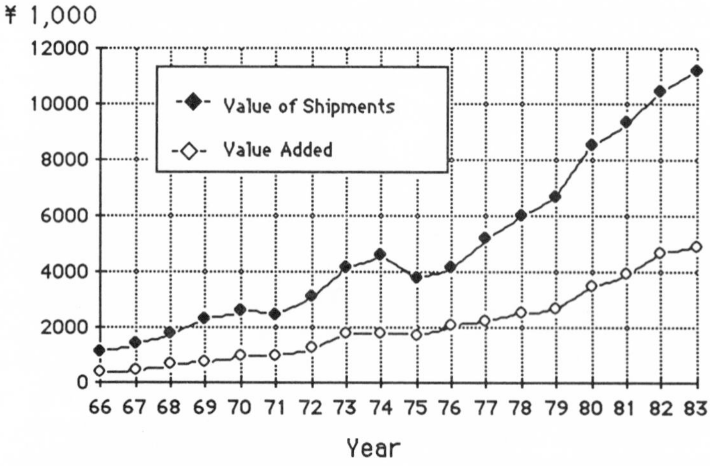

Figure 5.1. Manufacturing Value Added and Shipments, Sakaki, 1966–1983
SOURCE: Sakaki Machi Shōkōkai (Sakaki Chamber of Commerce), *Sakaki matchi shōkigyō keiei shihyō* (Indicators of Sakaki small enterprise performance) (Nagano Prefecture, 1983), p. 4.

township's available land space was occupied.[4] In comparison, Japanese value added in manufacturing industries during the height of the economic "miracle" rose 690 percent from 1966 to 1983; U.S. value added increased only 302 percent, and that amid high inflation, from 1963 to 1977.[5]

The economic development of the township has been marked by several stages in which different industries predominated (see Figure 5.2). The first wave of expansion, from immediately after the war to the mid-1960s, was in general machinery, paced by auto parts production. In the 1970s new firms in electronics and plastics predominated. Many of the older auto parts firms also shifted production to new industries.

Extremely small manufacturers accounted for most of Sakaki's industrial achievements. In 1982 only four of its companies employed more than three hundred workers. The township's firms were managed, for the most part, by former blue-collar workers who had begun their careers in other local factories. Indeed, in 1982 the vast majority of firms had fewer than ten employees (see Figure 5.3). Of 330 manufacturing firms in 1982, 257 were in the 1–9 employee category and 41 percent had three or fewer employees. All but eleven of Sakaki's factories were enterprises of 99 or fewer workers; average size was about 18 employees. Small and medium-sized firms accounted for

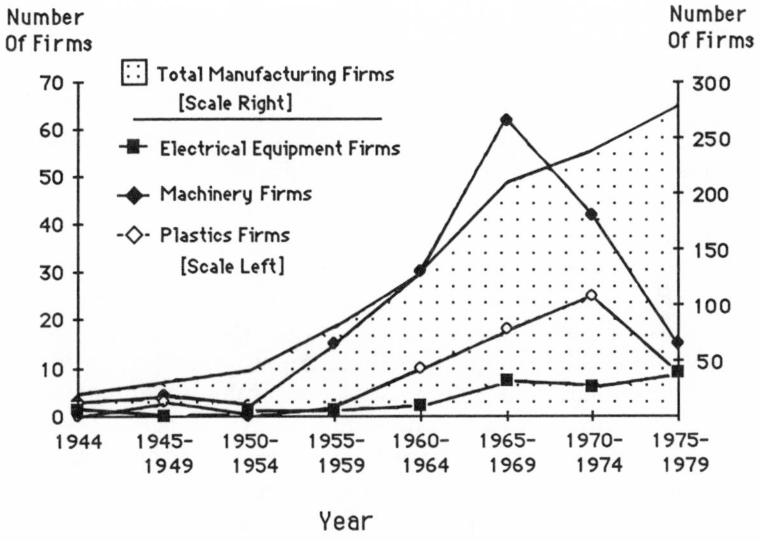

Figure 5.2. Growth of Manufacturing Firms in Sakaki, 1944–1979
Source: From Naganoken Chūshōkigyō Sōgōshidōjō (Nagano Prefecture Bureau for Assisting Small and Medium Enterprises), *Sakaki machi kikai kōgyō sanchi shindan hōkokushō* (Report of the study of Sakaki's regional machinery industry) (Nagano Prefecture, 1983), pp. 1–3. Confidential document provided by the Sakaki *shōkōkai,* December 18, 1984, p. 4.

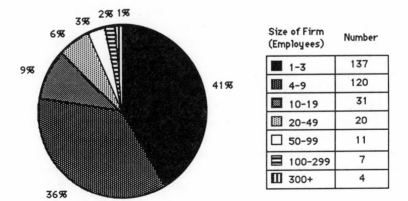

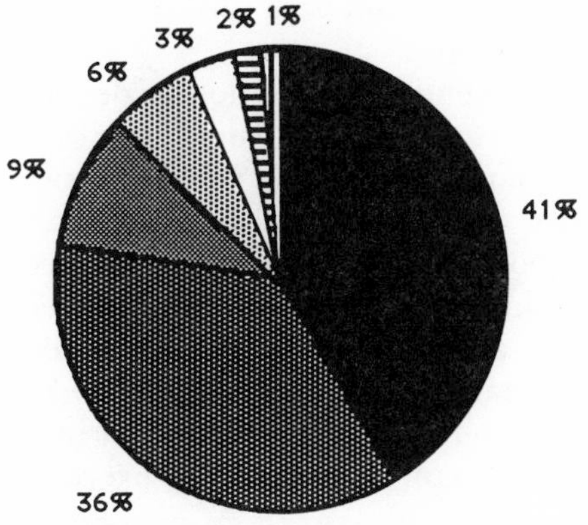

Size of Firm (Employees)	Number
1-3	137
4-9	120
10-19	31
20-49	20
50-99	11
100-299	7
300+	4

Figure 5.3. Firm sizes in Sakaki, 1982
Source: Same as for Figure 5.1.

over 60 percent of the value of shipments from the township, a figure that almost certainly understates their contribution because shipments from large firms always have a large subcontracting component. Yet Sakaki is extremely productive despite the small size of its firms; although the township ranked ninth in Nagano Prefecture—itself a peripheral region—in terms of average firm size in 1983, it was first in shipments per population and fourth in value added per employee. In fact Sakaki's wealth is such that it is one of only two municipalities in the prefecture that does not receive a local tax rebate.[6]

The few large firms in Sakaki were once small; they gradually became finished goods producers on a larger scale. They typically capitalized on unique technical skills or knowledge to formulate specialized products for specific uses. Many came to dominate world markets. By the early 1980s one local firm, Nissei, held 65 percent of the global market for blood pressure testers; another, Nakajima All Precision, captured 20 percent of the world market for manual typewriter keyboards and 35 percent of the U.S. market for electric models; Takeuchi led the world in the production of mini-backhoe construction equipment; and Soar, a marker of portable, sophisticated electrical testers, in ten years grew from a family operation to an enterprise operating throughout the world.[7]

The small size of manufacturing enterprises in Sakaki and their dispersal throughout the township can deceive the casual observer. The town's industrial activity is concealed in small, often shabby, corrugated metal structures that look like storage sheds or garages. Inside these unimposing buildings, however, are complexes of integrated NC lathes and mills—high-tech factories of the first order. Some of the world's most sophisticated computer-controlled machine tools can be found in the front gardens and back yards of what were formerly marginal agricultural holdings.

Sakaki's small factories are independent. They do not depend on large firms for technical or capital support, nor do they offer contractors cheap labor rates and inexpensive parts. This independence developed gradually. Its explosive growth in the 1960s was based on auto subcontracting. In the 1970s auto work declined, but specialty parts supply in general machining, electronics, and plastics became much more important. By 1983 auto subcontracting accounted for less than 15 percent of Sakaki's total production (see Figure 5.4). The movement away from auto parts subcontracting began to increase independence, because auto manufacturers customarily exert strong pressure on their suppliers.

Sakaki's manufacturers actively pursued subcontracting strategies that would increase their autonomy. When groups of subcontractors

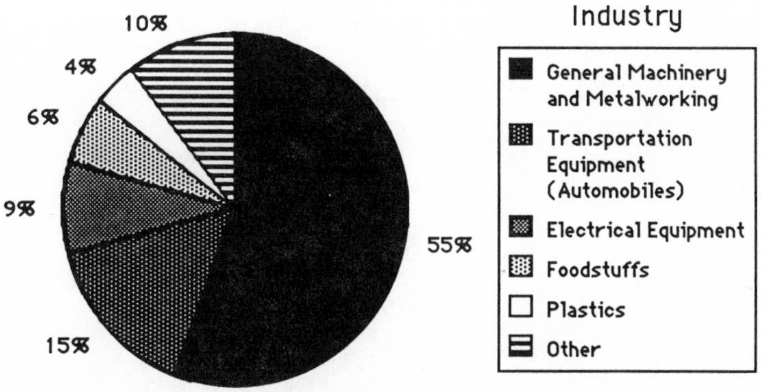

Figure 5.4. Manufacturing Product Composition in Sakaki, 1983
SOURCE: Same as for Figure 5.1, p. 6.

rely on one local manufacturer for their business, the probability of direct price or product pressure is very high; the region, in effect, is a company town. Where small firms rely on orders from outside the local area, and the local large firms purchase their parts elsewhere, on the other hand, the degree of domination is very low, because for the large firms direct coordination over a distance brings with it transaction costs that undermine the rationale (low production cost) of maintaining tight control in the first place.

In Sakaki the larger, finished goods producers go outside the township for their parts, while small firms manufacture for companies throughout the Kantō plain. Local large firms direct only 14 percent of their orders to companies in Sakaki (see Table 5.1). They rely on manufacturers in other cities in Nagano Prefecture or in the Kantō region for their parts. The small subcontractors, in contrast, receive over 51 percent of their orders from the Kantō area and about 23 percent from other locations in Nagano Prefecture. Just 11 percent of their business comes from within Sakaki, and much of it occurs when one subcontractor relets an order to another: local subcontractors placed 44 percent of their outside orders with other Sakaki companies.

The wage structure in Sakaki further illustrates the independent character of the region's manufacturers. If the township's firms were low-cost suppliers for larger concerns, one would expect to see a wage differential between local subcontractors and contracting firms at least as large as the Japanese average. Indeed, because the costs for Kantō firms of doing business with companies in isolated mountain communities would be high, one might expect Sakaki's wages to be below the average to compensate. But Sakaki's wages are the highest

Table 5.1. Regional Location of Subcontracting Orders in Sakaki, 1982

Firm	Regions	Percent of total
Larger firms: Regions in which outside orders are placed	Sakaki	14
	Northern Nagano	10
	Eastern Nagano	30
	Kantō	17
	Other	29
Subcontractors: Regions from which subcontracting comes	Sakaki	11
	Northern Nagano	12
	Eastern Nagano	11
	Kantō	51
	Kansai	5.5
	Other	9.5
Subcontractors: Regions in which outside orders are placed	Sakaki	44
	Northern Nagano	23
	Eastern Nagano	26
	Kantō	2
	Other	5

SOURCE: Same as for Figure 5.2, pp. 10–11.

in Nagano Prefecture; in 1983 blue-collar compensation per employee was 10 percent greater than in the next closest municipalities, the much larger cities of Okatani and Suwa.[8] Moreover, in comparison with averages throughout Japan, wages in Sakaki have historically been much higher than payment offered in comparable firms elsewhere. In fact, by 1983 workers in the township were paid almost exactly the same as blue-collar employees in manufacturing firms with five hundred employees or more nationwide. Over time, moreover, Sakaki's relative wages rose, from 82 percent of that for manufacturing firms of five hundred or more workers in 1968 to 93 percent by 1983 (see Figure 5.5). Such high wages are consistent with the fact that the town's firms are independent manufacturing specialists; the firms can support high wages by supplying high-quality, unique products to contractors and charge premium prices for them.

The first factories were established in the township in 1941 under the military's strategy of dispersing armament contracts throughout the countryside, a policy that, as we saw, arose from its anti-*zaibatsu* preoccupations as well as from a desire to avoid concentrating industry in regions vulnerable to bombing. By 1945 four metalworking factories and one plastics firm had been diverted to Sakaki or had opened in conjunction with military procurement. Until the end of the war Sakaki's few factories made airplane parts and communications equipment. With Japan's defeat the firms shifted production to such nonmilitary markets as agricultural implements, metal casting, and household goods. A small group of subcontractors associated with aircraft production did move into the manufacture of machinery

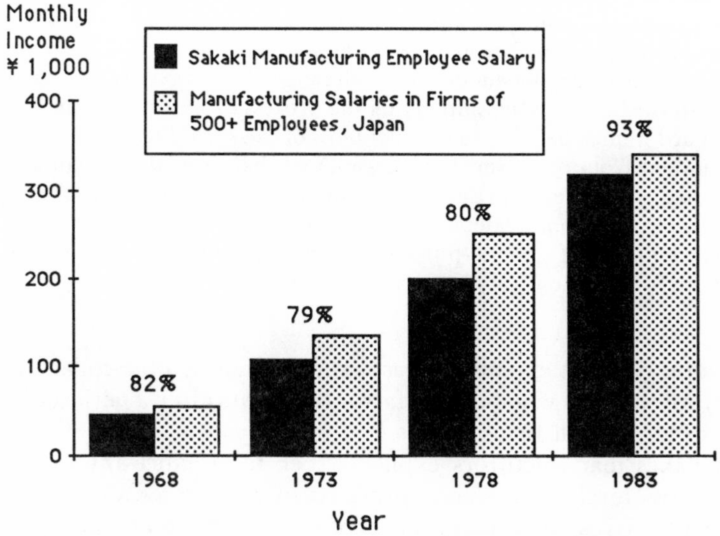

Figure 5.5. Wages in Sakaki versus Wages in Manufacturing Firms of More Than 500 Employees Nationwide, 1968–1983
SOURCE: For Sakaki, same as for Figure 5.1, p. 4; for Japan, *Monthly Wage Surveys* (1968, 1973, 1978, 1983).

parts, but until the late 1950s production in Sakaki was uneven, plagued by high startup costs, a lack of financing, and uncertain markets.[9]

Sakaki's fortunes began to change in 1957 when the township passed the Sakaki Township Factory Promotion Ordinance (Sakaki Machi Kōjō Yūchi Jōrei). This measure focused the town's efforts to apply the newly created national institutions for small-firm development to the benefit of factory operators in the township. In fact, Sakaki was successful; well over 90 percent of all companies subsequently established in Sakaki originated within the town, and 80 percent were started by workers who had left other Sakaki enterprises to start their own independent operation. The remaining 20 percent were managed by individuals who had switched careers from agriculture to manufacturing.[10]

Sakaki's development was thus shaped by the expansion of careers for Japanese blue-collar workers, discussed in chapter 4. As a Nagano Prefecture report indicates, one of the strengths of the Sakaki system was that potential factory managers and operators could gain expertise in other small firms and then begin their own company:

> There are no dominating large firms in the township. Rather, it is a typically small enterprise town. The vast majority of the managerial staff

> of these small enterprises learned their craft by taking employment in the township's small firms, mastering a certain set of technology, and then becoming independent. The full range of managerial skills can thus be studied in this way, simplifying the process of starting a firm. In this regard it must be pointed out that most of the small firms became independent from other small businesses, and that firms that began as offshoots of huge enterprises are extremely rare. Moreover, in Sakaki it is possible to become independent with just a single lathe or through the development of general-purpose, advanced technology—a fact that is thought to make it easy to open new firms.

In sum, Sakaki's expansion was accomplished by blue-collar or agricultural workers who became factor operators after a period of training in local small firms.

Sakaki's manufacturers explicitly seek to enhance their independence by developing unique products or techniques. Over the years since the 1940s, three main routes of success have emerged. The first, prominent in the 1940s and 1950s, was to become expert in particular manufacturing techniques. After a firm became independent, it would seek to apply the most advanced techniques to production or assembly processes, enabling Sakaki firms to increase the accuracy and reliability of various operations. Sakaki became known for the mastery of specific production techniques, attracting specialty work from afar into the township.

The second route, prevalent in the late 1950s and 1960s, was first to become independent as a parts supplier for a larger firm and then, by applying the techniques learned in parts production, to develop unique products. From there, several choices were possible. The new part could be supplied to the original contractors, resulting in design or quality advances in the final assembled product. Or by marketing the new product, innovative firms might seek to create new markets, expanding the range of sectors for which they produced. When successful, such design breakthroughs led to the growth of parts firms into final goods manufacturers.

In the latter 1970s a third route emerged. Sakaki's manufacturers developed expertise in electronics and electronic applications and then marketed their skill independently. This involved the application of special skills to a variety of manufacturing problems and designs. A firm might use its skill in connector technology, for instance, to increase the quality of keyboard, communication, or gauging equipment. Then, through earlier contacts with national and overseas users, many firms were able to supply larger computer and high-tech markets.

Sakaki's success became a model for local planners throughout Japan. In 1984 close to forty regional authorities visited the township, as did observers from the Korean Small Business Authority.[11] But how did the broad developments discussed in earlier chapters lead in the specific case of Sakaki to such remarkable industrial results? Part of the answer is that regionalism reduced the costs of flexible production while protecting Sakaki's firms from external price pressures. For regionalism to work, however, industrial interests in the township had to find a way to coordinate interfirm activities and allocate power between private and public actors. The next section sketches how local bureaucrats in the Sakaki Chamber of Commerce, or *shōkōkai,* helped administer a system of small-firm support which enhanced producer flexibility. The following sections describe private accommodations that permitted effective organization in the township.

The Role of the *Shōkōkai*

In Japan the *shōkōkai* is responsible for administering the entire range of small-business financing, recommending particular firms for specific sources of capital. The *shōkōkai,* except in the largest metropolitan areas, is directly supervised by the prefecture, which pays staff salaries and makes annual assessments.[12] This apparently vertical hierarchy conceals a substantial degree of local autonomy. An organizational map of the Sakaki *shōkōkai* would show it to be at the bottom of a chain of command that starts with MITI, passes through MITI's Small Business Bureau, continues through the bureau's five Commerce Bureaus (Tsùyō Kyoku), which are dispersed throughout the country, then to the prefecture, and finally to the local *shōkōkai* itself.[13] However, prefectural authorities are notoriously independent from MITI, frequently subverting or at least blunting national bureaucratic initiatives to fit their own needs. The same degree of functional autonomy exists between the local *shōkōkai* and the prefectural authorities.

In the 1960s, for example, MITI sponsored legislation aimed at rationalizing small businesses as a countermeasure to capital liberalization (described in detail in chapter 4). Its initiative provided a set of financial incentives to form cartels; what the central bureaucracy wanted was to combine the small firms into larger ones and then supply them with capital so they could compete with foreign firms. The policy was a failure. MITI could not possibly regulate the activities of hundred of thousands of manufacturers, nor were prefectural bureaucrats able to manage producers in their regions. Instead, the *shōkōkai* handled the distribution of resources mandated by the "rationalization" scheme. In most cases, however, the *shōkōkai,* acting at the express request of local manufacturers, interpreted rationalization to mean "technical advance." Using this standard they authorized funds not for firms that had consolidated, but rather for firms that were eager to buy new equipment. Instead of leading to mergers, the rationalization program helped protect small factories, and the *shōkōkai* actually increased the power of local industrialists relative to the central bureaucracy.

In Sakaki the *shōkōkai* is housed in a small public building in the center of town. About 80 percent of its operating expenses come directly from the prefecture; of this, 50 percent is supplied by the prefecture's tax base, and the other half is a subsidy provided by MITI's Small Business Bureau to the prefecture. The rest is secured by charging local firms a membership fee and a service fee for any work done by the *shōkōkai.* Most companies join; the rare one that does not is ineligible to participate in purely local programs, although support provided through national policies will still be available.

Shōkōkai staff are usually not former businessmen but rather career bureaucrats. In Sakaki they typically first study engineering or a related profession at university and then take a civil service exam. Successful applicants—the pass rate on the test is only about 10 percent in Nagano Prefecture—become junior staffers at *shōkōkai* dispersed across the prefecture. These employees have considerable discretion. Most of the staff at Sakaki was born and raised in the town, and generally *shōkōkai* employees tend to identify strongly with the area where they work, in effect championing the district's needs.

The most important role of the *shōkōkai* in industry is to secure financial support for local entrepreneurs. In Sakaki 33 percent of the manufacturing enterprises in the township have some form of direct capital assistance from government. The remaining firms, though funded by private sources, often have their loans guaranteed by the locality or receive approval based on the recommendation of the *shōkōkai.* The *shōkōkai*'s influence is especially important when firms are smaller; close to 100 percent of the companies with fewer than twenty employees received some form of government assistance.

Most of this assistance goes to purchase equipment. Usually small firms in Sakaki already own or have mortgages on the land they will use for their operations, and manufacturing tools and machinery are their greatest expense. The *shōkōkai* is instrumental in providing blue-collar employees with the capital to get their own machines; without assistance, prospective entrepreneurs would not be able to bear the investment burden, especially where expensive NC machines are involved. By reducing equipment startup costs, in most cases eliminating them, the *shōkōkai* is extremely important in the creation of small businesses.

For prospective factory operators, *shōkōkai* input is essential in securing a loan. First, the *shōkōkai* acts as expert counsel on what funds are available. Each of the small-business financial institutions have dozens of separate funds, and the decision of which to apply to is important. In 1984, for instance, the *shōkōkai*'s annual publication on finance for small and medium enterprises listed sixty-three major financing programs carried out by national and local governments and private institutions, and many of these programs were divided into more specialized funds.[14] To be successful, a firm must tailor its application to the specific grant agency. Often equipment is funded under seemingly unlikely programs, such as pollution reduction, and a new addition to a factory might be financed through loans offered to encourage agricultural conversions in rural areas.

The *shōkōkai* is also an important resource for lenders. It is an influential judge of whether an applicant is worthy of receiving support of any kind. In Sakaki 30 percent of direct government aid to small and medium-sized enterprises comes from national sources, 40 percent from the prefecture, 20 percent from programs administered by the township itself, and 10 percent from joint insurance of loans.[15] In the case of prefectural and township programs, prospective industrialists must apply through the *shōkōkai,* whose recommendations determine the outcome of the application. In the case of national sources, such as the People's Finance Corporation, the situation is more complex. Up to a certain amount, usually about $40,000, the *shōkōkai* has independent authority to write a loan against the reserves of the national institution. For larger sums it must send an application to central office in Tokyo. Theoretically a prospective small-business client can apply directly for these larger loans, because the final decision is made at the headquarters, but local officials' evaluation of the application is extremely influential—the absence of a *shōkōkai* recommendation reduces the chance for aid. Of all government financing, in practice 99 percent is accomplished through the *shōkōkai.*

Private lending to very small firms is also influenced by the *shōkōkai,* because banks and other lenders often seek loan guarantees. In rural Sakaki the large City Banks make very few loans, but the Regional Banks can be induced to lend to small firms if their investments are insured. Usually the bank's involvement represents 30 percent or 40 percent of a firm's total investment needs. When a firm seeks a loan guarantee, the *shōkōkai* determines whether it is stable enough to merit insurance and then commits the prefecture to cover the bank's equity in the event the firm fails. The bank's portion of the loan is risk-free, and the guarantee program increases lending activity in the region—provided, of course, the rate of failure is low.

Applications for government and insured loans are accompanied by a detailed account of the production, growth, marketing, income, and employment strategies of the proposed venture. Even an applicant funded by private sources alone may consult the *shōkōkai* for its expertise in evaluating proposals in particular areas. The staff is responsible for checking the plans and often will request that an applicant modify them. The *shōkōkai* therefore has intimate knowledge of the operating histories of most of the firms in the township, giving it a base against which to evaluate new proposals. As we shall see, however, its ability to assess ventures is conditioned on the cooperation of the local manufacturers; the *shōkōkai* does not have autonomous authority. Industrial evaluations that ran counter to the expectations of the town's industrialists would soon result in the *shōkōkai*'s being forced to adopt new criteria for judgment.

Under the national and local system of loan distribution, the *shōkōkai* has strong incentives to select firms that will succeed. If its recommendations lead to failures, it will lose influence with the national funds, and the township as a whole will suffer as it gains a reputation as a poor risk. Moreover, the commitment of funds to companies that fail will lead to pressure from the prefecture, reducing future funding and local autonomy. And even with loan guarantees, of course, the banks will be unlikely to participate in further proposals if the *shōkōkai*'s predictions prove untrustworthy.

To reduce the possibility of financing failures, the *shōkōkai* has undertaken initiatives and developed strategies that have influenced industrial development in the township. It provides expert advice to newly funded firms, in practice by seeking the opinion of experienced local manufacturers. The ability to refer troubled new enterprises to more senior managers provides smaller firms with access to detailed industrial assistance, including financial, marketing, and production information.

One effect of these subsidiary support programs has been to enhance the marketing abilities of smaller firms, especially in securing orders from outside the town. Startup firms in Sakaki usually obtain their initial orders from the companies where their managers formerly worked. A worker in a small firm making plastic electronics holders, for instance, might want to contract independently to build a small part of the product. His supervisors then negotiate with their main contractor to obtain additional orders; if they are successful, the worker opens a new firm on the strength of the new business secured.

Additional work may also come through the old company, and as we shall see, firms have incentives to keep their former employees solvent.

New firms also draw on family ties. Like most of Japan, Sakaki has historically lost population to the largest cities. Frequently, family members of Sakaki workers rise in large firms to positions from which they can influence decisions on parts sourcing. They act on behalf of relatives or friends in Sakaki, and local firms can expand sales on the basis of these contacts. And, of course, there is a multiplier effect; a good contact may benefit not only the immediate recipient but also companies with ties to the favored firm.

Private connections thus lead to many marketing arrangements, but the *shōkōkai* can also find parts contracts for firms that want to move into new fields in which their network of contacts is sparse. The *shōkōkai* staff seeks to build contacts throughout Japanese industry, and it uses the resources of the prefecture to do so, matching manufacturers who have particular skills with clients who have the same needs. Moreover, the *shōkōkai* carefully keeps track of the export and extraprefectural sales of local firms. It can thus advise smaller firms, on the basis of successful experience, about how to create independent product niches in Japan and abroad.

The *shōkōkai* also provides technical support, which can range from classes in computer programming and NC use to individualized production support from specialists brought in to assist a problem company. Classes of various sorts have been held in Sakaki since at least the 1960s, and they are supplemented by frequent special presentations and seminars designed to acquaint local managers and workers with new production techniques. Instruction is extremely detailed, frequently tuned to the manufacture of specific parts that concern Sakaki enterprises. The prefecture also sponsors materials research and programming and engineering courses outside the township, at universities and colleges; Sakaki firms may attend these courses or call on the staff for help. In response to NC machinery developments the *shōkōkai* created the Sakaki Small and Medium Enterprise Skill Development Center, which offers year-round instruction in NC programming, computing skills, and general business practice. Courses for the latter half of 1984 included quality control for small firms, producing plastic parts for computers, drafting on computers, business English, tax reporting, and wholesale marketing.[16]

The *shōkōkai* has helped build a working knowledge of computers among both managers and workers, thereby raising the overall ability of the manufacturing population in the township. This training has been an important resource for firms to learn about new technology.

Because Sakaki's factories are independent (the dual structure argument does not provide an accurate account of Japanese manufacturers, as we have seen), they do not receive outside guidance for most of their manufacturing tasks.[17] A subcontractor is given a blueprint, specifications regarding tolerances, and a contract for production and delivery. All decisions about how to make the part, how to manage raw metal stock, the best programming routine for NC machinery, and even modifications to the basic design to enhance product qualities are the responsibility of the small firm itself. But though the design of cutting routines is extremely complicated machine tool manufacturers provide only a basic introductory course.[18] The *shōkōkai*'s technical support programs enhance this basic training, enabling firms to learn how to make various classes of products that they can use as reference points when programming the cutting paths for new products. *Shōkōkai*-sponsored technological training has therefore been important in giving smaller manufacturers sophisticated information, in effect by socializing the costs of training.

As a supplement to financial and technical support, the *shōkōkai* runs bankruptcy guarantee programs. Even with careful screening and substantial support, regional companies encounter cyclical and management problems that threaten their existence. To protect its reputation, and that of the township, the *shōkōkai* administers a Bankruptcy Prevention Fund (Tōsan Bōshi Shikkin) and a Factory Conversion Fund (Kōjō Iten Shikkin).[19] The Bankruptcy Fund supports smaller firms experiencing cyclical shortfalls in demand. These companies carry an especially high debt load, and short-term business interruptions can be catastrophic; the fund provides for temporary payments to cover investments until orders recover. The fund also guarantees payment to equipment suppliers and subcontractors, assuring creditors that a troubled firm will be able to meet its contracted obligations. The Factor Conversion Fund works the same way. These programs cushion vulnerable firms from the consequences of adverse market shifts.

The success of such support programs for small manufacturers is attested to by very low bankruptcy rates among firms that made investments in heavy equipment. Although statistics show a high failure rate for startup firms, regional protection funds tend to prevent outright bankruptcy for firms like those in Sakaki, preserving continuity between equipment suppliers, parts orders, and subcontractors. Of the 20,841 firms that went bankrupt in Japan in 1984, only 25 percent were in the category "Metal Industries," which includes general machining, electronics, transportation, and precision equipment, the fields that account for most of Japanese manufacturing output. Investments were higher for firms in these sectors and were protected more fully by local funds. Bankruptcies involving firms that had more than $50,000 worth of assets, the lowest possible cost for a single NC tool, amounted to less than 10 percent of total failures in all industries. Independent construction contractors—mainly labor suppliers—and service firms accounted for 81 percent of Japanese bankruptcies.[20] Such statistics show that firms with large equipment costs received heavy support, which reduces the possibility of failure due to temporary market reversals.

Indeed, bankruptcy has been quite rare in Sakaki. The number of firms in the township has declined only when companies moved to other districts, usually for lack of land.[21] *Shōkōkai* support policies have systematically enabled blue-collar workers in the township to begin independent operations and to stay in business once established. These efforts were important in the extension of NC and other advanced production technology in Sakaki. Without the *shōkōkai*'s skillful manipulation of loan sources, firms might not have been able to introduce the new technology. Education about NC machines for operators permitted the rapid deployment of advanced production technologies. And measures to ensure that startup firms would not be wiped out by cyclical reversals increased the confidence of equipment suppliers and contractors with regard to Sakaki.

The NC machinery industry demonstrates the importance of local programs in national economic developments. The JMTBA publishes an annual pamphlet entitled "Guide to Obtaining a Machine Tool."[22] This publication is almost entirely geared toward small-scale purchasers, and it lists public sources of assistance together with addresses and telephone numbers of local administrators all over Japan. Machinery producers thus encourage small and medium-sized equipment users to contact their *shōkōkai* for information about machinery financing.[23]

Thus intensive local assistance to finance equipment purchases is not limited to Sakaki; the same pattern has been documented for other areas of Nagano Prefecture. Even in the 1960s, when startup costs were not so high for metals manufacturers, Kiyonari Tadao, writing about Suwa, a large town in Nagano Prefecture, showed that localities would supplement personal savings so that an operator could purchase or lease needed machinery. As most new firms were housed in a room of an existing home or an addition to the lot, most entrepreneurs could open small manufacturing enterprises in Suwa by financing equipment purchases with local support funds.[24] Ikeda Masayoshi, in his study of Ueda and Maruko townships in Nagano, showed that in the 1970s and 1980s the introduction of new, expensive computer equipment into firms with four or fewer employees was conditioned on *shōkōkai* support. He documented ten instances of NC diffusion; in every case locally administered financial programs defrayed almost the entire cost. Ikeda concluded that only the special capital assistance programs for Japanese small and medium-sized enterprises allowed the high-tech factory revolution to happen in small-scale enterprises:

> An NC lathe costs about [$60,000] and a machining center costs [between $60,000 and $165,000]. Consequently, it is impossible for very small enterprises which rely on family labor to obtain this machinery through normal channels. As a result the vast majority of these firms obtain their capital by using such funds as the National Small and Medium Enterprise Equipment Modernization Fund, the Small and Medium Enterprise Equipment Loan System or local lending assistance, the City, Town, and Village Small and Medium Enterprise Promotion Fund, or the Equipment Fund of the People's Finance Corporation. Moreover, many of the firms are part-time farmers, and members of Agricultural Cooperative Unions, so there are cases where equipment purchases were funded by money from this institution. Thus, Japan's small and medium enterprise finance system is much more extensive than in the United States or Europe. This is especially true of equipment modernization funds, which firms may rely on through a variety of national, regional, and local programs. Consequently, even in the case of extremely small firms that have amassed no capital of their own whatsoever, obtaining very expensive machinery becomes possible. . . . By using these public financial organs, most very small firms can rely on loans to obtain NC equipment. Their reliance on personal funds approaches zero.[25]

This discussion of the *shōkōkai*'s activities may suggest that the local government, in contrast to the national bureaucracy, has significant power. Where MITI struggled for decades to reshape the economy, local officials seem to have been much more effective in inducing industrial change. Such a conclusion would tend to support the bureaucratic regulation thesis; Japanese industry was transformed because local bureaucrats guided the behavior of firms under their jurisdiction. In fact, however, the *shōkōkai* enjoys only limited authority, and its programs depend on the cooperation and support of local manufacturers.

Though the *shōkōkai* is a contact point for banks and government funding sources, its potential to regulate funding is reduced by several compensating circumstances. Indeed, the extent of local financial support is particularly pronounced in Sakaki; for Japan as a whole the percentage of manufacturers relying on such assistance is much lower, and 30–40 percent are entirely self-financed. In general the *shōkōkai*'s ability to affect regional manufacturing is slight when a large number of local firms do not rely on it for support. This is the same constraint that we saw vitiating the efforts of MITI and the *gyōkai* as they tried to coordinate machinery production in the face of "outsider" firms.

Furthermore, it is local manufacturers themselves who evaluate loan applications to the *shōkōkai*. The *shōkōkai* depends on the insight of local industrialists, and so its decisions actually reflect the market vision of local manufacturers. Indeed, the single most important item in any application is evidence of solid production contracts. In the majority of cases an applicant obtains its first orders through an existing company, usually one where the operator was an employee. The *shōkōkai* is frequently in the position of asking local firms to assess the merits of an application that they are already backing with contracts, a situation that further undercuts its independent authority.[26]

In any case, the *shōkōkai*'s activities can explain only part of the reason that Sakaki's companies grew as fast as they did. The existence of financial support programs cannot tell us why the township's manufacturers moved into machinery sectors, nor can it account for the introduction of large quantities of NC machine tools into an isolated mountain hamlet. Monetary assistance alone cannot guarantee the growth of a high-tech, small-scale manufacturing region. In an economy in which giant enterprises interact with extremely small ones to produce final goods, some means needs to be established to protect flexible enterprises from wage and profit sweating. Sakaki developed such a mechanism, which transformed it from a well-financed collection of independent factories into what can properly be called a manufacturing community, and to understand how it did so we must look to the relations between firms. NC tools were not only attractive as responses to production problems, I shall show, but also crucial in restraining wage and profit pressures that would have destroyed the emergence of flexible, high-tech manufacturers. By reducing cost pressures, in turn, Sakaki's manufacturers were enabled to implement production strategies that increased their independence.

Regionalism and Small Firms in Sakaki

Startup companies in Sakaki universally seek independence. They want a global influence over manufacturing and they are motivated by an idealized vision that helps define their strategic choices. This vision affects their involvement with other firms; it affects their equipment purchases and their factory organization. In its basic form it involves a diversification from manufacturing *single products,* through the integration of various technologies to become a supplier of *assembled parts,* and then by exploiting assembly and technical expertise to create new markets and build *finished goods.*

Most firms in Sakaki are concerned with the first stage, diversification.[27] Single-product manufacturing makes the subcontractor totally reliant on the contractor. Business cycles can thus severely hurt the firm because it produces goods for only a limited market. Manufacturers in Sakaki often learned to diversify through painful experience; one family enterprise that owned four NC lathes in 1984 nearly closed down after the first oil shock (1973), when its auto parts business disintegrated. With assistance from the *shōkōkai,* the firm diversified extensively. It now makes construction equipment parts, cylinders, aircraft parts, oil pressure gauges, and agricultural implements.[28] This kind of diversification is the norm in Sakaki. One company of twenty employees makes both dies and molds for auto use and also sophisticated camera parts. Another, a firm of just five people, makes floppy disk drive parts, keyboards, and light fiber casings in a small workshop below the owner's home. Other firms combine large-scale work on auto parts with specialty machining for the electronics and computer industries.

Diversification has a number of benefits. It prevents reliance on a single industry, so if a slump should hit one field, another line of work may carry the firm through. It also helps reduce price pressure by making it possible for a firm to decline work from undesirable contractors. Finally, firms that experiment with new goods learn to integrate technologies into new products; for a firm seeking to define its own product niche, experience with a wide range of technologies and products is essential.

But moving into new fields is not easy. If machinery is dedicated to making one product, it cannot easily be converted to make another. Nor can workers be rapidly retrained. A firm may invest in additional equipment, but the operation of the new tools will take personnel away from primary production, putting established work at risk. An ambitious subcontractor must balance existing production needs against the chance to enter a potentially lucrative market and calculate the investment risks effectively.

In an effort to solve these problems and to increase flexibility, Sakaki's firms have established a system of cooperation that enables them to bid competitively on new work. Though cooperation is a phrase often used by students of Japan, Sakaki's cooperative spirit is in fact limited.[29] When asked, company managers deny that they receive technical help from other firms or even that they meet with fellow manufacturers at all. Indeed, Sakaki companies compete strongly, using their competitors' performance as a yardstick to measure their own accomplishments.[30] Surveys tend to confirm this view. One questionnaire in 1983 sought to measure the extent to which Sakaki firms were "cooperating" in joint ventures or research. Only 5 percent of respondents said they were doing so, whereas strongly negative responses were offered by 75 percent of Sakaki's manufacturers.[31]

This interfirm competition does *not,* however, preclude strategies designed to enhance the market strength of an individual company through collective action. To reduce new product costs, Sakaki's manufacturers began to share equipment; they frequently used machines in other companies to meet production deadlines or to make products that were impossible on their own equipment.[32] The difference between this form of cooperation and joint ventures is that the planning, bidding, and ultimate responsibility for production rested entirely with the manager of the firm holding the original contract; the assisting firm often contributed nothing but equipment.

Sharing machinery helped eliminate barriers to diversification. To expand business, a firm bids for work that it may not have the capacity or even the technical ability to produce. By relying on neighbor firms, the bidding company can confidently accept an order. If meeting a deadline is a problem, the firm can satisfy its contractual obligations by borrowing a neighbor's lathe or mill. Or if new products require new techniques, a neighbor's tooling and expertise may solve the problem. So was diversification facilitated by cooperation in the use of equipment.

As cooperation grew in Sakaki, NC tools became an essential part of the township's production equipment. Indeed, NC equipment might have been invented with Sakaki in mind. NC programmability makes it possible to design different cutting patterns for a wide range of materials. Once programmed, an NC tool can work automatically, which spares scarce employees for other tasks. By increasing productivity, NC tools can alleviate some of the cost pressures involved in diversification. Finally, NC tools are ideal for cooperative production. Instead of spending costly time setting up and calibrating a neighbor's general-purpose lathe or mill, a producer can carry a cutting-path tape to another firm and immediately produce goods to specification. NC tools provide flexibility within cost tolerances while enhancing the cooperative production arrangements that are essential to Sakaki's survival.

Equipment sharing has led to a redefinition of the way contractors perceive their relationship with the township. Large firms outside the region have come to realize that an order with one of Sakaki's manufacturers is in effect guaranteed by the whole regional network of factories. Individual firms are strengthened in bargaining with potential clients because they can assure clients that contractual requirements will, one way or another, be met. Indeed, the township has come to be known as "Sakaki, Inc.," an intentional parody of the stereotype of "Japan, Inc."[33]

Contractors' perceptions brought about an increased reliance on NC tooling. Larger firms were aware that Sakaki manufacturers could use each other's equipment to meet contracts. Those with NC tools were especially flexible. So to stimulate orders, even companies that did not really need additional flexibility or accuracy obtained computerized machine tools.[34] The need to meet the sales calculations involved in contracts thus fostered NC equipment usage in Sakaki to enhance equipment sharing.

Cooperative production arrangements also helped prevent downward price and wage squeezing in Sakaki. Price pressures were a factor in production contracts, of course, but management surveys consistently show that cost concerns are less important in Sakaki than "increasing parts quality," "retaining and educating employees," "moving into new fields," and "developing new products or technology."[35] The township's subcontractors avoided excessive cost demands from much larger contractors because regional identity precluded external pressure. In essence, Sakaki's firms had a tacit agreement to support one another's resistance to cost pressures. The smallest company in the town could resist pressures from the largest firm in Japan by threatening to cut off access to all of Sakaki. As one factor operator said, "We don't tolerate any excessive pressure to cut back our prices to get work. We tell our clients that. And if any company tried to get away with it, we wouldn't work for them. Nor would anyone else around here."[36] By limiting access to the region, Sakaki's firms enforced a floor price on the work they performed.

This resolve is necessary; manufacturers know that a price breaker would devastate the financial and strategic positions of the township's firms. Most companies carry huge loads of equipment debt (because of NC purchases); they need a reasonable profit to meet payments. They can obtain an adequate return only if they bid for contracts at fair prices, but their bidding strength is supported by the ability to use the machinery of other firms and by a collective resolve to resist cost squeezes. If a price war were to erupt, the cooperative structure would vanish, leading to downward pressure on wages and profits. Companies would become insolvent, shrinking the pool of machinery available for use. Owners would have to abandon their dreams of independence and move from high-tech production to low-cost manufacturing to obtain orders. To avoid this outcome, firms collaborated to maintain price floors.

There are further reasons for the commitment to maintain wages. Sakaki's labor system is predicated on high-skill, high-wage training. Indeed, firms could not recruit skilled workers if they did not offer high-tech training that holds out the promise of independence. NC tools in the United States were seen as labor replacement devices; in Sakaki, by contrast, they were welcomed by blue-collar workers who sought training on the best equipment. Throughout Japan, in fact, NC machine tools have been employed as a recruiting aid.[37]

NC machinery actually enhanced wages, by reducing price pressures through the cooperative sharing of equipment. Moreover, the redirection of competition away from price toward product quality or unique techniques required a work force extensively trained to meet a wide variety of demands. The labor-replacement potential of NC tools was subordinated in Japan to making a rapidly changing, technically innovative line of products. Such a strategy demands highly skilled operators, and throughout Sakati Township nearly all the workers in small firms (including female workers) can operate most of the machines.[38] The balance between factory power and labor recruitment was premised on maintaining worker autonomy and skill; price wars would destroy this equilibrium and reduce management's chances of achieving independence as well.

The interfirm cooperation facilitated by NC developments limited cost threats to the growth of flexible manufacturing in Sakaki. Joint action was also an essential complement to *shōkōkai* initiatives. As a result, Sakaki transformed itself from a marginal region to a globally recognized hamlet of high-tech manufacturers. This accomplishment was predicated on manufacturers reaching an accommodation with one another regarding the sharing of production equipment and the resistance to price pressures. Moreover, the balance of power between the *shōkōkai* and private firms had to be struck so as to make financial resources available to producers without either excessive state control or ineffective market speculation. The resolution of these issues ultimately depended on ideologies and the compromises made by the affected actors.

Conclusions

Sakaki illustrates how the general political developments identified in chapter 4, coupled with regional institutions, led to the adoption of flexible production in Japan. It also shows how producer strategies led to a demand for NC machine tools unique to the country. Sakaki's growth is more or less characteristic of Nagano Prefecture and of Japan. Individual regions vary, of course, in the degree to which local authorities have been able to direct funds to prospective new firms and to which companies have been able to coordinate to avoid cost pressures. In some locations, price squeezing did emerge, and patterns consistent with the dual structure argument have become the norm. Moreover, urban areas, involving many more firms with more direct ties to large contractors, may have developed solutions less effective than in Sakaki. But the many famous small machinery hamlets in the Kansai and Kantō regions are evidence that the Sakaki model is not confined to rural cases; the dramatic trends toward independence, increased technical skill, and specialized small and medium-sized enterprise support indicate the same kind of industrial outcome in even the largest metropolitan areas.

Collectively, urban and rural industrial hamlets have changed the shape of Japanese manufacturing, leading toward a decentralized economy of great flexibility. This outcome helps account for Japanese successes in the NC machinery industry. It also has important implications for our understanding of the Japanese political economy and of policy choices in other nations.

Chapter Six

Industrial Development and Political Change

At the outset of this book I proposed to examine the development of the Japanese machinery industry in order to test the value of competing explanations for the country's economic success. The results of that examination, I claimed, would have significance not only for our understanding of the Japanese political economy but for our interpretation of industrial options elsewhere as well. In this concluding chapter I first show that neither bureaucratic regulation nor market regulation can explain the pattern of development in the Japanese machinery industry. A consistent account can be achieved only by viewing developments in the sector as the product of political events throughout Japanese society and industry. Politics (in the sense used throughout this book) can change the character of a nation's industrial system. Even when resources and market constraints are similar, different political contingencies can produce a national economy organized toward flexible production *or* toward mass production. The idea that economic practices are limited by efficiency constraints alone, an assumption crucial to bureaucratic and market theories alike, is not supported. This finding highlights the limitations of conventional business-state analyses and of market explanations of differentials in international economic performance.

The Japanese case disconfirms not only theories of industrial development but also policies based on those theories. I focus on American experience because U.S. industrial initiatives, whether by firms or by national actors, offer a particularly clear example of strategies that seek primarily to enhance mass production efficiency. In current international markets, I will argue, such policies are very likely to fail, because they do little to stimulate, indeed may preclude, the flexible manufacturing option. Though American industrialists and policy makers often point to Japan in support of their vision of what should be done to stimulate growth, the Japanese case actually illustrates why current American strategies are likely to be ineffective.

Japan and the Bureaucratic and Market Regulation Theses

In previous chapters I have discussed at length the industrial behavior associated with developments in the Japanese machinery industry. Throughout the industry's history there has been extremely rapid firm entry into promising market segments. This market volatility results from the desire of machinery manufacturers to employ imported or domestically enhanced technologies to make new products. In turn, there has been strong demand for new machinery; by the 1970s, in particular, Japanese machinery users wanted smaller, sophisticated, NC manufacturing equipment. The interplay between unique product demand and the ability of Japanese producers to meet the needs of their customers led to the widespread introduction of special NC machine tools in the domestic economy. Then NC machinery was exported to countries that had overlooked or ignored the potential demand for small-scale machinery, which enabled Japanese manufacturers to exploit unique market niches profitably.

Bureaucratic Regulation

The bureaucratic regulation thesis is not able to explain the behavior of Japanese machinery firms, as chapters 2 and 3 showed. Indeed, from the 1930s onward the bureaucracy attempted to implement policies that would have reversed almost all of the activities associated with the rapid growth of the machine tool industry. In the prewar period the Machine Tool Industry Law and the *tōseikai* scheme attempted to limit the number of firms that could build machinery, generating economies of scale. These policies were failures. After the war MITI tried to promote consolidation, cartels, scale economies, and stable markets with various Special Measures laws. Its efforts did not transform the industry. Nor was private coordination successful; *gyōkai* production restraint programs failed to reduce firm entry or limit product development.

The idea that bureaucratic control fostered advances in efficiency rests partially on the assumption that the Japanese state could effectively plan and implement policies that changed the market behavior of firms. In the machine tool case, however, the state exhibited neither the ability to plan effectively or independently nor the capacity to force private interests into compliance. Furthermore, the pattern of development among machinery producers calls into question another assumption of the bureaucratic regulation thesis, that efficiency advances were the source of Japan's competitive advantage. Instead, consolidation schemes almost always gave way to strategies that facilitated production flexibility. In sum, the bureaucratic regulation thesis does not accurately describe Japanese economic organization, and it fails to provide a satisfactory account for the nation's economic successes.

Why, then, has the characterization of Japan as a "strong" or interventionist state enjoyed such wide acceptance? Part of the reason is that the methodological shortcomings of studies adopting the bureaucratic regulation thesis produce a tendency to confuse the promulgation of a policy with the policy's effectiveness. One good example is the machinery "cartel" episode of the 1960s. The cartels organized as part of MITI's countermeasures to trade liberalization have been portrayed as a success: researchers generally assumed that if MITI authorized cartelization, then the policy must have been carried out. But these "cartels," as we saw in chapter 3, were actually intended to *block* the bureaucracy's consolidation plan while satisfying the minimum requirements for obtaining support for demand stimulation. More generally, policy goals have not been compared to market outcomes in such a way that the government's effect upon the economy can be adequately assessed. On closer inspection, industrial policies that appeared at first blush to support the bureaucratic regulation thesis often flatly refute it.

The same problem exists in other cases. First, let us consider automobile industrial policy. Both the auto and the machinery industries involve shaping and combining metals, plastics, and other components to make sophisticated products. Also, traditional *zaibatsu* influence was low in the prewar auto industry, as in the machine tool case, and automobile sales registered exceptional gains only after the mid-1960s; exports did not become important until the late 1970s. These similarities make it no surprise that industrial policy for the auto sector was quite close to that for the machinery industry.

Prewar policies focused around a special industry law passed in 1936. Though intended to consolidate and coordinate vehicle production, the law was in fact dominated in its implementation by Toyota and Nissan. Both firms used financial programs intended to facilitate consolidation in order to fund individual corporate projects, and the MCI was unable to stop them. During the war, just as in the machinery case, automobile firms administered and controlled their own *tōseikai.*[1] One consequence we saw in chapter 2: even wartime objectives for the military transportation equipment were adversely affected by the individual calculations of *tōseikai* members.

Postwar support began with financial assistance; as in the machinery case, government-sponsored loans from the JDB defrayed a small fraction of overall capital costs. It is clear, however, that only the Korean War, which brought windfall American orders for trucks, ended the recession in the auto industry.[2] Japanese automotive firms were enabled to self-finance or borrow to pay for additional expansion.

The most significant episode in automobile policy occurred in connection with MITI's capital liberalization strategies of the 1960s. As we have seen, the bureaucracy felt that consolidation was the only effective means of preparing domestic producers for what it expected to be severe foreign competition in Japanese markets. But emergency laws giving MITI authority to dictate mergers were conclusively defeated in the mid-1960s. The bureaucracy tried to realize its objectives through other means. It tried to promote mergers between key producers in the auto industry to enhance scale economies; its goals were identical to those in the machinery cartel scheme.

To accomplish consolidation, MITI set up a special loan fund in the JDB to reward auto firms that merged according to plan.[3] Several consolidation schemes were proposed. First, there was a two-firm concept in which all auto companies would consolidate behind Nissan and Toyota. Severe opposition from the auto firms and their leading banks killed the proposal. Next, MITI attempted to implement a three-firm concept in which Toyota, Nissan, and a third new company (a combination of Toyo Kogyo, Fuji, and Isuzu) would make up the entire Japanese auto industry. Once again interfirm politics and banking interference led to the abandonment of the scheme. Finally, new combinations of companies making up the third firm in the three-group plan were discussed, but all of them failed because there was no agreement regarding which firms would be the dominant force in the consolidated industry.

The failures of these structural reorganization schemes were a much publicized embarrassment to MITI. The bureaucracy's weakness was further exploited when Nissan bought up struggling Prince Motors in 1966. MITI had opposed a Nissan/Prince merger on the grounds that it would not lead to the real integration envisioned by the consolidation program. Nissan nevertheless compelled the bureaucracy to provide an $11.1 million loan from the reserved JDB funds to "reward" the merger. The Nissan/Prince merger, sometimes presented as evidence of state control of the automobile industry, was actually a defeat for the bureaucracy. And afterward the JDB loan scheme and merger policy were abandoned. Not only had they not enhanced industrial consolidation, but new entrants, such as Suzuki and Honda, further fragmented the auto industry.

Automobile trade policy also illustrates how private firms thwarted or even reversed the deeply held objectives of bureaucrats. The primary goal of MITI's capital liberalization countermeasures was to prevent foreign ownership of domestic firms. Automobile producers attracted special attention because of the importance of transportation manufacturing in the economy. But in 1969 Mitsubishi Motors announced it would open a new auto manufacturing facility owned jointly with America's Chrysler. The bureaucracy, powerless to prevent Mitsubishi from carrying out its plans, was forced to carry out a hasty and very public redefinition of its foreign capital policies to align them with what *private* firms sought.[4]

These key episodes in automobile industrial policy disconfirm the bureaucratic regulation thesis. Prewar industrial policy was as ineffective in automobiles as it was in machinery. After the war capital liberalization countermeasures failed to induce consolidation; mergers that did result were neither planned by MITI nor effective in producing economies of scale. Even policies regulating foreign contacts, where the nationalism found in much of Japanese society probably maximized bureaucratic influence, were no barrier to the interests of private firms. The automobile case provides additional evidence of the bureaucracy's inability to regulate industrial outcomes in Japan.

Next, let us consider banking, and in particular the regulatory initiatives undertaken in the 1960s, when structural reforms and recovery policies were at their height. Private banks had expanded loans so rapidly that they were forced to draw additional funds from the central Bank of Japan (BOJ), which was controlled by the Ministry of Finance. This condition was referred to as an "overloan." Proponents of the bureaucratic regulation thesis have argued that Japanese bank regulators in this period directed loans to "key" industries chosen by the bureaucracy. The Ministry of Finance, they claim, was able to direct capital to selected industries because the banks, forced to rely on overloans to meet their lending obligations, were vulnerable to pressure from the BOJ.[5]

Overloan politics and the details of financial planning, however, contradict the bureaucratic regulation argument. If overloans were the source of the Ministry of Finance's regulatory power, and if the bureaucracy actually wanted to coordinate private lending, then we should expect to see overloans being actively promoted. However, from 1960, when the economy entered its high-speed growth period and overloans became common, the Ministry of Finance repeatedly tried to *abolish* the practice. In 1962, in fact, a new bond financing system was introduced to do away with overloans entirely; the BOJ would float public debentures to raise necessary capital. Overloans persisted, however, because they benefited *private* banks and borrowers.[6] The bureaucracy's attitude to the source of its hypothetical power—overloans—does not square with the bureaucratic regulation thesis.

Furthermore, if the bureaucracy were directing investment to key sectors, then the institutions associated with bank planning should have effectively influenced lending patterns in Japan. Banking regulation was first attempted in the Investment Finance Committee (IFC) of the Ministry of Finance between 1950 and 1968. The IFC was thereafter incorporated into the Industrial Rationalization Council (IRC) set up by MITI in the mid-1960s.[7] The IFC and the IRC were supposed to be institutions in which industrialists, bankers, and bureaucrats developed plans for coordinated investment and industrial growth. Did these committees in fact coordinate the allocation of capital?

The answer is that financial coordination was ineffective. The IFC was supposed to have produced one-year investment plans coordinating banking outlays with investment needs in industry, but in reality IFC plans had little effect on lending patterns. In the one-year period of the 1961 plan, for instance, lenders missed allocation targets by an average of nearly 6 percent in most industries and by 11 percent (cement) and 21 percent (paper) in others. In 1962 industries for which planned investment targets were missed by over 10 percent included petroleum, petrochemicals, ammonium sulfate, electronics, and paper, and in 1963 the average variance from targets was again 6 percent. The IFC never influenced financial allocation with any precision even within a one-year period; the wide discrepancies between planned and actual allocations indicate instead that banks made loans according to their own criteria.

The IRC was also ineffective. MITI incorporated the IFC into its rationalization program in the late 1960s to coordinate funding. Banks and industrialists treated the IRC as merely a forecasting service, duplicating the Economic Planning Agency and the JDB. In fact, when MITI spotted discrepancies between "planned" investment documents put out by the IFC and actual outlays, it was the amounts on the *planning* documents which were changed. The committee exercised no effective influence on private investment.

Banking, in sum, provides another example of government initiatives that apparently support the bureaucratic regulation thesis but actually cut against the argument. The bureaucracy opposed over-loans, undermining the supposed basis of its influence in Japanese banking. Moreover, it was unable to institute planning committees that could realize its objectives. These failures are consonant with what we have already observed in fiscal planning and policy implementation in the machine tool industry.

Finally, consider the Japanese oil industry. The Japanese energy sector raises acute problems for the bureaucratic regulation thesis. In most countries the government plays a direct, active role in petroleum development and allocation because the oil industry is of paramount importance to the national economy. But the Japanese state actually has *less* public presence in oil than any other major industrial power except the United States.[8] If Japan is a strong state, why has its bureaucracy been unable to achieve the degree of coordination exhibited by much weaker states? The reason is that private companies have frustrated government initiatives since before the war. The petroleum industry was the first industry licensed under the specific industry control laws of the 1930s. MCI policies were sacrificed to the private interests of the petroleum firms; even in wartime the oil industry resisted consolidation while receiving heavy subsidies.[9]

In the postwar period the attempt to consolidate the oil industry stands out as one of MITI's greatest policy failures. MITI first sought to enhance market coordination by creating a state oil company, a policy successfully pursued in most European countries. In 1955, partially because of the desire of "outsider" petroleum interests for a foothold in the market, the bureaucracy was able to create a state oil interest, called JAPEX. However, the recalcitrance of established oil interests severely restricted the scope of JAPEX. At best the company accounted for less than 2 percent of total Japanese demand, and its output never reached more than 50 percent of the amounts targeted. Ultimately Japanese oil firms, shareholders in the venture, abandoned their stake to cripple any further encroachment by JAPEX into their markets.[10]

Between 1961 and 1967 the creation of a new state oil company was proposed in connection with a planned Petroleum Industry Law, which MITI intended to consolidate the petroleum industry. Again the opposition of private firms, together with reservations voiced by other branches of the bureaucracy, led to difficulties. MITI did secure the promulgation of the law, but only after its plans for a state company had been eliminated. Later MITI would once again seek to expand its influence in the oil industry by creating a state equity institution that would hold shares in private firms, leading, it was hoped, to greater state control. The Ministry of Finance, fearing that

MITI might encroach into the financial sector, and petroleum firms vetoed the proposal. As Richard Samuels observes, the MOF "was willing to increase the JAPEX budget in the 1960s but it refused to accept the creation of a new public [equity] agency. Private industry was willing to accept new public funds but it resisted new public controls."[11]

Faced with strong bureaucratic and private opposition to its plans, MITI settled for the creation of the Japan Petroleum Development Corporation in 1967. MITI's original objective had been to coordinate petroleum production directly, through a state company. Then it tried to secure an equity position in private firms. Its final achievement, the Japan Petroleum Development Corporation, was permitted to do little more than provide exploration and drilling support for private firms. Existing companies used the corporation to defray their own research and development costs.

In oil MITI ultimately accepted the reverse of what it had initially sought. Though Japan is conventionally classified as a strong state, policy outcomes in its oil industry most closely resemble those in the United States, a very weak state. Like results in other sectors, the policy record in energy strongly disconfirms the bureaucratic regulation thesis. The government neither planned effectively nor possessed the power to shape the behavior of private firms. As in autos, banking, and machine tools, so in oil: policies suggesting state influence in fact masked government weakness.

Findings in the machine tool industry appear to be supported by a cursory examination of evidence from other sectors. If, then, the bureaucratic regulation thesis is incorrect, what should be our response? One possibility is to argue that we have made a *coding* error: Japan is not a strong state, and we need to categorize it so as to encompass both bureaucratic adventurism and significant constraints from private interests. This response would generate valuable research. However, it would ignore the more serious challenges the Japanese case poses to the basic concepts that inform the attempt to compare and classify business-state relations.

The study of political economy enjoyed a considerable revival in the 1970s and 1980s when economic dislocations demonstrated that industrial expansion could not be taken for granted; in an era in which most economies seemed moribund, observers sought for the social and political prerequisites for sustained growth. From this general perspective emerged an especially influential conviction: countries at different stages of development may require different degrees of state intervention. Another belief also gained currency: that certain forms of bureaucratic regulation could in the long run make a nation's economy more efficient. The perception of Japan as a strong state resulted from this approach. More generally, scholars tried to connect particular forms of state intervention to economic efficiency in different states.

This research scheme brought students of political economy to accept that politics in some form could affect industrial performance, but the degree to which political actions might affect economic change was nevertheless thought to be quite limited. The bureaucratic regulation thesis accepted a model of industrial development from neoclassical economists. Economic development is, in effect, a Darwinian struggle among producers who gradually discover and implement the most efficient practices. The process underlying industrial change was apolitical. But the state, it was thought, could adopt policies that would make producers more or less likely to apprehend more efficient techniques. In this view politics—the actions of the state in setting rules or allocating resources—can affect only the *speed* with which efficiency breakthroughs are made.

Comparative research in political economy was often refined to the coding of different forms of state regulation and the attempt to show which practices best enhanced efficiency. The problem, however, and one that the Japanese case highlights, is that politics may be much more significant than the conventional research scheme admits. The Japanese case demonstrates that significant political events affecting industrial development may not involve the state at all, but rather are shaped by worker ideologies, interfirm cooperation, and the like. The political resolution of conflicts in these areas may often be of importance equal to or greater than that of state actions. Moreover, politics can reshape a nation's economy by creating or destroying incentives to adopt different forms of production; its effects are considerably more important than merely regulating the speed of efficiency advances.

If my findings are correct, then the dominant business-state analytical scheme may frequently be irrelevant. It may also subtly distort our perceptions of political influence on industrial choice.

The preoccupation with classifying the character of business-state relations is irrelevant if government activities are at best one of many political influences on the economy and frequently among the least significant. Even when a state possesses a coherent policy, a comparatively rare case, we would be unable to assess the policy's economic results unless we understand the resolution of political conflicts elsewhere in society. The importance of state policies by themselves, and the implications of business-state relations in general, cannot be evaluated without situating them in the larger political context that surrounds industrial activity.

In Japan, for instance, the fact that capital markets were redirected toward smaller firms tells us little about the country's industrial organization in the absence of an awareness of politics between workers, between firms, and in regions. Policy might have induced large firms to force their subcontractors to accept the dual structure, with new, specialized loan programs defraying small-firm costs. The broader context, however, was shaped by the politics of worker careers, subcontractor coordination, regionalism, and the like, and so created opportunities for small-scale producers to claim independence through flexible manufacturing. State financial support in fact became part of a process in which the dual structure was rolled back. Indeed, as I argued in chapter 4, political events unrelated to the bureaucracy's initiatives generated a momentum so great that the dual structure would probably have been eroded even without state intervention in capital markets. In this example, government activity was only a part, and arguably not an especially important part, of a profound transformation of Japanese manufacturing which was rooted in politics. If one objective of political economic research is to understand the interplay between politics and industrial change, a single focus on business-state relations may well direct attention away from more significant research topics.

The preoccupation with developing categories for comparative business-state relations can also be misleading, because it subtly reinforces what may be an inaccurate picture of the influence politics can exert on industrial change. Japanese research in particular, and government and industry studies in general, have been shaped by the often implicit conviction that politics can affect only the speed of economic development. Indeed, business-state analysis is frequently undertaken to show that particular national policy styles produce efficiency gains.

Japan provides compelling evidence that this view is far too limited; political outcomes throughout society can transform a nation's economy completely. We are all, to some extent, prisoners of the categories and terminology we employ, however, and the attempt to describe Japanese government-industry interaction more accurately runs the risk of reaffirming implicit beliefs about politics and economic change which Japan's industrial experiences directly challenge.

I do not imply that researchers cannot focus on one political economic issue -government-business relations—without recognizing the limits of their study. Nor am I arguing that understanding and categorizing business-state relations are without value. Obviously there are many interesting questions and issues that can be resolved only by understanding bureaucracies and categorizing state institutions. But I do believe that a preoccupation with the character of state intervention can seriously distort research about politics and economic change. It is difficult to write within a tradition that treats "politics" as state activity alone and simultaneously accept that events elsewhere in society are equally political. Nor is it a simple matter to adopt a research agenda that has traditionally viewed politics as having only a limited effect on economic change and at the same time recognize that political conflict can profoundly transform industrial organization.

The results of this tension are exhibited in much of today's comparative research: arguments that purport to account for economic differentials by referring to the character of state intervention but that actually employ much of what I call politics as additional, necessary explanations. Indeed, Japanese business-state research is itself an excellent example of analytical preconceptions leading to significant misapprehensions about a country's industrial regulation. To respond to criticisms of the bureaucratic regulation thesis by simply reclassifying Japanese business-state relations would thus be an inadequate response. Rather, it is important to recognize that the Japanese case directly questions the reasons for attempting to characterize government-industry interaction in the first place.

Ultimately Japan sustains the idea that we must address politics throughout society if we are to assess a country's economic change. That is, the subject of political economy research should be broadened. Furthermore, we must recognize that the consequences of the specific political circumstances in each country will be to create more incentives to adopt either mass or flexible production. The range of possible outcomes is, in sum, greater than efficiency differentials alone. Such observations may preclude the creation of simple, precise theories of political and economic change, but the choice we are offered may be between theoretical parsimony achieved at the cost of comprehension and a less elegant but more insightful method.

Market Regulation

The Japanese case also poses problems for the market regulation thesis. The market approach, as we have seen, can explain Japanese industrial outcomes only if it can be assumed that market or resource constraints tightly shape economic behavior. If this is so, then the structure of Japanese industry, the character of machinery demand, and the responses of machinery producers can be interpreted as the "natural" consequence of market forces. But if, instead, efficiency constraints in Japan are looser, admitting of several possible responses, then a market explanation is at best incomplete, for we still require an account of the reasons why actual choices are made. Selection among industrial options must be a function of the power relations and ideologies of affected individuals or groups, I have argued; in short, it is *political* in nature. Any explanation of Japan's successes needs to focus on the politics that *created* the markets and market capacities of producers and consumers rather than on the market itself.

In the Japanese case, material and resource constraints did not determine the character and growth of manufacturing industries. Japanese industrialists, policy makers, workers, and regional authorities might have adopted a variety of responses to international and domestic circumstances. Indeed, the economy very nearly developed along dual structure lines in the 1950s, but instead political conflict and compromise among industrialists, government actors, laborers, and regions enhanced the role of flexible manufacturers in the economy.

This enhancement of flexible manufacturing in Japan helps in turn explain such successes as machinery. The structure of market demand for new NC machine tools and the capacity of Japanese machinery firms to compete vigorously and supply required equipment can be comprehended only in the context of the transformation of Japanese manufacturing. Japanese machinery users sought to employ new NC equipment because political circumstances (financial allocation, worker career expectations, small- and large-firm coordination, and regionalism) expanded opportunities for flexible production. The consequence was a large and growing market for special, high-tech machinery. Japanese machine tool makers could enter the market with new technology to try to meet the machinery demand from small firms because they too could take advantage of politically generated incentives for flexible manufacturing. Capital opportunities, large- and small-firm coordination, and regional cooperation affected the ability of often very small machinery firms to exploit new ideas or techniques and build unique products. Japanese machinery successes, therefore, cannot be comprehended without reference to the politics that have shaped Japanese industrial development.

Consider first how expanded opportunities for small-scale flexible producers in Japan after the 1950s created a unique Japanese market *demand*, especially for new, smaller NC products. NC machinery was especially suited to the production strategies and interfirm cooperation pursued by small-scale manufacturers seeking independence.

Such equipment was reprogrammable, with the general-purpose flexibility needed for continuous product development. It was also highly accurate, enhancing quality while providing even the smallest family operation with the ability to make extremely sophisticated goods. Finally, NC tooling, with its cutting path tapes, made it possible for one firm to use another firm's equipment to meet unforeseen output or new product requirements.

Unique machinery markets, therefore, were generated to the extent that the Japanese economy encouraged smaller, flexible producers. But the ability of smaller firms to become flexible, and to introduce new machinery, was conditioned on broader political circumstances. The politics of financial allocation, for instance, made it possible for potential users to purchase the equipment they sought. Even the smallest flexible factories could afford NC equipment, because national financial institutions existed to support the capital needs of small firms. Furthermore, as we saw in the case of Sakaki, the use of NC tooling was greatly stimulated by the regional practice of sharing machinery to advance into new markets and to reduce cost pressures from large firms. Small factories seeking to operate as independent high-tech manufacturers had to reach some accommodation between their individual corporate goals and the larger objectives better served by some degree of interfirm cooperation. Institutions and ideologies facilitating regional coordination were adopted, and the technical capacities of NC equipment meshed perfectly with small-firm strategies. Also, the search by blue-collar workers in small firms for eventual status as managers or independent producers, again a politically contingent event, promoted NC use; workers sought training on the most advanced machinery.

Because flexible producers were a significant force in the manufacturing economy, they stimulated unique demand for new NC equipment. But, as I have argued, the growth of flexible manufacturers was predicated on political events; their expansion was not inevitable. Different approaches to subcontractor coordination by large contractors, different ideologies regarding acceptable work conditions, and different abilities to foster regional cooperation might well have entrenched the dual structure. Small firms in Japan would have been closely integrated into the mass production network of large firms, and they would have sought much more specialized, single-purpose machinery to reduce the costs of standardized components. It was because political circumstances forestalled the dual structure that subcontractors could achieve a measure of independence through flexible production. And it was this development that stimulated demand for new machinery.[12]

Machinery *supply* was also conditioned by political factors. In chapter 4 I showed that the transformation of relations between large and small firms after the 1950s led to the decentralization of large firms and to new opportunities to create smaller, independent factories. To permit experimentation in factory organization, large firms created subsidiaries that were expected to become autonomous over time. At the same time they encouraged startup enterprises run by former blue-collar employees from small firms. These broad trends affected the growth of the Japanese machine tool industry. The best example of large-firm decentralization enhancing NC machinery expansion was, as we saw in chapter 4, the case of Fanuc. Fanuc was established by Fujitsu in the late 1950s; by the 1970s it had become completely independent. Its creation was important because the firm gave pioneer developers of Japanese small-scale NC machinery a continuity in basic controller design.[13] The small-scale flexible machinery users could not afford to develop or learn new manufacturing techniques with each piece of machinery, as was normal practice in the United States. Standard data entry protocols and controls were essential, and in the early phase of NC development, Fanuc, then the world's only dedicated NC controller producer, provided them. As a result, sophisticated manufacturing techniques could be supplied more readily to the smaller consumers of flexible equipment.

The same political factors that generated incentives toward flexible manufacturing in the economy as a whole also helped produce the rapid market entry and technological diffusion characteristic of Japanese machinery successes. Indeed, though several machinery firms had grown quite large by the late 1970s, only former *zaibatsu* affiliates had not been small producers at one time. In particular, many of the most important NC makers, among them Mori Seiki and Matsuura, a specialist in NC machining centers, had been very small subcontractor firms as late as the mid-1970s.

The capacity of Japanese machinery producers to organize new firms and enter promising markets was facilitated by the institutions and financial innovations associated with the transformation of Japanese manufacturing. Because the Japanese context in effect reduced the risks and costs associated with entering new markets or exploiting undeveloped technical ideas, entrepreneurial machinery firms could enter the NC market rapidly. The result was the market fragmentation and volatility noted in chapter 3: as firms reduced machinery size, developed new tool changers, and modified programming and other tooling parameters, NC market shares shifted. Indeed, so dramatic was the capacity to create new firms marketing unique products that foreign machine tool designers often came to Japan to manufacture ideas spurned in their own countries. Some machinery designs ignored abroad were built by very small Japanese firms such as Matsuura and Mori Seiki and exported successfully.[14] The ability to build and market small-scale NC tools was thus conditioned on the enhanced opportunities for flexible production that machinery builders and equipment consumers enjoyed.[15]

The dynamism of the Japanese machinery industry, then, must be understood in the context of the political events that promoted flexible manufacturing more generally. We can appreciate further this correspondence between industrial organization and machinery development with reference to the manufacturing strategies of U.S. and Japanese producers. The machine tool case provides an important test of explanations for Japanese success, I argued in chapter 1, because it provides a glimpse of the entire character of a national economy. In an ideal-typical world the machine tool industry would be organized according to manufacturing principles *inversely* related to the production strategy dominant in the economy as a whole. In a purely mass production economy, for instance, machinery would be so specialized that machine tool firms would have to make each tool separately, through craft techniques. In an economy of flexible small firms, by contrast, demand for general-purpose machines that permit rapid product shifts would be paramount. The machinery industry would make standard goods for use by flexible producers.

The relationship between the character of a nation's economy and its machine tool industry is indeed supported by developments in both the United States and Japan. Japanese NC tools are more standardized, general-purpose equipment; American firms tend to build highly specialized machinery. Indeed, many Japanese machine tool manufacturers build general purpose machinery in production runs and lot sizes that are from ten to one hundred times greater than those of firms in the United States.[16] They do so by building basic machine tool components in larger volumes and then augumenting these parts with specialized equipment purchased from outside vendors. In its main factory in Nara, for instance, Mori Seiki, Japan's largest NC lathe maker, concentrates on producing metal machine tool support frames. Most of the other parts, such as NC controllers, motors, air pressure equipment, and the like, it buys from subcontractors.[17] In contrast, American firms typically build NC machinery as one-of-a-kind equipment for use by mass or specialized producers. That Japanese firms build general-purpose NC machinery, unlike their counterparts in the United States, confirms the idea that flexible manufacturing has been more widely adopted in Japan.

The market behavior of Japanese machinery firms was intimately related to the growth of flexible production in the economy. Political circumstances not only generated a large group of small-scale firms seeking new equipment, they also affected the ability of Japanese machinery makers to meet their customers' needs. The structure of market demand and the capacity of Japanese producers to meet market imperatives, then, were preconditioned on the political transformation of the economy described throughout this book.

This finding illustrates the limitations of the market approach in explaining Japanese industrial development. Indeed, the very idea of a "market explanation" in the Japanese context is somewhat deceptive. In market theory, industrial outcomes are a function of competition generating efficient solutions to market imperatives. In Japan, however, we cannot define market demand or the capacities of machinery firms to meet demand without considering the political factors that shaped the economy. Consequently, a full account of Japanese machinery successes must refer to political factors in order to specify the character of the market itself. The market approach offers at best an insufficient method for discussing comparative economic performance.

To the extent that the market approach implies that industrial outcomes were all the product of efficiency pressures, moreover, it can be misleading. Markets are, in a fundamental sense, responses to ambiguous material circumstances. To provide a way of structuring action, industrial actors have to formulate ideas about proper economic behavior. The development of these ideas is politics; we saw the process at work in Japan during the prewar struggles between the military and small producers, and in the postwar definition of workplace morality, small-firm coordination, and regional cooperation. Once and if basic conceptions and rules regarding economic activity are fixed, it makes sense to talk about industrial outcomes as a function of the market. Where market ambiguity exists, however, a market explanation *conceals* the political roots of choice by suggesting that all results were inevitably produced by the rational enhancement of manufacturing efficiency.[18]

Market analysis can, of course, be extremely valuable in treating questions that do not implicate the basic market structure of an economy. Market studies have taught us a great deal about human behavior in certain contexts. But the explanation of international and historical performance must directly address the source of an economy's fundamental organization and so makes apparent the limitations and dangers of the market explanation.[19] The Japanese case shows that because there is no necessary congruence between "objective" material or resource constraints and outcome, market theory can say little about the way economies are structured. In sum, the market approach suggests a degree of continuity and absence of choice contradicted by Japanese experiences. Market explanations are of limited utility in explaining comparative performance because a considerable range of industrial outcomes can result even when resource or material constraints are similar. In the Japanese case, at least, the political sources of the market are important to understanding why the nation's economy grew so rapidly.

Competing Explanations for Japanese Success

In sum, a coherent account of Japanese industrial successes during the nation's high-growth period must make explicit reference to the politics structuring industrial behavior at all levels of the economy. Such an analysis indicates that Japanese achievements were due to the enhancement of flexible production in the country, permitting rapid product innovation and product competition in global markets. The case of Japan thus sustains the argument that the convergence hypotheses underlying both the bureaucratic regulation thesis and the market regulation thesis are mistaken. Material constraints cannot explain much about Japanese practices, and politics can transform a nation's economy as well as simply enhancing efficiency.

The alternative theoretical position, drawn from the work of Michael Piore and Charles Sabel, enjoys several advantages over both regulation theories. First, it directs research toward frequently ignored or misinterpreted areas of the Japanese economy because it rejects the notion that efficiency advances alone determine comparative economic performance. Furthermore, it suggests that politics is much more than just the actions of the state. Guided by these ideas, I have shown, for instance, that Japanese firms competed as much through product differentiation as through price; that conventional approaches have significantly misstated the role of Japanese small manufacturers in the economy and the power of the government; and that regions of small-scale firms in isolated mountain areas have played an unexpectedly large role in the high-tech resurgence of Japanese manufacturing.

Second, this approach offers an intellectually honest treatment of the political background factors that structure economic relationships. As I argued above, studies guided by either the bureaucratic regulation or the market regulation thesis need to be supplemented with additional explanations; indeed, this problem characterizes much of the literature in comparative political economics. The difficulty with such supplementary explanations lies in the profound tension that exists between the argument that particular outcomes result from certain factors and the need to offer additional explanations to account satisfactorily for any given case.

The alternative is to recognize at the outset that the politics affecting industrial change is, fundamentally, not reducible to a simplified, comprehensive theory. We cannot predict outcomes from structural or material conditions because politics at all levels of society conditions industrial strategies in unpredictable ways. The drawback to such a view is, of course, that it reduces ability to relate causal variables to specific outcomes. However, the comparative analysis of political economic systems is a problem in which attempts to create overarching explanation where none is possible can be more detrimental than the lack of a predictive theory. Indeed, as I have shown, widely accepted theoretical traditions have misjudged or ignored many important features of the Japanese economy. We need to trade scientific precision for the ability to interpret and account for comparative industrial development.

Finally, the alternative approach makes it possible to offer a new empirical explanation for Japanese success. Japan's high growth rate from the late 1950s to the mid-1970s was at least in part a product of competitive advantages resulting from increased opportunities to adopt flexible production. In the machine tool case, demand for new NC tools, the ability of machinery firms to build new equipment, and successes in international markets with unique goods were all based on the expansion of flexible manufacturers. Of course, in some industries price competition may well have been more important. By the mid-1980s, moreover, the high-growth pattern I described in chapters 4 and 5 may well have changed, affecting both the character of Japanese production and the nation's comparative performance.[20] Nevertheless, in automobiles, machinery, electronics, and other industries that were central to postwar Japanese achievements, the extensive adoption of flexible manufacturing enhanced Japan's competitive advantage.

This finding requires revision of the interpretation of the influences the Japanese government wields in the economy. At the same time, it exposes the limits of market explanations. It also shows the potential vitality of economic alternatives to mass production. My findings therefore affect more than our understanding of Japan or of theory development; they bear directly on interpretations of our own industrial options.

Japan, Flexible Production, and Economic Policy

My findings about Japanese economic experience affect how we understand our own circumstances. Japanese experiences do not support dominant ideas about why U.S manufacturing growth has been so poor or the strategies usually proposed to rectify the problem. American "industrial policy"—both government initiatives and the strategies of private industrialists—is likely to lead to continued adjustment difficulties, I shall suggest, because it does not adequately understand the value and genesis of flexible production under contemporary market conditions. Theoretical misperception can lead to ineffective policy.

American manufacturing during the Japanese high-growth period was in trouble; U.S. output growth was among the lowest of all industrial countries in the 1960s and 1970s, and by the mid-1980s nearly 110,000 manufacturing jobs were being lost each month.[21] The reasons for American difficulties have attracted considerable discussion, but there has been a substantial degree of congruence between apparently contradictory views. American industrial thought has been deeply influenced by what I have called convergence theory. Most government and industry observers tend to assume that international competition is an efficiency race; to succeed, a nation must match or exceed the efficiency standards set by the leading producers. Conversely, industrial failure is an inability to meet efficiency challenges. This general agreement concerning the fundamental nature of industrial development and U.S. problems has been masked by considerable debate over specific, appropriate responses.

Consider first the conventional interpretation of why American manufacturing performed poorly. The basic explanation is that U.S. producers did not implement the most effective and efficient techniques. At one time American industry was the global efficiency leader and thus prospered. Other nations, including Japan, rapidly "caught up"; they became able to produce goods at lower costs. At the broadest level there is agreement that each nation's economy is, in a sense, an efficiency machine dedicated to producing the lowest-cost goods; the American economic machine has, so to speak, been made obsolete by more advanced designs.

This basic understanding has led American policy makers in government and industry to try to isolate particular responses that might stimulate U.S. manufacturers to achieve global efficiency levels. The question most analysts ask is, What can the U.S. state or private industrialists do to rebuild American manufacturing and increase efficiency? It embraces the notion that efficiency advances are the principal basis of international competition. Particular policy responses differ mainly in the means suggested to increase American industrial efficiency.

In the realm of government policy, for instance, people who view the state as an essential player in promoting manufacturing advances have argued that American institutions must be modified to permit the state activism presumed to have been helpful in Japan.[22] Others, in consonance with the market approach, have come to precisely the opposite conclusion; they believe that government interference in the economy has distorted the market and reduced the implementation of efficient practices. One version insists that the state reject social demands that adversely affect production costs; for instance, the government should reduce its enforcement of pollution controls or minimum wage legislation. Another suggests that the state permit or enhance "natural" economic behavior through such policies as encouraging private savings or relaxing antitrust laws to permit the degree of market concentration and scale economies associated with rapid growth elsewhere.[23] A third approach argues that if all nations competed fairly, American firms would be competitive. Foreign trade restrictions and illegal subsidies therefore account for market reversals, and the government should protect domestic firms and punish American trading partners to equalize the position of U.S. producers in global competition.[24]

Private-sector initiatives reflect a similar diversity. In the wake of American manufacturing reversals, a considerable literature was generated arguing that U S. management techniques, corporate planning strategies, labor relations, and the like account for poor performance. Many observers argued that reform of industrial practices would put the United States back on track.[25] Another private reaction was that American factor costs, especially wage rates, were too high and that consequently U.S. goods were too expensive. Acting on this belief, producers sought to compensate by moving their plants to low-wage, anti-union states, employing foreign laborers, and moving operations abroad. Finally, in industries such as footwear, steel, textiles, and automobiles, industrialists sought government protection on the basis of perceived unfair competition from abroad; foreign governments, in this view, artificially reduced their domestic producers' costs through subsidies or other means.[26]

The responses I have mentioned are not exhaustive, and they suggest considerable policy diversity in the United States, but in fact they are substantially in agreement. Most view U.S. difficulties as a function of failure to meet overseas efficiency standards. Their solution is to try to isolate one factor or a set of factors that can rectify apparent reversals, that is, equalize the cost of American output with that of overseas producers. The real scope of policy debate in the United States, then, concerns what exactly should be done to enhance efficiency so that the manufacturing economy can become a formidable competitor once again.

Japan does not support this interpretation of poor American manufacturing performance. The primary difficulty with American manufacturing, as the machine tool and automobile cases show, is less an efficiency shortfall than the lack of *production flexibility* in manufacturing. The implication is that policies which seek to build ever-greater economies of scale, intensify coordination in mass production industries, and further rationalize U.S firms may well prove irrelevant or even counterproductive. I consider each proposition in turn.

Japanese successes in machinery and automobiles tend to confirm the view that the nation's competitive successes were based more on product differentiation than on a coordinated effort to reduce the costs of standard goods. Japanese machine tool firms, frequently using designs initially rejected by American producers, built unique products that created and captured specialized niches in world markets. The country's firms, after a disastrous attempt to compete on the basis of low-cost, standard goods, gradually learned to break up mass markets by modifying their products extensively and continuously. In contrast, American machinery producers did not take advantage of potential new NC markets because they perceived high-tech equipment as suitable only for large firms and specialized manufacturing problems; general-purpose, small-scale NC machinery seemed to them anomalous. U.S. auto firms never believed that mass markets might fragment to any great extent, and so either they attempted to meet foreign competition by making epochal manufacturing shifts to what they thought would be a new mass market—GM's $40 billion downsizing program is an example—or they tried to reduce costs by increasing scale economies through a "world car" strategy: components built in huge volumes at plants serving the needs of markets throughout the world.[27]

In the contrast between Japanese and American manufacturing, then, the major difference is the extent to which flexible strategies inform Japanese production. Producers in both nations have relied on mass production to build standardized products at low cost. But Japan adopted flexible manufacturing to a much greater degree; smaller, flexible firms played a large and increasing role in the economy during the high-growth period. In contrast, as we saw in chapter 1, the U.S. economy experienced precisely the reverse trend. Japanese mass producers were supplemented by a large number of flexible, specialist producers; in the case of machinery production, for instance, one firm might mass produce basic components, which would then be combined with high value added specialty items built by flexible subcontractors. In the United States some industries were organized to permit a degree of flexibility, but in general mass production strategies have been dominant.

Just as the growth of flexible production helps explain Japanese successes, so the commitment to mass production provides an insight into American manufacturing stagnation. U.S. production strategies became problematic during the 1960s and 1970s because overseas producers and changing global circumstances eroded the stability of mass markets. Mass producers, as I argued in chapter 1, tend over time to become inflexible; machinery, labor skills, and management become specialized in producing one, and only one, product. If mass markets for standard goods erode, a mass production economy will be unable to adjust. This problem accounts for a large part of U.S. manufacturing reversals.

Circumstances in the latter half of the twentieth century undercut the market stability essential for U.S. success. First, more flexible Japanese and European firms fragmented mass market tastes by creating and responding to specialized consumer needs. As consumers became aware of the possibility of distinctive products, they began to demand more carefully tailored goods. Increasingly, success came to depend on creating or catering to submarkets in what formerly had been homogeneous mass markets. Many U.S. firms tried to counter this trend through intensive marketing appeals or advertising, but pressure from flexible overseas producers made cosmetic market differentiation more difficult. The result was a decline in the size of mass markets and the creation of smaller, specialized submarkets.

Second, as mass production technology advanced, less developed nations found they could import manufacturing techniques more readily and produce complex products rapidly. In stable mass markets, countries with much lower wage rates or fewer restraints on firms could quickly copy standardized designs and offer comparable products at lower prices. Even when mass market demand remained stable, therefore, mass producers in the United States and elsewhere faced severe price competition that frequently reduced their profits to the point of operating losses.

Finally, global resource uncertainties destabilized mass markets. Shortages and surpluses of basic raw materials disrupted assembly operations; manufacturers were forced to become more flexible to respond to the varying availability of materials. Changing resource conditions also affected basic demand for mass market goods according to the comparative price of certain materials. For example, automakers had to contend with demand shifts toward fuel-efficient cars, then toward luxury autos, and finally to a mixed market as oil prices rose and fell. More flexible manufacturers could cope better with these rapid market shifts.

If Japan is our guide, then American manufacturing reversals are due more to a lack of flexibility than to retarded efficiency. Japanese producers benefited from a more widespread national adoption of flexible production; entrepreneurs, because of Japan's support for small-scale producers, could take advantage of new ideas and bring them into the market. They could also respond better both to competitive pressures and to market uncertainties that tended to break up mass markets. The American environment, in contrast, precluded such rapid responses, and ultimately profitable ideas went unexploited. In international competition, American firms could not readily respond to, and of course did not seek, market fragmentation, and so they suffered a competitive disadvantage relative to more flexible producers.

If this analysis is correct, many American policy proposals are, at best, irrelevant. Private or public strategies to increase mass production efficiency, if they were in fact successful, might marginally improve the competitive position of U.S. firms. Even so, competitive pressures would quickly erode any gains. No matter how far U. S. wages are reduced or economies of scale further enhanced, for instance, American prices in standard markets can always be met by foreign firms exploiting much lower factor costs. From this perspective, the only long-term solution is to institute trade regimes such as the Multifiber Agreement or import quotas that guarantee American mass producers a share of markets they would otherwise be unable to earn.[28]

At worst, however, many of the conventional policy proposals threaten severely to impede the ability of American firms to adjust to new market conditions. Flexible manufacturing, I argued in chapter 1, requires management ideologies, labor freedoms and skills, and interfirm cooperation and trust, all of which are undercut by mass production strategies. It is difficult to imagine a firm or a nation seeking efficiency advances without simultaneously reducing future flexibility. Should a government or an industry dedicate resources to building ever-greater scale economies, or coordinate economic behavior to reduce costs, the financial and market opportunities for flexible firms will decline. Furthermore, efforts to reduce production costs through wage pressures would destroy interfirm trust and labor cooperation. Indeed, as we saw in the case of Sakaki, Japan needed *restraint* on downward wage and price pressure so that flexible operations could flourish. In the worst case, then, American industrial policy may increase adjustment difficulties by eliminating opportunities for flexible production.

What strategies *does* the Japanese case support? It is not possible to use one nation's experiences as a precise guide for another; specific policy recommendations cannot be derived from individual cases because, as I have argued, political contingencies cumulatively define a nation's industrial organization. Indeed, it is impossible to say, other than in the broadest sense, that a particular national solution is "best."[29] Furthermore, quite different political contexts can lead to the same outcome. For instance, in Japan flexibility was in part the result of right-wing prewar and conservative postwar politics, whereas in Italy flexibility was associated with a left-wing ideology.[30]

Despite these limitations, and though Japanese experiences are unique, Japan accomplished its growth through the realization of certain basic principles that can inform the U.S. debate over industrial policy in particular and general adjustment concerns everywhere. To conclude this book, I examine three policy propositions derived from the Japanese case.

First, Japan shows that successful industrial adjustment cannot be achieved without comprehensive social and political change. As we saw in the machinery industry, complementary political events affecting industrial behavior in specific firms, workers' outlooks, interfirm coordination, regional cooperation, and financial allocation combined to enhance opportunities for flexible production. In Japan isolated initiatives would probably not have transformed manufacturing by themselves. Flexible production, like mass production, involves the systematic adjustment of *all* phases of industrial activity.

The American effort to isolate a particular factor that can reverse the country's manufacturing decline is thus unlikely to be effective. Financial support for small firms, for example, would not lead to greater flexibility if mass production principles continue to shape the environment affecting labor and interfirm relations. Nor would a transformation of labor attitudes toward managerial prerogatives lead to significant results if factory management policies and ideologies regarding the market do not also change. Unfortunately, American adjustment strategies conceive of the nation's task as simply identifying the particular reason why U.S. producers fell behind in the efficiency race—tune up the efficiency machine, it is thought, and once again the United States will be able to compete. But Japan's experiences show that even when government or industry policy makers recognize the problem of flexibility, such limited responses will fail. A comprehensive commitment to the reshaping of work, management, and finance according to flexible principles is required if U.S. industry is to regain its international competitiveness.

Second, Japan suggests that one major element of American policy is especially misguided: the conviction that to increase efficiency, social objectives must be sacrificed and individual freedoms limited.

Even liberal and radical observers have reluctantlv concluded that economic efficiency demands the subordination of goals of equality, wage support, and the like. As a result, policy debate frequently focuses on reforms designed to curb political or social freedoms or to limit economic rights that, it is feared, may restrict business activity.

Japanese experience challenges this view. First, in flexible production some of the perceived tradeoffs between efficiency and specific social objectives are reduced. As we saw in Sakaki, a competitive flexible industry is not inconsistent with either equality or wage support goals. Indeed, high wages and increased managerial or self-employment opportunities were crucial to the labor and interfirm trust that made flexibility possible. Firms could offer higher wages because they were building products for consumers with specialized needs who were willing to pay more for individually tailored goods. Equality of opportunity in the factory and between firms was essential to the high skill and worker autonomy that facilitated rapid production shifts. To the extent that American policies sacrifice social objectives consistent with flexibility, they reduce the potential for manufacturing revival.

Ironically, the notion that increased discipline and reduced freedom are necessary to stimulate growth is often justified by the widespread perception that the Japanese make enormous personal and social sacrifices for their work. Whether or not Japanese work conditions really differ from those in other nations, industrial actors in Japan enjoy more freedom than those in America. In the high-growth period, manufacturing entrepreneurs had considerably more opportunities to open firms and to finance the purchase of new equipment; they were supported more fully by other manufacturers through regional cooperation; and in the event of reversals, a comprehensive network of support reduced the personal and professional consequences of failure. Thus Japanese manufacturers took advantage of new designs or techniques more readily to create new markets and products. Enhanced freedom, not additional restrictions, were necessary to foster flexible production in Japan.

Industrial policies that increase social and economic restrictions will run the risk of destroying the political basis on which flexible production is built. One common thread unites Japanese and European experience: the provision of comprehensive opportunities through financial and cooperative support is essential to the promotion of flexible manufacturing.[31] American policies may be particularly wrong-headed because they usually seek to restrict rather than to expand economic freedom.

Finally, the Japanese case hints at the promise of regional promotion strategies for stimulating American flexibility and manufacturing revival. American manufacturing is attuned to mass production principles, as I have argued; nevertheless, there are important industries in which industrial practices consistent with flexible production have emerged. In Japan flexible firms were promoted because political events gradually strengthened areas of the economy (small-scale manufacturers in particular) where the potential for alternative styles of production was high. In the same way an effective American strategy would reinforce industrial activities that adhere to flexible principles.

In the United States, high-tech regions displaying many of the attributes of flexible manufacturing have played a major role in stimulating such industries as computers.[32] Initially these regions emerged from the interplay between the development of new technologies, frequently in local universities, and the ability of ambitious entrepreneurs to open small firms. In the early phases of the computer industry entrepreneurs, though quite competitive, had to rely on one another extensively. A new chip design or hardware innovation would be useless without supporting software or product innovations. Individual designers could not possibly be aware of all the potential applications of new technologies, and they depended on contacts with other innovators to complement their own new ideas. To a significant degree, therefore, the computer industry in America resonated with the regional cooperative institutions prevalent in Japan. If this American pattern could be sustained more generally, it might provide a basis for the promotion of flexibility.

The experiences of the early computer industry are not, however, widespread in the United States; nor, over time, does the U.S. economy support the cooperative yet competitive behavior of entrepreneurs. Financiers and industrialists expect that, eventually, all products will evolve toward mass markets. As a consequence, even industries that initially exhibit flexibility are usually reorganized according to mass production principles.

One way to avoid this problem would be consciously to create regions dedicated to flexible production. Regional coordination would facilitate the comprehensive social and political change that the promotion of flexible production appears to require; unlike broad national strategies, regions encourage a personal commitment by involved industrial actors. At the regional level it should be possible to provide finance and articulate labor and management principles to support flexibility. In this way the gap between the generation of technology in universities and private foundations (the special strength of the United States) and the ability to exploit potential markets (the particular problem of American manufacturing) would be bridged. The ultimate goal would be networks of regions dedicated to continual product innovation throughout the country, supplementing the nation's mass producers.

Such an outcome is not a fanciful dream. American industrial "regions" already exist—San Jose and Boston were built, often unconsciously, on much the same principles as those that informed Japanese economic behavior. I see no reason why American industrialists or government policy makers should not foster the same result deliberately and sustain a region's dynamism. If they do so, the United States would be enabled to meet global competition more successfully than it has in the last few decades. Indeed, should American manufacturers learn to exploit more effectively the tremendous number of potential technologies and techniques U.S. researchers generate—as Japanese manufacturers have through technology imports and licenses—the country could well regain its industrial preeminence. But the United States will not achieve flexibility unless it actively promotes the industrial freedoms and comprehensive ideological and social changes that were associated with Japanese high-growth success.[33]

If we look to Japan to support policies that would reduce industrial opportunities and seek only refinements in mass production efficiency, we tragically mistake the import of Japanese achievements. Such a view profoundly misinterprets Japanese economic history. The result would be unnecessary foreclosure of options that could revive U.S. manufacturing. The Japanese case shows that to enhance the flexible alternative to mass production is to enhance the overall strength of a national economy. Of course, policy makers in America, Europe, even Japan, may fail to appreciate the implications of Japanese achievements and blindly seek only to "perfect" the mass production economy in response to industrial dislocations. If so, the future will be bleak for global trade harmony and for millions of individuals caught up in what will almost certainly be chronic manufacturing adjustment difficulties. But nothing in Japanese experience justifies this outcome. And the Japanese case shows that if we can harness the appropriate political will, there is a better alternative.

Notes

CHAPTER 1. *Explaining the Japanese Miracle*

1. Recently there has been an attempt to combine the features of both market regulation and bureaucratic regulation explanations into a single argument. Though my comments here anticipate discussion of these approaches, I explain briefly why the "mixed regulation" thesis cannot stand on its own.

The mixed regulation thesis is that in response to discrete stages of economic development, the Japanese resorted to different combinations of market and bureaucratic regulation. As an industry matures, it has different industrial requirements; in one stage, government intervention is particularly important, in another, market regulation produces the best outcome. In Japan either market or bureaucratic regulation was matched at various times to the particular needs of the country's manufacturing industries. Hence, greater efficiency was generated in Japan than elsewhere.

The mixed regulation thesis provides a much more nuanced way of describing Japanese industrial and regulatory behavior than is possible with either regulation thesis alone. But it also combines most of the problems of both arguments. We still need to know, in periods when the bureaucracy is thought to have preeminent industrial power, whether state initiatives were independently effective or whether they were superfluous or forced on bureaucrats by industrialists. In the absence of careful evaluation of how the bureaucracy developed its policies and whether such measures in fact induced beneficial industrial responses, we cannot judge whether the state had any independent effect at all. Furthermore, if it is thought that responses to the demands generated by the lifecycle of particular industries is the source of Japanese success, then it is still necessary to explain why Japan was able to meet these demands better than other countries could.

Moreover, the mixed regulation thesis seems in the final analysis to reduce to either a market or a bureaucratic argument. If product cycles determine necessary responses, and the Japanese met these imperatives with more skill than elsewhere, the argument is market theory, that, in its elaboration of the stages of sector development, provides a more detailed account of what the "market" consists of. If it is thought that the ability of bureaucrats to fashion efficient Japanese responses to sectoral crises led to industrial success, then the argument is substantially similar to the bureaucratic regulation thesis.

The mixed regulation theory is also premised on much the same industrial assumptions as support the bureaucratic and market arguments. It assumes that in all countries, industrial imperatives are essentially the same in similar sectors; economic success is the product of a nation's ability to meet these demands. That is, all of the theses adopt in general terms the same basic model of industrial growth and competition, but they diverge over what factors led to presumed Japanese advantages, whether bureaucracy, "natural" market cues, or some combination thereof.

Because the mixed regulation thesis imports but does not solve most of the problems in the bureaucratic regulation and the market regulation theses, I treat it in this book as a subset of these two theories. Indeed, in practice the proponents of the mixed thesis have tended to look favorably on the bureaucratic regulation approach and may be interpreted as enhancing the idea that the state should play a role in economic development. See, for a well developed account, Daniel Okimoto, *Between MITI and the Market* (forthcoming), especially chap. 1.

I also exclude from consideration two other common arguments about Japanese success, those based on culture and on unique institutions or circumstances. The cultural argument cannot stand serious scrutiny; for culture to explain industrial success, national character or values have to be linked to some theory of competitive advantage. That theory is the convergence hypothesis I discuss later in this chapter: all nations are engaged in roughly the same economic enterprise. In this case, culture explains greater efficiency, but used in this way, cultural factors are just another variant of the two theories. Second, the cultural claim chokes off any comparative study; the Japanese had a higher growth rate because, in effect, they are Japanese. Such a hypothesis suggests a fundamental distinction between Japan and everywhere else, even though many recognizable features of the Japanese economy call out for comparative analysis. Economic advances in states such as South Korea have undercut much of the appeal of uniqueness. An excellent review of the problem is in Chalmers Johnson, *MITI and the Japanese Miracle: The Growth of Japanese Industrial Policy, 1925–1975* (Stanford: Stanford University Press, 1982), pp. 7–8.

Can special circumstances—the lack of a military budget commitment, for instance, or a high savings rate—explain Japanese growth? Most such claims boil down to the market argument; the proponents merely focus on a single factor to account for industrial outcomes. Nearly all of the efforts to explain comparative growth rates by virtue of such limited factors have failed because the economic effects are not clearly identifiable. High savings may create some capital advantages, for example, but they also reduce the degree of investment available from other sources—maybe not a convincing advantage. Furthermore, this type of argument has most often been employed to attack the Japanese, ascribing the country's achievements to some illicit or unfair advantage such as reduced military obligations or technology imports. Again, careful study has never shown such factors to be clearly advantageous. Military spending may well induce growth; the import of technology raises more questions about why Americans did not make use of designs the Japanese seized on. Such explanations are not powerful enough to merit individual scrutiny. Again, see Johnson (1982), pp. 11–17, for a comprehensive discussion.

2. Examples of scholarship in this vein include T. J. Pempel, "The Bureaucratization of Policy Making in Japan," *American Journal of Political Science*, November 1974, pp. 647–664; Daniel Okimoto, ed., *Competitive Edge: The Semiconductor Industry in the U.S. and Japan* (Stanford: Stanford University Press, 1984), pp. 78–133; John Zysman, *Governments, Markets and Growth: Financial Systems and the Politics of Industrial Change* (Ithaca: Cornell University Press, 1983); and Ezra Vogel, *Japan as Number 1: Lessons for America* (New York: Harper, 1979), and *Comeback: Case by Case* (New York: Simon & Schuster, 1985).

3. The best articulated version is Johnson (1982), a book distinguished from most other accounts by the comprehensive theoretical context the author provides. See his introduction, pp. 17–34.

4. This idea was first put forward by Alexander Gerschenkron and subsequently has inspired a vast literature. See Alexander Gerschenkron, *Economic Backwardness in Historical Perspective* (New York: Praeger, 1965). Note that Gerschenkron's objective was to show that economic and political *diversity* characterized industrial cases; he was seeking to refute the more deterministic economic and social models of development in vogue in the late 1950s and 1960s. But those who followed Gerschenkron frequently generated a new kind of determinism from his work. Thus Johnson argues that late developers *must* generate an interventionist state. See Johnson (1982), p. 19. An even more illuminating example is James Kurth, "The Political Consequences of the Product Cycle: Industrial History and Political Outcomes," *International Organization* 33 (Winter 1979), pp. 1–34.

5. Comparative literature associating Japanese development with a "strong state" includes the influential book edited by Peter Katzenstein, *Between Power and Plenty* (Madison: University of Wisconsin Press, 1978), pp. 3–22, and Zysman (1983), who relies heavily on Chalmers Johnson's work for comparison with other "strong" states such as France.

6. See Johnson (1982), pp. 23–34, for a summary of industry policy initiatives undertaken by MITI since the Depression.

7. Johnson (1982), p. 24.

8. An extended discussion of this problem appears later in this chapter.

9. This conclusion was offered, for instance, in Ronald Dore, *British Factory—Japanese Factory* (Berkeley: University of California Press, 1973), pp. 404–420. Dore's influential comparative study of labor practices illustrated many fascinating ways that British and Japanese workers differed in their approach to their employment and work. He accounted for his findings by citing Japan's late development: with the experience of other nations as a guide, Japan could choose efficient practices, avoiding the confrontational labor strategies of early-developing England. He speculated that as countries such as Britain found themselves in a state of comparative underdevelopment, they would converge toward the newer states such as Japan. Thus Dore viewed differences in labor practices as variations within a single industrial model, more advanced practices being those which were more disciplined. In this way he reiterated the link between efficiency, control, and economic convergence, a link that also informs the "strong state" tradition of Japanese political economy. See also Johnson (1982), pp. 305–323.

10. See, for a typical account, *Wall Street Journal,* September 13, 1984, p. 26.

11. A concise statement of this position, rejecting the role of the state as a primary factor in Japanese development, is Hugh Patrick, "The Future of the Japanese Economy: Output and Labor Productivity," *Journal of Japanese Studies,* Summer 1977.

12. The literature includes such pathbreaking works as William W. Lockwood, *The Economic Development of Japan: Growth and Structural Change, 1868–1938* (Princeton: Princeton University Press, 1954), and Elizabeth Schumpeter and G. C. Allen, *The Industrialization of Japan and Manchukuo* (New York: Macmillan, 1940). More recent economic treatments include Lockwood, ed., *The State and Economic Enterprise in Japan: Essays on the Political Economy of Growth* (Princeton: Princeton University Press, 1965); Allen, *Japan's Economic Recovery* (London: Oxford University Press, 1958); Allen, *Japan's Economic Expansion* (London: Oxford University Press, 1965); Phillip Trezise, "Politics, Government, and Economic Growth," in Patrick and Henry Rosovsky, eds., *Asia's New Giant: How the Japanese Economy Works* (Washington, D.C.: Brookings, 1976); Ohkawa Kazushi and Rosovsky, *Japanese Economic Growth: Trend Acceleration in the Twentieth Century* (Stanford: Stanford University Press, 1983); James Wheeler et al., *Japanese Industrial Policy in the 1980s* (Croton on Hudson, N.Y.: Hudson Institute, October 1982); Gary Saxonhouse and Kozo Yamamura, eds., *Law and Trade Issues of the American Economy* (Seattle: University of Washington Press, 1986), which contains several essays criticizing the bureaucratic regulation approach; Yamamura, ed., *Policy and Trade Issues of the Japanese Economy* (Seattle: University of Washington Press, 1982); and Yamamura, *Economic Policy in Postwar Japan: Growth versus Economic Democracy* (Seattle: University of Washington Press, 1967).

13. An excellent critique of the market approach—characterized as the "no miracle occurred" argument (Japanese growth was the natural result of market forces)—can be found in Johnson (1982), pp. 9–11. In general I agree with his critique, though, of course, I differ in the view that the bureaucratic regulation model is any better.

14. Interestingly, the propensity to obscure the details of Japanese or other national industrial cases through macroeconomic or generically descriptive accounts was not typical of the earlier economics literature. For instance, both Lockwood and Schumpeter and Allen were acutely aware of the remarkable, vibrant role of smaller firms in the prewar economy (see chaps. 2 and 4). More recent efforts, though perhaps better grounded in economic theory, have tended less to study examples of Japanese divergence than to assume a continuity in the economic logic informing all countries' behavior. That in all cases individuals or groups maximize wealth may indeed be true, but the range of potential outcomes is nonetheless very significant.

15. An excellent review of convergence theory and its influence in modern political economic research appears in Michael Piore and Charles Sabel, *The Second Industrial Divide* (New York: Basic Books, 1984), especially pp. 7–11.

16. The relationship between timing of development and state responses is discussed above. See especially notes 3 and 4.

17. In economics literature the perception is growing that the applicability of neoclassical categories to all cases and in all times necessarily requires that all countries develop in the same way. A problem arises if one assumes or concludes from empirical observation that human choice, politics, social con-

texts, and the like—that is, nonmaterial factors—may profoundly reshape the rules and objectives governing economic behavior. Economists who appreciate this problem either limit the range to which conventional analyses can apply or propose an additional explanation for market structures themselves. An example of the former approach can be seen in the debate regarding Verdoorn's Law, named for the Italian economist who proposed that productivity and output are linearly related. Critical scholars and eventually Verdoorn himself were forced to conclude that under identical technical conditions, cultural and political forces could lead to dramatically different outcomes. Hence the law itself was valid only under very special circumstances—when cultural and political constraints were similar. See R. E. Rowthorn, "What Remains of Kaldor's Law." *Economic Journal* 85, no. 357 (1975), pp. 10–19, and P. J. Verdoorn, "Verdoorn's Law in Retrospect: A Comment," ibid. 90, no. 337 (1980), pp. 382–385. Efforts to account for background factors presumed to affect market structures include Nicholas Kaldor, "The Irrelevance of Equilibrium Economics" ibid. 82, no. 328 (1972), pp. 1237–1255, which argues that purely market explanations of action are inadequate; T. Lawson, "Uncertainty and Economic Analysis," ibid. 95, no. 380 (1985), pp. 909–927, arguing that economists must apply a "socially interactive" analysis to understand the contingency of much economic behavior; and Douglass North, *Structure and Change in Economic History* (New York: Norton, 1981), which argues that neoclassical analysis is limited to understanding choices *within* established systems of rules and proposes a theory of transaction costs to understand long-term systemic change. These examples underscore the often implicit role that convergence theory must play in market explanations; if all countries do not respond to resource or material constraints identically, then we need additional explanations for why subsequent market responses took the form they did.

18. Statistics for Japan for the years cited from Tsūsanshō (MITI), *Kōgyō tōkei nenpō (Annual industrial statistics);* for the United States from Bureau of the Census, "Summary Statistics," *Census of Manufactures.*

19. The Japanese were able to enter American auto markets successfully only after they abandoned price strategies and moved to new products. For an account see David Friedman, "Beyond the Age of Ford," in John Zysman and Laura Tyson, eds., *American Industry in International Competition* (Ithaca: Cornell University Press, 1983), esp. pp. 363–369.

20. See Friedman (1983) for details of the first and second import waves.

21. This section draws on a number of works by Piore and Sabel. The link between politics as they describe it and industrial alternatives is treated in Charles Sabel, *Work and Politics* (Cambridge: Cambridge University Press, 1981), especially the final chapter, "The End of Fordism?" and Piore and Sabel (1984), esp. chaps. 1 and 2, where they refine this thesis and show how the idea of mass production as the "blind destiny" of economic development has informed both Marxist and liberal research, thus dominating the intellectual landscape. The distinction between mass production and flexible production is also made in Piore and Sabel, "Italian Small Business Development: Lessons for U.S. Industrial Policy," in Zysman and Tyson (1983), pp. 391–425, and in a presentation that owes much to their approach, Friedman (1983), pp. 354–356.

22. For an application of this approach to defining strategies for the U.S.

automobile unions see Harry Katz and Charles Sabel, "Industrial Relations and Industrial Adjustment in the Car Industry," *International Relations* 24 (Fall 1984).

23. See, for example, Koike Kazuo, "Japan's Industrial Relations: Characteristics and Problems," *Japanese Economic Studies,* Fall 1978, pp. 42–90.

24. American flexible manufacturing is discussed in Sabel (1981), in the final chapter; Italian developments in Piore and Sabel (1983); and for the German case see Gary Herrigel, "German Machinery Industry Developments" (forthcoming).

25. Piore and Sabel (1984), pp. 19–48.

26. Machine tools are what other manufacturers use to make their products; they shape raw materials into finished parts. Typical machine tools are lathes, which enable an operator to cut a symmetrical part while the material is being spun rapidly; boring machines, which drill or tap materials; and mills, which apply a high-speed cutting tool to stationary workpieces in order to cut grooves or faces.

27. An excellent history of NC machinery development is David Nobel, *Forces of Production: A Social History of Industrial Automation* (New York: Knopf, 1984). NC machine tools are automated versions of basic machines. They are named for the system of digital controls or "numbers" that manipulate the workpiece mount, the cutter, and the tool changer on the machine itself. When the tools were first developed in 1957, by the Massachussetts Institute of Technology under a Defense Department program, machine tools were automated much like a player piano; a role of punched tape was fed into an adjacent reader, which then translated the codes represented by the punches into directions that guided the cutter and the material mount. Gradually, computers have substituted for the tapes; a machine tool can now be linked directly to a computer on which parts are designed and receive an automatically generated cutting plan via digital interface. This kind of equipment is sometimes called Direct Number Controlled (DNC), although in general any machine tool that can be programmed using tapes or on-line commands is now designated NC. NC tools are the basic building blocks for all advanced, automated manufacturing; sets of NC or DNC machines that are linked to perform successive tasks on a group of parts, sometimes serviced by materials-loading robots, are known as flexible manufacturing systems (FMS) or FMS cells; and a whole factory composed of integrated FMS units is an automated or "manless" factory.

The machinery's latent production potential affects the strategies of the firms studied in this book. For example, consider a vertical machining center. A "machining center" gets its name from the fact that it can perform a multitude of cutting tasks and can automatically mount its own cutting tools; it is like a mini-automated factory. To operate an NC machine tool, the planned cutting routine must be entered into the machine's central processing device, which can be done in two different ways. If the part under construction is composed of simple rectangular (XYZ coordinate) or circular shapes, commands can be sent to the machine via a programmable computer attached to the machine. More complex parts involve either punching a tape or setting up a computer routine that must then be fed to the machine.

Once cutting instructions are coded, the workpiece, raw metal stock for instance, in clamped to the workpiece mount. A hydraulic base underneath the mount can rotate the metal, move it up and down, or combine rotation and vertical movement by means of servomotors controlled by digital commands. Most modern machines use air pressure motors, although some still depend on oil hydraulics. The machine, following instructions, can select the cutting tool required for a given task, such as a drill for boring or a cutter for facing. A cutting-tool storage wheel rotates the necessary tool into place, where a hooklike automatic tool changer grasps it and spins to put the tool into the chuck holder. At the chuck precision motors are used to rotate the tool, causing a drill or cutter to spin so it shaves away material and makes a part. The chuck can be moved in this example up and down a metal shaft (hence "vertical" machining center). This motion, affecting the cutting tool, and the complex, hydraulically controlled movements of the base on which the part is clamped are carefully coordinated through digitized commands to result in a part conforming to desired specifications.

NC machine tools offer enormous advantages for producers facing certain sorts of manufacturing challenges. Once programmed, they can automatically produce parts within high tolerances, thus promising productivity gains (because manual setup time and operator attention are reduced). However, NC tools are also programmable; once they have made one part, they can be recoded to manufacture something completely different. Finally, because the equipment can be programmed to make extremely accurate, difficult cuts that are impossible on normal machines, NC tools hold out the possibility of constructing new products; indeed, one of their first tasks in the United States was to contour jet fighter wings in shapes not previously possible.

NC tools are thus ideal for manufacturers engaged in changing lot production rather than mass or extremely specialized work. The mass producer does not need the flexibility NC programmable capabilities provide and instead uses dedicated machinery. In terms of manufacturing capability, NC tools permit their operators to make parts that are impossible with ordinary equipment, and to do so within exacting tolerance limits.

28. Calculated from Nihon Kōsaku Kikai Kōgyōkai (Japan Machine Tool Builders Association) *Hahanaru kikai: San-jū nen no ayumi* (Mother machines: a thirty-year history) (Tokyo: Seisanzai Marketing, 1982), pp. 121, 133.

29. This fundamental distinction between U.S. and Japanese NC products was recognized by interested machinery users, including the U.S. military. See Defense Industry Analysis, "The Machine Tool Industry," Industrial College of the Armed Forces (May 1983), p. 7.

30. See Richard Copaken et al., *Petition to the President of the United States through the Office of the United States Special Trade Representative for the Exercise of Presidential Discretion as Authorized by Sec. 103 of the Revenue Act of 1971, 26 U.S.C. 48(a)(7)(D),* May 1982.

31. Marvin Wolf, *The Japanese Conspiracy* (New York: Empire, 1983).

32. See the account in Johnson (1982), p. 133.

33. Johnson (1982), pp. 24–25, 20.

34. See generally Johnson (1982): on cartels, pp. 162–163; on the defeat of the military, p. 168. The auto industry case is detailed on pp. 287–289; the failure of the Special Measures Laws is described on pp. 265–266.

35. Japan Machine Tool Builders Association, *Machine Tool Industry, Japan, 1984,* (Tokyo: 1984), page 7.

36. "NC kōsaku kikai seisan: Shitchinen buri ni" (NC production: Seven year's retrospective), in *Seisanzai Marketing,* October 1983, p. A-114.

37. The use of the term "dual structure" in Japan was first popularized in

Arisawa Hiromi, "Nihon ni okeru kōyō mondai no kihonteki kangaekata" (Basic thinking about Japan's employment problem), in Japan Productivity Center, ed., *Nihon no kōzō mondai to kōyō mondai* (Tokyo, 1957). It was incorporated into a small business White Paper the same year and became a basic analytical idea in small business throughout the postwar era.

CHAPTER 2. *Early Regulation of the Machine Tool Industry*

1. An excellent account of the internal history of the MCI and the bureaucratic maneuvering that led to its creation is Chalmers Johnson, *MITI and the Japanese Miracle: The Growth of Japanese Industrial Policy, 1925–1975* (Stanford: Stanford University Press, 1982), pp. 83–115.

2. See E. B. Schumpeter and G. C. Allen, eds., *The Industrialization of Japan and Manchukuo* (New York: Macmillan, 1940), pp. 686–691; also Johnson (1982), pp. 109–111, for background about the laws.

3. The learning thesis is proposed by Johnson (1982), pp. 23, 33. The idea that MITI was a reincarnation of the MCI and thus that there is a logical, developmental continuity between prewar and postwar regulation comes from Nakamura Takafusa, *Nihon no keizai tōsei* (Control of the Japanese economy) (Tokyo: Nihon Keizai Shinbunsha, 1974), p. 164.

4. The effects of the Depression in stimulating interventionist economic planning are discussed in Nakamura Takafusa, *The Prewar Japanese Economy* (New Haven: Yale University Press 1983), pp. 231–233; see also Schumpeter and Allen (1940), p. 686, and Johnson (1982), pp. 83–115.

5. The split between the Yoshino, "soft" faction and the harder, Kishi faction in the economic bureaucracy is described by Johnson (1982), pp. 123–125; the "new bureaucrats" are treated in Nakamura (1983), pp. 30–31.

6. See Johnson (1982), pp. 116–119.

7. The policy of anti-*zaibatsu* decentralization as a part of military strategy is discussed in Schumpeter and Allen (1940), pp. 760–772, esp. p. 770, and also in Isoshi Asahi, *The Economic Strength of Japan* (Tokyo: Houseido, 1939), pp. 108–109.

8. See Nakamura (1983), pp. 195–210.

9. Descriptions of inter-*zaibatsu* competition can be found in William Lockwood, *The Economic Development of Japan* (Princeton: Princeton University Press, 1954), pp. 228–235; an excellent revision of the view that *zaibatsu* achieved dominant power in manufacturing can be found in Nakamura (1983), pp. 230–235.

10. See Nihon Kōsaku Kikai Kōgyōkai (Japan Machine Tool Builders Association), *Hahanaru kikai: San-jū nen no ayumi* (Mother machines: A 30 year history) (Tokyo: Seisanzai Marketing, 1982), p. 47.

11. For a description for prewar machinery producers see Chokki Toshiaki, *Kōsaku kikai gyōkai; Sangyōkai series 67* (The machine tool industry; industrial sector series 67) (Tokyo: Kyoikusha, 1978), pp. 42–44.

12. Chokki (1978), pp. 45–50.

13. The founding of the resources bureau is described in Johnson (1982), p. 118. Its creation was a direct result of military pressure, although to appease private interests it was made semi-autonomous.

14. Nihon Kōsaku Kikai Kōgyōkai, *Nihon kōsaku kikai kōgyō hattatsū no katei*

(The development of Japan's machine tool industry) (Tokyo, 1951), p. 111. I rely on this source for the next several paragraphs.

15. The politics of the S-Type machine tool episode is described in Nihon Kōsaku Kikai Kōgyōkai (1951), pp. 112–113.

16. Nihon Kōsaku Kikai Kōgyōkai (1951), pp. 114–115.

17. See Johnson (1982), p. 133.

18. See Schumpeter and Allen (1940), pp. 686–691.

19. See Johnson's excellent treatment (1982), pp. 109–111.

20. Eleanor Hadley, *Antitrust in Japan* (Princeton: Princeton University Press, 1970), p. 330.

21. See Schumpeter and Allen (1940), p. 687, and Johnson (1982), p. 110.

22. See Schumpeter and Allen (1940), pp. 719–723, for details concerning insider and outsider firms in various cartel arrangements.

23. Schumpeter and Allen (1940), p. 691. See also Fujita, "Cartels and Their Conflicts in Japan," *Journal of the Osaka University of Commerce, No. 111,* December 1935: cartels were ineffective instruments not only of state control but of private restraint as well. Indeed, Fujita criticizes the MCI for overstating the usefulness of the cartels.

24. See Johnson (1982), p. 111, for details of public outrage over cartel abuses.

25. See Nakamura (1983), p. 301.

26. Richard Samuels, *MITI and the Market: The Japanese Oil Industry in Transition,* MIT EL 84-016 WP (Cambridge: MIT Energy Laboratory, International Energy Studies Program, October 1984), p. 15.

27. See Johnson (1982), p. 131.

28. The poor quality of Japanese stock was a constant problem for the military. Growth in autos stagnated but rose in trucks during 1936–1941. Thus the industry became a producer of poor-quality trucks and sacrificed production of all other vehicles. Total vehicle output in 1936 was 31,000 units, of which 5,000 were trucks; in 1941 it was 49,000 units, and all but 42,800 vehicles were trucks. See "Senzen ni Okeru Nihon no Kikai Kōgyō no Hatten no Tokushusei" (Special Qualities of Japanese Machinery Industry Development in the Prewar), in Gendai Nihon Sangyō Hattatsū Shi Kenkyū Kai, (The Contemporary Japanese Industrial Development History Research Group), *Gendai Nihon sangyō hattatsū shi* (Contemporary Japanese industrial development history) (Tokyo, 1967), pp. 55–56.

29. Nihon Kōsaku Kikai Kōgyōkai (1951), pp. 114–115.

30. See Chokki Toshiaki, "Nihon no kōsaku kikai kōgyō no hatten: Katei no bunseki" (An analysis of the development of the Japanese machine tool industry) (diss., Tokyo University, 1963), pp. 129–130.

31. In the prewar the MCI continually addressed the problem of small machinery production scale. See Chokki (1963), p. 127.

32. Chokki (1963), p. 131.

33. See Kato, "Kosaku kikai kōgyō no kōzō to kadai" (The structure and selected topics of the machine tool industry), in Gendai Nihon Sangyō Hattatsū Shi Kenkyū Kai (1967), p. 340.

34. See Johnson (1982), p. 23.

35. Chokki (1963), p. 131.

36. Chokki (1963), p. 162.

37. As quoted in Chokki (1963), p. 136, note 8.

38. Chokki (1963), pp. 154–158.

39. "Senzen ni okeru nihon no kikai kōgyō no hatten no tokushusei" (Special qualities of Japanese machinery industry development in the prewar), in *Gendai nihon sangyō hattatsū shi* (1967), p. 59.

40. See Chūshōkigyō Chōsakai Hen (Small and Medium Enterprise Survey Group), *Chūshōkigyō no hattatsū (2): Chūshōkigyō kenkyū vol. VII* (The development of small and medium enterprises (2): Small and medium enterprise research vol. VII) (Tokyo, 1962), pp. 64–66.

41. Nihon Kōsaku Kikai Kōgyōkai (1982), p. 46.

42. See Nakamura (1983), pp. 266–301.

43. See Byron Marshall, *Capitalism and Nationalism in Prewar Japan: The Ideology of the Business Elite, 1868–1941* (Stanford: Stanford University Press, 1967).

44. Johnson (1982), pp. 153–154.

45. T. A. Bisson, *Japan's Wartime Economy* (New York: Institute of Pacific Relations, 1945), pp. 202–203.

46. The metals distribution system is described in Nihon Kōsaku Kikai Kōgyōkai (1951), pp. 125–126.

47. A good account is in Chūshōkigyō Chōsakai Hen (1962), pp. 57–59.

48. Nihon Kōsaku Kikai Kōgyōkai (1951), p. 128.

49. Chūshōkigyō Chōsakai Hen (1962), pp. 57–59.

50. Nihon Kōsaku Kikai Kōgyōkai (1951), p. 130.

51. Nihon Kōsaku Kikai Kōgyōkai (1951), p. 131.

52. See Johnson (1982), p. 139.

53. Nihon Kōsaku Kikai Kōgyōkai (1951), pp. 132–133. "External organ" is a translation of *"gaikaku kikan,"* as the machinery *tōseikai* described itself. See, for the following paragraphs generally, Nihon Kōsaku Kikai Kōgyōkai (1951), p. 133–136.

54. Chokki (1963), p. 149.

55. Chokki (1978), p. 75–76.

56. Nihon Kōsaku Kikai Kōgyōkai (1982), p. 47.

57. Edwin Reubens, "Small Scale Industry in Japan," *Quarterly Journal of Economics* 61 (August 1947), p. 592. Damage statistics and Reubens's evaluation of the causes are on p. 589.

58. Figures for Japan from Nakamura (1983), p. 197; for the United States from *Census of Manufactures* data for 1938.

Chapter 3. *Economic Regulation and the Postwar Machine Tool Industry*

1. See, for example, Chalmers Johnson, *MITI and the Japanese Miracle: The Growth of Japanese Industrial Policy, 1925–1975* (Stanford: Stanford University Press, 1982), chap. 1; Daniel Okimoto, *Between MITI and the Market* (forthcoming), Conclusion; Ezra Vogel, *Comeback: Case by Case* (New York: Simon & Schuster, 1985), pp. 69–74; and John Zysman *Governments, Markets and Growth: Financial Systems and the Politics of Industrial Change* (Ithaca: Cornell University Press, 1983).

2. See Nihon Kōsaku Kikai Kōgyōkai (Japan Machine Tool Builders Association), *Hahanaru kikai: San-jū nen no ayumi* (Mother machines: A 30 year history) (Tokyo: Seisanzai Marketing, 1982), p. 48.

3. Nihon Kōsaku Kikai Kōgyōkai (1982), p. 48.

4. Nihon Kōsaku Kikai Kōgyōkai (1982), p. 99.
5. Nihon Kōsaku Kikai Kōgyōkai (1982), p. 121.
6. However, several firms continued operations in other fields, waiting for production opportunities to develop. See the description and statistics in Nihon Kōsaku Kikai Kōgyōkai (1982), p. 48.
7. The best account is by a former staffer of the JMTBA, Sugiyama Kazuo, who was active in the creation of the *gyōkai*. See Sugiyama, "Kōgyōkai hassoku ni itaru made o kaikō shite" (Recalling the creation of the JMTBA) in Nihon Kōsaku Kikai Kōgyōkai (1982), pp. 25–26.
8. The record of movements by firms into and out of the *gyōkai* in 1951–1981 is detailed in Nihon Kōsaku Kikai Kōgyōkai (1982), p. 58.
9. Membership figures from Nihon Kōsaku Kikai Kōgyōkai (1982), p. 58; industry figures from Ministry of International Trade and Industry, *Nihon no kōgyō tōkei* (Industrial statistics of Japan) (Tokyo), for the years specified.
10. Nihon Kōsaku Kikai Kōgyōkai (1982), p. 50.
11. The consolidated groups moved again in 1966 to their present location in Kamiyacho, near Shiba Koen (park) in Tokyo. See Nihon Kōsaku Kikai Kōgyōkai (1982), p. 53.
12. The entire document is reproduced as *Kōsaku kikai kōgyō no genjo to ikusei no michi* in Nihon Kōsaku Kikai Kōgyōkai (1982), *shiryō* section, pp. 10–15.
13. Nihon Kōsaku Kikai Kōgyōkai (1982), pp. 62–63.
14. "Rationalization" (*gōrika*) and "modernization" (*kindaika*) continually appear in MCI and MITI reports and legislation. They suggest different ideas in different contexts. Sometimes, particularly in bureaucratic application, rationalization has the meaning "concentration" or central direction. In other settings it means improving the quality of firms' operations rather than increasing scale; this was the dominant interpretation among smaller firms, for instance, which understood rationalization policies as encouragement to buy advanced equipment. In the case of the 1953 policy statement, pressure by machinery makers eventually caused the second meaning to be adopted; rationalization strategies would promote the substitution of new tools for old. See Nihon Kōsaku Kikai Kōgyōkai (1982), p. 63.
15. Nihon Kōsaku Kikai Kōgyōkai (1982), p. 68.
16. The subsidies are described in Nihon Kōsaku Kikai Kōgyōkai (1982), p. 63. Capital spending for the period is calculated from data supplied in Wender, Murase, and White, et al., "Investigation of Imports of Metal Cutting and Metal Forming Machine Tools under Section 232 of the Trade Expansion Act of 1962" (submitted to the International Trade Administration, U.S. Department of Commerce, Washington D.C., 1983), p. 104.
17. See Johnson (1982), pp. 191–242.
18. Nihon Kōsaku Kikai Kōgyōkai (1982), p. 64.
19. The Machinery Promotion Law is registered as Law Number 452 of 1957 of the Japanese Diet.
20. Details of the various plans can be found in Nihon Kōsaku Kikai Kōgyōkai (1982), p. 64.
21. See Nihon Ginkō Chōsabu (Bank of Japan Research Bureau), *Waga kuni no kinyū seido* (Our country's financial system) (Tokyo, 1976), p. 347.
22. Confidential JDB loan data were made available to the author by MITI's Industrial Machinery Bureau in a chart, "Nihon kaihatsu ginkō kara

no kōsaku kikai sangyō e no yūshi suii" (The Disbursement of Funds from the Japan Development Bank to the Machine Tool Industry). The chart covers the period 1956–1983.

23. Nihon Kōsaku Kikai Kōgyōkai (1982), p. 63.

24. The following paragraphs rely on statistical material from *Nihon kōsaku kikai Kōgyōkai* (1982), pp. 104–111 for production cost data and p. 121 output and export volume goals.

25. Nihon Kōsaku Kikai Kōgyōkai (1982), *shiryō* sec., pp. 25–26.

26. See for instance Johnson (1982), pp. 63–73. It has yet to be shown whether *amakudari* increases the power of the bureaucrats or of the firms they are supposed to be regulating. Large enterprises develop government contacts in all industrial countries; a change in administration in the United States, for instance, is often accompanied by a "fire sale" of former cabinet officials. Few would argue that the placement of these officials increases state control; rather, it provides the enterprise involved with a potentially useful pipeline into policy decisions. The same is almost certainly true of Japan; large enterprises may find that their *amakudari* appointments pressure them to comply with what the bureaucracy wants, but it is inconceivable that these same employees do not lobby regulators on behalf of their new employers.

27. MITI, *Nihon no kōgyō tōkei* (Industrial statistics of Japan) (Tokyo, 1957).

28. Nor could veteran *gyōkai* officials recall one in the history of the machine tool industry. Interview, Kawashima Yuzo, director of the JMTBA Technology Division, November 29, 1984.

29. JMTBA interview, November 29, 1984; interviews with Sugiyama Kazuo, former director of the JMTBA, November 20, 1984, and January 15, 1985.

30. Interview, MITI Industrial Machinery Bureau, October 17, 1984.

31. To my knowledge, the regular rotation of officials has not been discussed in analyses of MITI. My observations are based on interviews within the Bureau in October 1984. For instance, younger staff were perplexed by questions about machine tool policies in the 1950s to the 1970s; middle-level staff could sometimes recall the measures but generally had the details wrong; and the contribution of senior staff was to supply me with the names of former employees who might know what I was talking about. In addition, I worked for a two-week period in MITI; I interviewed officials informally and from those conversations learned about the effects of the two-year rotations.

32. Interview, MITI Industrial Machinery Division, October 17, 1984.

33. Both MITI and the *gyōkai* confirm that the machine tool industry organization was the source of the ideas and data used in the Rationalization and Recovery Plans. All product specifications and other statistical data were compiled by the *gyōkai*. These were transmitted to MITI in discussion groups; in turn, the Industrial Machinery Bureau wrote the reports into a final document. MITI interview, October 17, 1984; JMTBA interview, November 29, 1984.

34. MITI interview, October 17, 1984.

35. Many machine tool firm leaders expressed a lack of confidence in the *gyōkai*. The most pronounced opinion came from a representative from Mori Seiki, who stated flatly that "no one speaks the truth there." Interview, December 26, 1985.

36. See Johnson (1982), pp. 209–211; also Eisuke Sakakibara, ed., *The*

Japanese Financial System in Comparative Perspective (Washington, D.C.: Joint Economic Committee, U.S. Congress, March 1982), p. 21.

37. Data regarding the number of loans were supplied by MITI's Industrial Machinery Bureau from confidential data made available to the author in February 1985; industry data from MITI, *Nihon no kōgyō tōkei, 1957*.

38. These observations can be strengthened with statistical measures of the relationship of government investment to changes in machine tool industry output. There is no significant correlation between government assistance in a given year and industry development. The coefficient is very weak (R = .330) and the probability measure, ρ = .0825, is quite high, indicating that the observed connection between JDB outlays and annual production is close to random. If the relationship between the timing of JDB support and output is staggered, on the assumption that the effects of investment might lag behind annual results, the correlation coefficients actually weaken: for a one year-lag, R = .223; for a two-year lag, R = .158. Such findings support the claim that government financial assistance to the machine tool industry was ineffective.

39. See Vogel (1985), pp. 70–71.

40. Confidential data supplied to the author by the Industrial Machinery Bureau (see note 22 above).

41. See Ministry of International Trade and Industry, *Growth Factors of the Machine Tool Industry* (Tokyo, 1983), pp. 10–13, for details of U.S. spending; also Wender, Murase, and White, et al. (1983).

42. For example, Riken Seiko, a small manufacturer of spark discharge and milling machines based in Niigata, twice received development subsidies from MITI. The firm never had direct contact with the bureaucracy. Rather, it first negotiated with the Niigata prefectural government for assistance under a regional scheme for subsidizing the technical advancement of local firms. Then, in an effort to offset proposed outlays to Riken Seiko, Niigata officials applied under MITI's assistance program. Eventually MITI split the cost of the subsidy with Niigata. Interview, Riken Seiko, November 22, 1984.

43. Nihon Kōsaku Kikai Kōgyōkai (1982), p. 70.

44. MITI officials asked to describe their recollections of the period smiled wistfully and suggested they just paid out money while specifying fanciful goals taken from, as one official put it, "thin air." Interview, Industrial Machinery Bureau, October 17, 1984.

45. See Johnson (1982), pp. 274–281, for an excellent account of the bureaucracy's response to the capital liberalization crisis.

46. See Kozo Yamamura, "Success That Soured: Administrative Guidance and Cartels in Japan," in Yamamura, ed., *Policy and Trade Issues of the Japanese Economy* (Seattle: University of Washington, 1982), p. 82. Yamamura cites over one thousand cartels as evidence of consolidation. However, even if such cartelization occurred—if these were more than sham agreements—the huge number of cartels strips the effort of effectiveness. The larger the number of cartels, the less coordinated production becomes. Further, as Yamamura recognized, the huge majority of these cartels were really organizations of smaller firms seeking a defensive position against larger ones. The cartels in fact promoted the survival of the smaller firms that mergers were supposed to eliminate.

47. See Okimoto (forthcoming), final chap.; Vogel (1985), pp. 70–71.

48. Johnson (1982), p. 278.

49. Yamamura (1982), p. 82.

50. See "Kōsaku kikai seizōgyō kōzō kaizen keikaku" (Machine tool industry structural reform plans), in *Kōsaku Kikai News,* October 1969), p. 9. *Machine Tool Industry News* is published by the JMTBA from Tokyo as the industry's in-house newsletter.

51. Kōsaku kikai seizōgyō kōzō kaizen keikaku, *Kōsaku Kikai News,* October 1969, pp. 9–10.

52. Nihon Kōsaku Kikai Kōgyōkai (1982), pp. 67–68.

53. Expenditure data supplied to author by the MITI Industrial Machinery Bureau in January 1985. See note 22, above.

54. Data supplied to author by the MITI Industrial Machinery Bureau in January 1985. See note 22 above.

55. This history is described in "Shūchūseisan ni kan suru mōshiawase no kaitei ni tsuite" (Concerning the consolidated production agreement), in *Kōsaku Kikai News,* January 1968, p. 8.

56. *Kōsaku Kikai News,* January 1968, p. 8. Also interview with Sugiyama Kazuo, November 11, 1984.

57. In Industrial Equipment Division discussion groups MITI was, of course, aware of the machine tool industry's activity. But officials recall MITI's role as that of a cheerleader, urging the participants on but having no direct influence on the application or definition of the restraint scheme. Interview, Sugiyama, November 20, 1984; see also "Kōsaku kikai seizōgyō kōzō kaizen keikaku," *Kōsaku Kikai News,* October 1969, p. 10.

58. "Kōsaku kikai seizōgyō kōzō kaizen keikaku," *Kōsaku Kikai News,* October 1969, p. 10.

59. Nihon Kōsaku Kikai Kōgyōkai (1982), p. 58.

60. As calculated in Yano Securities, *The Machine Tool Industry* (Tokyo, 1982), p. 57.

61. "Shūchūseisan ni kan suru mōshiawase no kaitei ni tsuite," *Kōsaku Kikai News,* January 1968, p. 8; also "Kōsaku kikai seizōgyō kōzō kaizen keikaku," ibid., October 1969, pp. 9–10.

62. "Shūchūseisan ni kan suru mōshiawase no kaitei ni tsuite," *Kōsaku Kikai News,* January 1968, p. 8.

63. Based on Nihon Kōsaku Kikai Kōgyōkai (1982), pp. 72, 121.

64. Interview with "Morys" Imada, president, Hamai International, October 24, 1984.

65. The entire text appears in Nihon Kōsaku Kikai Kōgyōkai (1982), *shiryō* sec., pp. 19–21.

66. Interview, Sugiyama, November 11, 1984. "Group" was actually an English loan word employed to distinguish the arrangements from cartels.

67. Nihon Kōsaku Kikai Kōgyōkai (1982), pp. 72–73.

68. The most comprehensive treatment of the group scheme is "Kōsaku kikai gurupu no "ayumi" to genjō" (The current condition and "development" of machine tool groups), reprinted in Nihon Kōsaku Kikai Kōgyōkai, *Ni-ju nen no bijaku* (Twenty years of growth) (Tokyo: Seisanzai Marketing, 1972), pp. 489–500; quotation p. 491.

69. Nihon Kōsaku Kikai Kōgyōkai (1972), p. 491.

70. Interview, Sugiyama, November 11, 1984; Nihon Kōsaku Kikai Kōgyōkai (1982), p. 72.

71. Interview, Imada, October 24, 1984.

72. Interview, Sugiyama, November 11, 1984, and Nihon Kōsaku Kikai Kōgyōkai (1982), p. 72.

73. Interview, Sugiyama, November 11, 1984; Nihon Kōsaku Kikai Kōgyōkai (1982), p. 72.

74. This and following quotations are from Nihon Kōsaku Kikai Kōgyōkai (1972), pp. 498–499.

75. During interviews, company officials who participated in various groups and *gyōkai* staff active during the group program indicated that the groups were not utterly without effect. Many noted apparent examples of useful cooperation in technical and other business areas. But no one could suggest how the groups systematically affected the tangible position of the participant firms. *Gyōkai* staff, who were perhaps the industrial actors most receptive to the idea of coordination, seemed especially eager to link the emergence of groups to a concrete market outcome. But they concluded with a weak suggestion, that perhaps the group episode deepened the feeling of friendship or common destiny among JMTBA members. Interviews, Sugiyama, November 1984 and January 1985.

76. Nihon Kōsaku Kikai Kōgyōkai (1982), p. 121.

77. Nihon Kōsaku Kikai Kōgyōkai (1972), p. 499.

78. "Kōsaku kikai seizōgyō kōzō kaizen keikaku," *Kōsaku Kikai News,* October 1969, pp. 9–10, on which the next few paragraphs draw.

79. Interviews, Sugiyama, November 1984.

80. See, for example, the account of the FTC and steel in Johnson (1982), pp. 299–303.

81. See the text of the agreement in "Kōsaku kikai seizōgyō kōzō kaizen keikaku," *Kōsaku Kikai News,* October 1969, pp. 10–12.

82. "Shūchūseisan ni kan suru mōshiawase no haishi to shinseihin todokede ni kan suru kijun no seitei ni tsuite" (Concerning the repeal of the concentrated production agreement and the standards for reporting new products), *Kōsaku Kikai News,* February 1971, pp. 24–25.

83. NC output data from Nihon Kōsaku Kikai Kōgyōkai (1982), p. 133; NC firm and machine type data collected from annual "Suchi seigyo kōsaku kikai sangyō jisseki nado chōsa" (Surveys of aspects of the current NC machine tool industry), *Kōsaku Kikai News,* July 1975, 1979, 1984.

84. For example, faced with growing import pressure, the American National Machine Tool Builders Association (NMTBA) mounted a concerted effort to show that trade reversals were the product of unfair practices. Its president, James Gray, argued that "while the association has long been a proponent of free trade and has one of the most active international trade promotion efforts in the trade association field, we cannot stand idly by while key segments of the American machine tool industry are decimated by targeted sales of foreign machine tools. Frequently assisted by subsidies and a variety of preferential programs sponsored by their respective governments, foreign builders have come to dominate certain key sectors of the domestic machine tool market, a fact we find inconsistent with our vital national interests. America is the defender of the industrial west and machine tools are the foundation of our industrial defense preparedness." The NMTBA view identifies many beliefs about Japanese export policies that are consistent with the bureaucratic regulation thesis, in particular that Japanese export suc-

cesses are due to targeting and to explicit state promotion. See James Gray in NMTBA, *1984–1985 Economic Handbook of the Machine Tool Industry*, (Maclean, Va., 1983), pp. ii–iii.

85. Import data from Nihon Kōsaku Kikai Kōgyōkai (1982), pp. 121, 112–113.

86. Nihon Kōsaku Kikai Kōgyōkai (1982), p. 133.

87. Nihon Kōsaku Kikai Kōgyōkai (1982), pp. 63, 121.

88. Nihon Kōsaku Kikai Kōgyōkai (1982), p. 65.

89. As presented in MITI (1983), pp. 15–16. See note 41 above.

90. This analysis is based on data and import records in Nihon Kōsaku Kikai Kōgyōkai (1982), p. 121.

91. The *gyōkai* arranged to have its U.S. offices funded by the Japanese External Trade Association (JETRO). Though JETRO was set up by MITI to promote Japanese trade, the incorporation of the research offices into the organization did not signal growing state control. Rather, the *gyōkai* was able to obtain funding for weak research activities by inducing JETRO to sponsor them. Later, as we shall see, JETRO actually became the center of a state effort to *restrain* Japanese exports in response to foreign criticism. See Nihon Kōsaku Kikai Kōgyōkai (1982), pp. 70–71.

92. Yano Securities (1979), p. 14. See note 60, above.

93. Interview with Mochizuki Yutaka, Shizuoka Machine Tool Co., December 8, 1984.

94. Interview with "Morys" Imada, Hamai Machinery, October 24, 1984.

95. See Johnson (1982), p. 217.

96. Privately, Japanese firms and international lawyers admit that MITI is sometimes used as a bargaining device to extract favorable terms from prospective partners. The Japanese side can claim that license fees, or the right to use technology, or other aspects of a contract will not be approved by the bureaucracy. In some cases firms will argue that they are legally prohibited from contracting at certain terms. But in a small industry, such as machine tools, as long as the capital input of the foreign enterprise was limited to less than 50 percent—a requirement formally dropped in 1973 but still a subject of concern for the nationalistic bureaucracy—MITI would approve the license as a matter of course.

97. From confidential industrial Machinery Bureau documents made available to the author in January 1984.

98. See Nukui Ken, *Kiiroi roboto* (Yellow robots) (Tokyo: Yomiuri, 1982), pp. 46–55. This book is a firm biography of Fanuc, whose robots are noted for their yellow color.

99. This equipment was essential to provide the NC controller with information that the part to be moved had reached its destination; it was critical to the feedback loop necessary for accurate automatic machining. See Nihon Kōsaku Kikai Kōgyōkai (1982), pp. 90–91.

100. Nukui (1982), p. 35.

101. Interview, Mori Seki, December 25, 1984.

102. Nihon Kōsaku Kikai Kōgyōkai (1982), pp. 128–129.

Chapter 4. *Flexible Production and Small-Scale Manufacturing*

1. The use of this term dates from Japan's 1957 White Paper, which popularized the idea that small firms were inferior to larger ones and subject

to the control of bigger producers through contracting arrangements. See Nakamura Takafusa, *The Postwar Japanese Economy* (Tokyo: University of Tokyo Press, 1981), pp. 174–175, for a useful summary of this development. But recognizable elements of the dual structure hypothesis can be found in Japanese literature since at least the 1920s, when MCI bureaucrats wanted to consolidate "backward" or "traditional" firms into "modern" factories. In the 1930s Japanese export successes prompted foreign countries to criticize what they felt was the highly exploitative use of low-wage labor in small firms to undercut global prices; intense scrutiny of labor conditions in Japanese small firms led to the conviction that smaller factories were technically and managerially deficient, dependent on sweating for their survival. Chalmers Johnson, *MITI and the Japanese Miracle: The Growth of Japanese Industrial Policy, 1925–1975* (Stanford: Stanford University Press, 1982), p. 98, offers a good account of the early position of Yoshino Shinji and other MITI officials regarding small enterprises in prewar Japan. Following the war, recession once again produced wage differentials; the expansion of Marxist analysis in Japan helped lead to the widespread adoption of dual structure analysis. Though the Japanese literature often treats the dual structure as one more manifestation of Japanese "uniqueness," the argument resembles work dealing with America and Europe. For a summary see Michael Piore's account of technological dualism, in Piore and Suzanne Berger, *Dualism and Discontinuity in Industrial Societies* (Cambridge: Cambridge University Press, 1982).

2. This process is called "burden shifting" or *shiwayose;* when demand turns down and orders dry up, even small firms that are lucky enough to obtain orders may have their payments delayed as large companies use resources internally. Such perceived abuses (and as we shall see quite real abuses in the 1950s) were part of the political climate that led to the creation of the small-firm financial institutions discussed below.

3. Nakamura (1981), p. 175.

4. See Johnson (1982), p. 13, for a brief summary of the way American academics have absorbed the dual structure argument.

5. Johnson (1982), p. 13, summarizes the standard treatment of the dual structure in American literature. A "benign" tradition of analysis in Japan views high wages in large firms as the result of inherent Japanese cultural traits; benevolent paternalism led to a wage gap because smaller firms could not afford to match the largess of larger firms. But recent studies show conclusively that neither paternalistic large-firm management nor wage differentials existed in Japan until the Russo-Japanese War, 1905 at the earliest. Throughout the Meiji period factory wages appear to have been uniform and low. See Umemura, "Chingin kakusa to rōdō shiryō" (Wage differentials and labor materials), in *Nihon keizai no bunseki* (An analysis of the Japanese economy), vol. 2 (Tokyo: Keiso, 1955). Because the idea of "lifetime employment" in large firms and other paternalistic practices developed in comparatively recent times, it is highly unlikely they grew out of some immutable part of Japanese culture. See the excellent discussion by Yasukichi Yasuba, "The Evolution of Dualistic Wage Structure," in Hugh Patrick et al., *Conference on Japanese Industrialization and Its Social Consequences* (Berkeley: University of California Press, 1976), p. 253. Treating the historical development of interindustry wage gaps but not wage differentials by firm size is Koji Taira, *Economic Development and the Labor Market in Japan* (New York: Columbia University Press, 1970), pp. 13–93.

6. See Yasuba (1976), p. 253.
7. Yasuba (1976), p. 286.
8. There is, however, no conclusive proof; the pattern of prewar wage rates in different-sized firms is unclear because monthly and yearly surveys were not undertaken. See the discussion by Morishima Michio, *Why Has Japan Succeeded?* (Cambridge: Cambridge University Press, 1982), pp. 110–111.
9. A good discussion is in Ronald Dore, *British Factory—Japanese Factory* (Berkeley: University of California Press, 1973), pp. 380–385.
10. All labor/wage surveys below are from Rōdōshō (Ministry of Labor), *Maigestu tsurō tōkei chōsa* (Monthly wage statistics), for the periods cited. Hereafter these surveys are cited as Ministry of Labor, *Monthly Wage Statistics*. The size classes used here are the standard references for compensation surveys undertaken by the Ministry of Labor. I focus on male wages, which comprise the bulk of manufacturing compensation; movements in male wages are indicative of general trends.
11. See Nakamura (1981), p. 174.
12. Ministry of Labor, *Monthly Wage Statistics* (1975).
13. No one has yet explained why supposedly technically advanced, dominant large firms in Japan should be such poor performers in contrast to the smaller firms they are commonly thought to exploit. See Yasuba (1976), pp. 249–280, for fascinating data about inverse profitability differentials.
14. Yasuba (1976), p. 287.
15. Kiyonari's classic work is Kiyonari Tadao, *Nihon chūshō kigyō no kōzō hendō* (Small business structural changes) (Tokyo: Shin Hyoron, 1970), which presented the first comprehensive challenge to the postwar dual structure theory. Kiyonari became a leading academic spokesman for financial and support organizations for small-scale firms and has frequently elaborated the view that postwar small firms relied not on exploited labor but on skilled use of capital-intensive machinery. See Kiyonari (1970), p. 245.
16. See Kiyonari, *Chūshōkigyō dokuhon* (An introduction to small and medium enterprises) (Tokyo: Toyo Keizai, 1984), pp. 95–98. Privately Kiyonari has argued the rate may be even higher.
17. Koike Kazuo, *Chūshōkigyō no jukuren* (Small and medium enterprise training) (Tokyo: Dōbunkan, 1981), pp. 89–90.
18. Compiled from Tsūsanshō (Ministry of Trade and Industry), *Nihon no kōgyō tōkei* (Tokyo, for the periods cited). Hereafter cited as *Industrial Statistics of Japan*.
19. Figures on U.S. start-up firms are not regularly covered in U.S. surveys. However, a special report by Joel Popkin & Co., "Measuring Gross Product Originating in Small Business: Methodology and Annual Estimates, 1955–1976," Small Business Administration SBA no. 2624-OA-79 (Washington, D.C., 1981), suggests that small business manufacturing had declined about 50 percent in the period covered. Census figures show that smaller firms have declined in absolute numbers during the postwar period.
20. Kiyonari (1984), pp. 80, 98.
21. Koike (1981), p. 96.
22. The principal sources for detailed information about postwar small business are surveys taken at irregular intervals by MITI's Statistical Survey Department. Tsūsanshō, Chūshōkigyō Chō [Ministry of Trade and Industry, Small and Medium Enterprise Bureau], *Kōgyō jittai kihon chōsa hōkoku shō* (The basic survey of manufacturing conditions) (Tokyo, 1960, 1964, 1968). After

1972, Tsūsanshō, Chūshōkigyō Chō, *Chūshō kigyō sōgō kihon chōsa* (The basic general survey of small and medium industry) (Tokyo, 1972, 1976, 1983). Hereafter cited as Small Business Survey. Statistics in the previous paragraph for the general machinery and manufacturing sectors were calculated from the 1983 survey.

23. Small Business Survey (1983). Kiyonari, using a different methodology, estimated in 1966 that small firms doing no subcontracting amounted to about 47 percent of all firms engaged in manufacturing; those doing no or only partial subcontracting amounted to over 57 percent. Kiyonari (1970), p. 166.

24. Kiyonari (1970), p. 166.

25. Kiyonari (1970), p. 171, showed that even in the early 1960s "business contact" (*torihiki kankei*) was the only form of relationship between suppliers and contractors for over 60 percent of Japanese small firms doing subcontracting.

26. See Richard J. Samuels, *The Business of the Japanese State* (Ithaca: Cornell University Press, 1987), chap. 3, for details.

27. Nakamura argues that in most manufacturing industries in the prewar period, Japanese small firms were exporters, producing consumer goods from intermediate products made by larger firms. He describes this relationship as one of the "interdependence of the modern and traditional (small scale) sector." See Nakamura Takafusa, *The Prewar Japanese Economy* (New Haven: Yale University Press, 1983), pp. 83–94.

28. On silk see Elizabeth Schumpeter and G. C. Allen, *The Industrialization of Japan and Manchukuo* (New York: Macmillan, 1940), pp. 655–675. A good account of prewar small-scale manufacturers is Teijiro Ueda, ed., *The Small Scale Industries of Japan* (Tokyo: Japanese Council, 1936), which describes the ceramics, electronics, and transportation manufacturing industries throughout the 1920s and 1930s. Ueda shows the smaller firms had considerable technical and marketing expertise. More generally, William Lockwood, *The Economic Development of Japan* (Princeton: Princeton University Press, 1954), pp. 201–214, discusses the role of smaller prewar firms. Both works suggest the prewar small firm in Japan was considerably more dynamic than generally thought.

29. See Nakamura (1983), pp. 83–94, and Kiyonari (1970), p. 171.

30. Nakamura (1983), pp. 83–94.

31. Much of this discussion was suggested by intriguing observations on Japan in Michael Piore and Charles Sabel, *The Second Industrial Divide* (New York: Basic Books, 1984), pp. 229–250.

32. On Nissan see Michael Cusumano, *The Japanese Automobile Industry* (Cambridge: Harvard University Press, 1985); also, for an extremely useful survey of postwar manufacturing strategies in larger firms and their relations with smaller ones, see Juzo Wada, "A Case History of Guidance and Upgrading of Subcontracting Firms," in Asia Productivity Organization, *Intra-National Transfer of Technology* (Tokyo, 1975), pp. 87–119.

33. Wada (1975), pp. 102–103. Experiences in the auto industry were matched in other machinery sectors. For example, Japan's largest bearing manufacturer, which played a dominant role in the industrialization of Nagano Prefecture, also attempted to set up an integrated mass production network in the 1950s. But as the firm's coordinator of outside orders recalled, by the latter fifties the company was offering little or no technical or manage-

ment guidance to its suppliers. Though the firm had made the attempt to direct suppliers centrally, cost pressures related to a lack of time and manpower led to rapid retrenchment by the early 1960s. In any case, he said, "there isn't a lot we can tell them [now] anyway." Interview, Mechanical Section Manager of Minebea Inc., November 18, 1984.

34. See David Friedman, "Beyond the Age of Ford," in John Zysman and Laura Tyson, eds., *American Industry in International Competition* (Cornell: Cornell University Press, 1983), pp. 364–367: Toyota tried to export and learned that if it did not change its products and seek unfilled niches, U.S. firms would be able to defend their markets with price reductions.

35. Rodney Clark, *The Japanese Company* (New Haven: Yale University Press, 1979), pp. 56, 60–61. Some scholars suggest this reshaping of industry resulted from the influence of the older *zaibatsu* system of investment, updated to the postwar marketplace; the Japanese *zaibatsu* initiated the practice of using centralized capital to create increasingly autonomous production units under nominal central direction, and this became the Japanese norm. See Piore and Sabel (1984), pp. 133–164, for an interesting discussion.

36. Koike (1981), pp. 98–113.

37. Interview, Shizuoka Machinery, November 9, 1984.

38. Interview, Minebea, November 18, 1984.

39. Interview, Mori Seki, December 25, 1984.

40. Yano Securities, *The Machine Tool Industry* (Tokyo, 1982), p. 20.

41. Kiyonari (1984), p. 90.

42. Johnson (1982), pp. 98–99.

43. For an English account of the *mujin* see Fuji Bank, *Banking in Modern Japan* (Tokyo, 1967), pp. 73–74.

44. Schumpeter and Allen (1940), pp. 530–537 and 556–566, brilliantly describe the manipulations of the *toiya* in the context of textiles. The rest of this paragraph is based on their description at pp. 761–762, 765.

45. Johnson (1982), p. 99.

46. See Schumpeter and Allen (1940), p. 768.

47. See the excellent discussion by Johnson (1982), pp. 104–107.

48. See Nakamura (1983), p. 232.

49. See the account in Isoshi Asahi, *The Economic Strength of Japan* (Tokyo: Houseido Press, 1939), pp. 109–116.

50. The excellent account in Nakamura (1983), pp. 232–240, explains Takahashi's activities in detail.

51. Fuji Bank (1967), pp. 128–129.

52. Fuji Bank (1967), p. 147.

53. See the account in Nakamura (1981), pp. 175–176.

54. Nakamura (1981), p. 177.

55. Surveys on the proportion of lending to enterprises broken out by the size of the recipient are extremely rare in Japan; most studies are highly aggregated and do not show the internal lending structure of the institutions. One notable exception is Kokumin Kinyū Kōkō (People's Finance Corp.), *Nihon no shō reisai kigyō* (Japanese small and very small enterprises) (Tokyo: Toyo Keizai, 1968), p. 124, which is used here. Since 1966 the general pattern has changed little except to emphasize the role of small business–lending institutions in the economy.

56. The history of City and Regional banks may be gleaned from Nihon Ginkō (Bank of Japan), *Waga kuni no kinyūseidō,* (Japan's financial system) (Tokyo, 1979), pp. 156–197.

57. Fuji Bank (1967), p. 226.
58. Fuji Bank (1967), p. 225.
59. Horiuchi Akiyoshi, "Economic Growth and Financial Allocation in Postwar Japan," University of Tokyo research paper 84-F-3 (Tokyo, August 1984), pp. 6–8.
60. Fuji Bank (1967), p. 225.
61. In 1958 the credit insurance role originally intended for the Corporation was shifted to a new institution, the Small Business Credit Insurance Corporation (Chūshō Kigyō Shinyō Hoken Kōkō). Since the late prewar period, localities themselves had been the main guarantors of small enterprise loans. This burden gradually shifted to the national government, sometimes as national banks reinsured the local-level guarantees. In 1953 the government passed the Credit Insurance Law (Shinyō Hoken Kyokai Hō), which, among other provisions, made available special funds to lending institutions that suffered losses on long-term loans to small businesses. In 1957 the law was extended to local insuring bodies as well. These functions were all incorporated into the Credit Insurance Corporation and represent additional state support for small business credit because they reduce lending risks. See Fuji Bank (1967), pp. 266–267.
62. Fuji Bank (1967), pp. 266–267.

CHAPTER 5. *Industrial Regionalism: Sakaki Township*

1. See Michael Piore and Charles Sabel, "Italian Small Business Development: Lessons for U.S. Industrial Policy," in John Zysman and Laura Tyson, eds., *American Industry in International Competition* (Ithaca: Cornell University Press, 1983); they highlight the importance of regional institutions. Also Piore and Sabel, *The Second Industrial Divide* (New York: Basic Books, 1984), pp. 281–308, discusses the regional foundations of flexible manufacturing.
2. A general account of Sakaki in English is "Silkworms First, Then Shoehorns and Now Robots," *Far Eastern Economic Review,* December 20, 1984, pp. 70–71. A much more detailed review in Japanese is "Semai totchi, seikodanbane ni" (Small area, but it has become a hot topic of success), *Shinō Mainitchi Shimbun,* September 12, 1984, p. 6.
3. I visited several factories and the Sakaki *Shōkōkai* during December 18–19, 1984. Interviews are cited as Sakaki *Shōkōkai* Interviews in the event the sources were local bureaucrats, Sakaki Factory Interviews in the event the sources were private industrialists.
4. The best account is a study of Sakaki by the Naganoken Chūshōkigyō Sōgōshidōjō (Nagano Prefecture Bureau for Assisting Small and Medium Enterprises), *Sakaki machi kikai kōgyō sanchi shindan hōkokushō* (Report of the study of Sakaki's regional machinery industry) (Nagano, 1983), pp. 1–3. This confidential document was provided to me by the Sakaki *Shōkōkai,* December 18, 1984.
5. Data for the years cited from *Japanese Industrial Statistics* and the U.S. *Census of Manufacturers.*
6. Statistics from materials provided by the Sakaki *Shōkōkai,* "Naganoken kōgyō jōi ranking" (Top ranking industrial regions in Nagano Prefecture) for 1983; tax information is from Sakaki *Shōkōkai,* December 18, 1984.
7. See *Shinō Mainitchi Shimbun,* September 12, 1984, p. 6; material on Soar from Sakaki Factory Interviews, December 18, 1984.

8. From materials provided by the Sakaki *Shōkōkai,* "Naganoken kōgyō jōi ranking" (Top ranking industrial regions in Nagano Prefecture) for 1983.

9. Naganoken Chūshōkigyō Sōgōshidōjō (1983), pp. 1–3.

10. Information in this and the next four paragraphs is from Sakaki *Shōkōkai* Interviews, December 18–19, 1984. The quoted passage is from Naganoken Chūshōkigyō Sōgōhidōjō (1983), p. 4. See note 4 above.

11. *Shinō Mainitchi Shimbun,* September 12, 1984, p. 6.

12. In these cases supervision is vested in an urban institution called the *kuyakushō.* Greater Tokyo, for instance, is made up of some twenty-eight *kuyakushō,* which resemble a board of supervisors or a city council.

13. Information in this and the next four paragraphs is from Sakaki *Shōkōkai* Interviews, December 18–19, 1984.

14. See Sakaki Shōkōkai, *Chūshō kigyō kinyū no shiori* (Finance for small and medium enterprises) (Nagano, 1984).

15. Information in this and the next six paragraphs is from Sakaki *Shōkōkai* Interviews, December 18–19, 1984.

16. Class information from the circular Sakaki *Shōkōkai, hai-teku jidai ni kotaeru* (Responding to the high-tech era) (Nagano, 1984).

17. Indeed, factory operators frequently suggested that in particular production tasks, large firms knew less than they did. Sakaki Factory Interviews, December 18–19, 1984.

18. Sakaki Factory Interviews, December 18–19, 1984.

19. Sakaki *Shōkōkai, Shōkōgyō shinkō no shiori* (Programs for the promotion of commerce and manufacturing) (Nagano, 1984).

20. Bankruptcy statistics as compiled by Tokyo Shōkō Research, *Gurafu de miru tōsan* (Bankruptcies as Depicted in Graphs) (Tokyo, December 1984).

21. Indeed, no one at the *shōkōkai* could remember a single case of a manufacturing bankruptcy. Sakaki *Shōkōkai* Interviews, December 18–19, 1984.

22. Nihon Kōsaku Kikai Kōgyōkai, *Kōsaku kikai konyū no tebiki: Setsubi gōrika no ōsusume* (Guide to obtaining a machine tool: All about equipment rationalization) (Tokyo, October 1984).

23. The pamphlet is filled with illustrative cartoons. One shows a manager, a worker, and a samurai holding aloft a small factory beneath the word "Rationalization!" The samurai bears the inscription "public funds," and his face is shaped like the yen character (¥). Another shows a man waking up in the morning, his head shaped like a factory. He is stretching as though weak and tired. On a table nearby is a vial of tonic medicine bearing the label "National and Prefectural finance"; drinking from the vial will lead, the cartoon suggests, to the "strengthening of enterprise quality." Nihon Kōsaku Kikai Kōgyōkai (October 1984), pp. 5 and 17.

24. Kiyonari Tadao, *Chiki no henkaku to chūshō kigyō (shita)* (The regional revolution and small and medium enterprises, vol. II) (Tokyo: Nihon Keizai Hyoron, 1975), pp. 205–207.

25. Ikeda Masayoshi "Shō-reisai kigyō no ME-ka" (The "mechatronization" of small and very small enterprises), in Kokomin Kinyū Kōkō, *Chōsa Geppō* no. 283 (November 1984), pp. 19–21.

26. In practice it is very difficult to assess the relations between the *shōkōkai* and the local firms. Each side tends to take most of the credit for industrial successes while downplaying the contribution of the other. In field interviews, moreover, and perhaps especially in Japan, it is very hard to delve into resentments or conflicts that individual bureaucrats or factory owners might have

experienced. The *shōkōkai* and local company managers view themselves as part of a single team competing for resources against other prefectural and national groups. And, as I have indicated above, the two groups are mutually dependent, so they avoid potential conflicts as much as possible. Sakaki *Shōkōkai* and Factory Interviews, December 18–19, 1984.

27. Every manager I spoke with brought up the danger of becoming a single part supplier to a single firm or industry. Sakaki Factory Interviews, December 18–19, 1984.

28. Sakaki Factory Interviews, December 18–19, 1984.

29. "Cooperation" is a repeated theme in Japanese studies. In Sakaki, the *shōkōkai* gives visitors glowing accounts of how leaders of various firms offer technical assistance to smaller companies, and how after work blue- and white-collar staff meet and discuss production problems in restaurants or *nomiya* (neighborhood bars). Prefectural reports even tie this supposed spirit of cooperation to ancient traditions forged during planting or harvest times. In fact factory managers and workers compete strongly with each other, and most regard the *shōkōkai*'s claims as wildly inflated. See Naganoken Chūshōkigyō Sōgōshidōjō (1983); also Sakaki *Shōkōkai* and Factory Interviews, December 18–19, 1984.

30. Sakaki Factory Interviews, December 18–19, 1984.

31. Naganoken Chūshōkigyō Sōgōshidōjō (1983), p. 37.

32. Sakaki Factory Interviews, December 18–19, 1984.

33. Sakaki *Shōkōkai* Interviews, December 18–19, 1984.

34. Many *shōkōkai* officials lamented that expensive equipment, involving large public loans, was often introduced into factories or workshops without compelling technical reasons. Sakaki *Shōkōkai* Interviews, December 18–19, 1984.

35. Naganoken Chūshōkigyō Sōgōshidōjō (1983), p. 14.

36. Sakaki Factory Interviews, December 18–19, 1984.

37. See Mori Kiyo, *Machi kōjō* (Village factories) (Tokyo: Keizai Hyoron, 1982), pp. 61–91, for NC introduction as seen by a literate technical employee in a small firm.

38. Typically in Sakaki most of the work force could enter cutting instructions via the cathode ray tube interface attached to most NC tools. Programming via tape, which involves a special punching machine, or the making of computerized cutting routines was more restricted, and there was some variation among factories. A usual case was a firm of six employees, three of whom could create digitized programs on tape. Sometimes all of the workers were trained to program in the most sophisticated manner, and a company might have a special programming room in which young workers could experiment with different ideas. In other cases, the owner would be the primary programmer. Sakaki Factory Interviews, December 18–19, 1984.

Chapter 6. *Industrial Development and Political Change*

1. For a brief English account of the prewar Automobile Industry Law of 1936 see Chalmers Johnson, *MITI and the Japanese Miracle: The Growth of Japanese Industrial Policy, 1925–1975* (Stanford: Stanford University Press, 1982), p. 131.

2. Indeed, Japanese auto firms were increasingly pessimistic about gov-

ernment policies for ending the recession and thought the Korean War, as one executive recalls, a "godsend." See the appendix to Shotaro Kamiya, *My Life with Toyota* (Tokyo: Toyota Motor Sales, 1976).

3. The best account of the merger scheme and the resulting failure of the bureaucracy's strategy is in William Duncan, *U.S.-Japan Automobile Diplomacy* (Cambridge, Mass.: Ballinger, 1973), pp. 142–145.

4. Johnson (1982), pp. 287–288, provides an excellent account of the *failure* of the bureaucracy to limit foreign participation in the auto industry. To salvage his view that MITI directed industrial activity in Japan, however, Johnson argues that the lack of an *amakudari* placement in Mitsubishi reduced MITI's influence. This is an unlikely claim; Mitsubishi, originally part of a powerful *zaibatsu,* had extensive contacts with MITI. The real reason for the company's defiance is that Mitsubishi stood to benefit from foreign contacts because it had no foothold in the domestic market; foreign ventures gave it a growth opportunity. That these private concerns overrode national policy exhibits the powerlessness of the bureaucracy.

5. See John Zysman, *Government, Markets, and Growth* (Ithaca: Cornell University Press, 1983), pp. 247–250.

6. Structurally, the only way for the Japanese economy to provide flexible credit was for the BOJ to adjust its loan ratios. Thus, in a period of high investment, overloans would occur as banks extended more credit. As a result, overloans were a convenient, cheap source of capital for private lenders; above a certain level, in effect, the government was providing public funds to private banks for their own loans. Thus the *banks* lobbied for the overloan program, to increase their own profitability. See Horiuchi Akiyoshi, "Economic Growth and Financial Allocation in Postwar Japan," University of Tokyo research paper 84-F-3 (Tokyo, August 1984), pp. 29–33.

7. See Horiuchi (1984), pp. 50–53, 55–56, for details.

8. My account of the oil industry relies heavily on Richard J. Samuels, *The Business of the Japanese State* (Ithaca: Cornell University Press, 1987) which juxtaposes market outcomes in oil with perceptions of Japan as a strong state. Samuels reaches conclusions very similar to my critique of the bureaucratic regulation argument.

9. The best account of the prewar period and the failures of the state is in Samuels (1987).

10. Richard Samuels, *MITI and the Market: The Japanese Oil Industry In Transition,* MIT Energy Laboratory International Energy Studies Program, MIT EL 84-016 WP (Cambridge, October 1984), pp. 20–21.

11. Samuels (1984), p. 23.

12. Compare, for example, Japanese and U.S. experiences affecting machinery demand. Several studies have argued that, due to politics (as I use the term here), the United States adopted mass production more extensively. Historically, early U.S. industrialists did not have to contend with a huge sector of smaller producers, as did the Japanese in the prewar period. Further, U.S. mass producers could expand into midwestern farming regions and use farm laborers who had a different conception of factory work from those in Japan. Additionally, consumer demand pliability in U.S. markets differed from Japan's, where export and domestic demand differentials, regional variation, and foreign competition constrained the ability of firms to create mass markets. American tastes may have been more easily shaped. When Japanese firms attempted to institute mass production, as a result, they

faced severe political constraints. Conflict with smaller firms and factory workers, and even ideological struggles over optimal production practices, forced the retrenchment of mass production and led to a greatly expanded flexible sector. In America, firms could institute mass production with much less difficulty. In shaping tastes and building ideologies they in effect institutionalized a national manufacturing system that tended to reduce opportunities for flexible production. See Michael Piore and Charles Sabel, *The Second Industrial Divide* (New York: Basic Books, 1984), chap. 5. Also see David Hounshell, *From the American System to Mass Production, 1800–1932* (Baltimore: Johns Hopkins University Press, 1983). For an excellent account of how American mass production ideology has constrained the ability of U.S. firms to use flexible manufacturing systems (robots, NC tools, and the like) effectively, in contrast to Japanese firms, see Ramchandran Jaikumar, "Postindustrial Manufacturing," *Harvard Business Review* no. 6 (November–December 1986), pp. 69–76.

Whatever the reasons for the comparatively widespread U.S. adoption of mass production, the outcome was a different NC machinery market from Japan's. NC development in the United States was largely confined to building very expensive specialty equipment for military-related enterprises such as aircraft firms or for use by giant private companies engaged in mass production; large mass production firms purchased 75–80 percent of U.S. NC output. Japanese machine tool companies also serviced the needs of mass producers with highly specialized equipment; but the flourishing smaller factories, as we saw in Chapter 4, accounted for 70 percent of Japanese NC demand by the 1970s. Demand for Japan's NC products was more diverse than in America because the politics transforming industry varied.

13. Interview, Nihon Kōsaku Kikai Kōgyōkai, November 17, 1984.

14. The technical development of Matsuura and Mori Seki products from U.S. designs was confirmed for me in confidential interviews in Japan and the United States, December 1984.

15. The rapid entry of new firms exploiting new technologies, characteristic of Japanese NC developments, did not take place in the United States. Indeed, though Japanese market volatility and the numerical growth of machinery producers, as I showed in Chapter 3, was significant, the total number of U.S. machine tool firms was almost constant from the mid-1960s to the 1980s, and in absolute levels less than half that of Japan. Most of the major manufacturers had dominated production in the 1950s, or for that matter in the 1920s. As a result, new technical ideas and designs were frequently ignored. Observers of American industry excoriated U.S. machinery development as being "in the Stone Age"; others observed that "in some cases, [U.S. machine tool makers'] methods have changed very little in the last century." See "Are Machine Tool Builders Cutting It with Industry?" *Iron Age,* August 24, 1981, p. 87, and Clifford W. Fawcett, "Factors and Issues in the Survival and Growth of the U.S. Machine Tool Industry" (diss., George Washington University, 1976), pp. 2–5.

16. See Paul Ong, "NC Machine Tools," in *Industry and Trade Strategies,* Office of Technology Assessment Report no. 333-2840 (Washington, D.C., 1983).

17. Interview, Mori Seki, December 24, 1984. A careful reader might be bothered that it appears I am attributing Japanese machinery successes to an apparent commitment to *mass production.* If Japanese firms manufactured

products in higher volumes than U.S. producers, surely their competitive advantage lay in lower prices? This argument must be rejected, however, for several reasons. The first, and most important, is that Japanese NC machine tools were developed for the *domestic* market; they succeeded as new products for smaller firms rather than as cheaper versions of tools that were, in any case, unavailable elsewhere. Indeed, this differentiation was the basis of export successes; because they were distinct from the U.S. norm, Japanese products occupied a secure niche. Price differentials were not the primary factor in the country's machinery advances. Further, it is somewhat misleading to speak of the NC market as a mass market at all. The total number of Japanese NC machine tools produced in 1983 was 26,398 units; in the United States, about 8,945 units. For NC lathes and NC machining centers, Japanese output was 10,020 and 7,833 units respectively in 1983, while the totals were 1,203 and 893 units for America. See National Machine Tool Builders Association, *Economic Handbook of the Machine Tool Industry* (Maclean, Va. 1983), pp. 106, 111, 198. Even if one firm manufactured these products for each country, the total output would fall far below the annual production level associated with economies of scale in such industries as automobiles and consumer electronics. But Japanese NC producers were much more numerous than in the United States. Where a handful of firms dominated American NC manufacturing, Japanese NC markets were fragmented as new entrants flooded into promising sectors. Thus Mori Seki, the leader in NC lathe output, made about 2,000 NC units in 1983. And the firm's products were not all standardized; the 2,000 unit total includes specialized machinery. The distinction between U.S. and Japanese production, therefore, is in the purposes for which the machines were designed. Because American NC machinery was developed for use by mass producers, it was much more specialized. Japanese production was attuned to the needs of smaller-scale firms seeking general purpose machinery; to some extent, basic designs were standardized. But even in its capacity to combine products made by subcontractors to differentiate basic patterns, the Japanese machinery industry exhibits some of the flexibility of the economy as a whole. Thus if machinery manufacturing is inversely related to the dominant manufacturing style of an economy, we can infer from Japanese and U.S. machinery divergence that flexible operations were much more widely diffused in Japan.

18. To say that material conditions may be ambiguous is not to say that at all times anything is possible. When global or national conditions are relatively fixed, one production style may appear self-evidently best suited to market demands. However, my findings support the idea that the background conditions in all cases *do* change; we cannot define one particular industrial solution that is best for all time. Further, as I discuss below, even when such broad categories as "mass" or "flexible" production seem to define appropriate strategies in any given period, we cannot say that a particular response is best. There are many different ways of instituting flexible strategies, for instance, and, in accordance with the politics of each case, different outcomes will constrain or enhance future possibilities in different ways.

19. I discuss the preconditions required for successful market analyses in Chapter 1; see especially note 17.

20. The Japanese manufacturing system may have undergone significant changes from the late 1970s to the 1980s. First, international pressures (ironically) strengthened the hand of the bureaucracy. Although MITI still could

not dictate outcomes, industries that relied on export earnings became more accepting of the idea that some entity should regulate foreign trade so as to avoid severe sanctions. In automobiles and machinery, for example, overseas market allocation schemes were forced on the Japanese by trading partners such as the United States in the form of export quotas. One effect was to restrict opportunities for new firm entry and to reduce incentives toward product innovations. With a fixed overseas quota, Japanese producers did not need to change products rapidly. In turn, relations with subcontractors may have been transformed to meet more limited, standardized production goals—some of the freedom of the high growth period may have been attenuated.

Second, the political coalition supporting small business steadily eroded under the Nakasone cabinet. The opposition parties were in disarray, reducing the need to make large transfer payments to small-firm constituents in order to secure safe conservative seats. Consequently, small- and medium-enterprise support was cut severely in the budgets of the mid-1980s. At the same time financial deregulation, fostered by falling banking profits and foreign complaints, put pressure on the small-firm banking institutions. The result was a considerable slowdown in public and private support for small business.

Finally, for the first time in postwar Japanese history, major segments of Japanese manufacturing were integrated into military production, especially in computer and other high-tech sectors. In effect, the Japanese military and allied manufacturers began to create a new industrial system fostered by state aid justified on the grounds of national defense. Industries that developed under the new system differed greatly from the old, high-growth practices. Large firms centralized operations internally, much as U.S. firms had done.

Have these developments had a major impact on contemporary Japanese manufacturing? Any answer remains speculative. But I believe that the differences between, for instance, machinery and autos in the 1970s and semiconductors in the 1980s can be partially explained by transformations in the Japanese political economy. The Japanese may inadvertently destroy the basis of their postwar economic successes by instituting an industrial system that bears much more resemblance to American manufacturing. If so, the country's economic performance will be much less spectacular in the years ahead.

21. See Oswald Johnson, "Jobless Rate Climbs to 7% in Month—Slump in Manufacturing Cited," *Los Angeles Times,* February 1987, pt. IV, p. 1.

22. In the mid-1980s the idea that government intervention could foster efficiency had declined in appeal because of the more conservative mood in America. Still, industries and government analysts alike did debate the relative merits of protectionism and other state responses. Currently, proponents of some form of government intervention to generate greater efficiency usually offer the more modest suggestion that state activity should supplement the market; thus intervention of some sort is part of the overall competitive advantage that countries develop. Further, they attempt to distinguish state influence in the form of direct ownership or taxes from pervasive *policy* power. See Johnson (1983), pp. 306–323; the last chapter of Daniel Okimoto, *Between MITI and the Market* (forthcoming); and John Zysman and Laura Tyson, eds., *American Industry in International Competition* (Ithaca: Cornell University Press, 1983), pp. 28–32.

23. Perhaps the most intriguing version of this approach came from the

"ungovernability" school of thought regarding economic decline. The idea was that efficiency advances often required states and societies to sacrifice other objectives, such as pollution control or equality. But modern governments, for reasons tied to the development of the welfare state and the maintenance of social order, were unable to resist social demands by interest groups. Over time the efficient operation of the economy was increasingly burdened by costly, intrusive policies that artificially stimulated high wages and increased production costs. Generally, then, the industrial world was experiencing stagnation because political interference had reached the point where economies and markets no longer functioned efficiently; but if states withdrew from the market, they would sacrifice social order. The solution was to retrench and let the market arbitrate among competing claims. These views, of course, were the intellectual precursors of national policies followed by the Reagan and Thatcher governments.

Scholars both on the left and on the right offered essentially the same interpretation of the global crisis of the late 1970s and 1980s. Leftists saw the problem in terms of legitimation: in order to restrain class conflict, governments had to make concessions to the middle and lower classes. But these payoffs in effect reduced efficiency to the point that the economy stagnated. This congruence between left and right suggests, I think, the degree to which convergence theory is embedded in our political economic theories. It provides a particularly stark example of the more general conviction in policy debate that to foster economic growth, "natural" market efficiency must be unimpeded. See, generally, Piore and Sabel (1984), chaps. 1 and 7. On trade-offs between efficiency and social concerns, and the ungovernability thesis, see Arthur Okun, *Efficiency versus Equality* (Washington, D.C.: Brookings, 1975); Michel Crozier, Samuel Huntington, and Joji Watanuki, *The Crisis of Democracy: Report on the Governability of Democracies to the Trilateral Commission* (New York: New York University Press, 1975); Paul McCracken, et al., *Towards Full Employment and Price Stability* (Paris: OECD, 1977); and John H. Goldthorpe, "The Current Inflation: Towards a Sociological Approach," in Fred Hirsh and John H. Goldthorpe, eds., *The Political Economy of Inflation* (Cambridge: Harvard University Press, 1979). Examples of the convergent neo-Marxist approach are James O'Connor, *The Fiscal Crisis of the State* (New York: St. Martin's, 1973), and Claus Offe, "Competitive Party Democracy and the Keynesian Welfare State: Factors of Stability and Disorganization," in Thomas Ferguson and Joel Rogers, eds., *The Political Economy* (Armonk, N.Y.: Sharpe, 1984), pp. 349–367. In addition, for an example of the tendency to view democracy and efficiency as incompatible, because political representatives meddle in the economy to secure votes, see Samuel Brittain, *The Economic Consequences of Democracy* (London: Temple Smith, 1977), pp. 237–238.

24. A good example is the U.S. congressional debate in 1987 concerning an omnibus trade bill. Instead of focusing on remedial measures for U.S. firms (apart from worker retraining), the proposed legislation called for tough sanctions against unfair trading partners and a broader interpretation of unfair practice. See, for example, Oswald Johnson, "House Panel Votes Tough Trade Bill," *Los Angeles Times*, March 26, 1987, pt. 1, p. 15.

25. Indeed, "fad" business advice books became a growth industry in the 1970s and 1980s; authors drew on everything from arcane Japanese culture to pseudo-psychological "theories" to suggest appropriate U.S. managerial responses to manufacturing crises. The popularity of such works indicates the

degree to which U.S. industrialists thought they could solve their problems by isolating a single, debilitating factor that cut against efficiency. Simply reform management, it was believed, and all would be well. A general critique of this conviction is offered below.

26. An excellent treatment of the protectionist responses of several industries to foreign competition can be found in Zysman and Tyson (1983).

27. For details of responses by U.S. auto firms to market fragmentation challenges, and a critique, see David Friedman, "Beyond the Age of Ford," in Zysman and Tyson, (1983), pp. 367–369 and 386–390.

28. The U.S. trade deficit of the 1980s illustrates this point well. Between 1985 and 1987 the U.S. dollar declined about 57 percent against the yen. The volume of Japanese imports to the United States and the U.S. trade deficit nevertheless *increased.* It is difficult to imagine efficiency reforms cutting costs by more than the amount achieved by these currency fluctuations. So it is possible to conclude that lowering American costs by enhancing efficiency will do little by itself to stimulate U.S. manufacturing. Thus though the American trade deficit is no doubt the product of complex factors, and may yet respond to more dramatic changes in exchange rates, U.S. price differentials in 1985–87 indicate that American producers face *product competition* as much as price challenges from flexible manufacturers. See Sam Jameson, "U.S., British Answer Japan's Plea to Boost Sagging Dollar," *Los Angeles Times,* May 3, 1987, pt. IV, p. 1; Oswald Johnson, "February Trade Deficit Soars to $15.1 Billion," *Los Angeles Times,* April 15, 1987, pt. 1, p. 1.

29. Market circumstances, for example, might shift so as to make apparently ineffective strategies suddenly more suitable. For instance, if the United States is indeed a case in which mass production is particularly dominant, the country might well emerge as a predominant producer should global markets become fixed again. I believe that destabilizing influences are likely to increase, so this outcome is remote. As a matter of logic, however, future American manufacturing successes based on mass production strategies cannot be ruled out. In addition, as I argue above, it is very difficult to distinguish more or less effective national responses within broad categories of flexibility and standardization. The Japanese solution is only one way of achieving manufacturing flexibility; Japanese producers first tried to copy American mass production techniques but had to retreat, in the process creating new opportunities for smaller firms. In parts of Europe, however, flexible firms have emerged which were not shaped by an initial experience with mass production. In contrast to these producers it is Japanese firms that appear more inflexible. In the 1960s and 1970s, during the period of Japanese high growth, the ability to fragment mass markets into smaller but often quite large submarkets was enough to provide firms with a competitive advantage. But should markets fragment even more—should the small group of European manufacturers exert more influence on the global economy, for instance, as tastes become more refined—Japanese flexibility may prove insufficient. Political circumstances create latent production possibilities that are impossible to predict. Hence they cannot provide a detailed example for focusing policy debate.

30. See Piore and Sabel (1983).

31. The notion that political and social freedom is essential to foster flexible production has been referred to as "yeoman democracy." The idea is that flexible operations combine individual self-interest with cooperation. Part of

the cooperation is to reduce downward price and wage pressures; another is to facilitate equal opportunities to obtain capital and to enter the market with new ideas. Here again, the notion that economic adjustment necessarily involves a restriction on freedom is contradicted. See Piore and Sabel (1984), chap. 11.

32. For a discussion that focuses on the resonance of American high-tech firms with flexible operations in Europe, see Piore and Sabel (1984), chap. 11.

33. For the idea that American manufacturing ideology—Taylorism—has precluded American productivity advances through the use of computerized machinery, see Jaikumar (1986), p. 71. See also Harry Katz and Charles Sabel, "Industrial Relations and Industrial Adjustment," *Industrial Relations* 24 (Fall 1985), for an argument suggesting the relationship of labor reforms to a flexible production adjustment strategy in the United States.

Index

Library of Congress Cataloging-in-Publication Data

Friedman, David (David Bennett)
The misunderstood miracle.

(Cornell studies in political economy)
Bibliography: p.
Includes index.
1. Industry and state—Japan. 2. Machine-tool industry—Government policy—Japan. 3. Small business—Government policy—Japan. 4. Japan—Economic policy—1945– . 5. Japan—Politics and government—1945– . I. Title. II. Series.
HD3616.J33F75 1988 338.952 87-447855
ISBN 0-8014-2073-3 (alk. paper)
ISBN 0-8014-9479-6 (pbk.: alk. paper)